PRAISE FOR UNQUIET V

"Rob and Nonie Douglas provide the reader with ⸻
by their many years in the field and magical practice. The book has much to
recommend it; from its brief history of necromancy and its misunderstanding
in the Western tradition, to its technical classification of deceased human
spirits. There is too a concise and exceptionally helpful discussion of
Aristotelian philosophy and its enmeshment with later occultism....The
authors' emphasis on precise language is linked to the need for prospective
sciomancers to be able to communicate effectively with those in need who
do not necessarily share their worldview, and this adds a level of reason and
compassion to the work which is very welcome. This is a highly readable and
clear exploration of necromancy or sciomancy, both in the past and present,
enlivened by the authors' Scottish folk magic roots."

—**DR. PETER HEWITT,** Folklore Museums Network founder and Museums
 Officer, Dumfries & Galloway, Scotland

"This book is a concrete step-by-step overview of the laying of spirits and the
various tools, rituals, and approaches one can employ. More importantly, this
book stresses relationship with spirits so that you do not inadvertently disrupt
a spirit minding its own business. This volume breaks down this sometimes-
overwhelming field for all who have ever been curious about what goes into
paranormal work. A thoroughly enjoyable read!"

—**BEN STIMPSON,** author of *Ancestral Whispers*

"*Unquiet Voices* is a guidebook steeped in tradition and culture. The reader
is instantly transported to a fireplace in Scotland where the practice of laying
ghosts has been passed on for hundreds of years—and now it's our turn to
learn! Using both science and ancestral lore, Rob and Nonie Douglas impart
their years of experience and research in ways that are easy to incorporate into
any spiritual practice. They teach both a deep respect for the tradition and
the mechanics needed should the reader find themselves in need of action.
From investigating a disturbance to choosing a method of resolution and
everything in between, this book is a must-have addition to your spiritual

library or paranormal investigation toolkit. Rob and Nonie's passion for magic and working with the spiritual realm bleed off every page and leaves the reader hungry for more."

—**COURTNEY BUCKLEY**, professional paranormal investigator, educator, and
   "ghost bait" on *Scared and Alone* YouTube series

"The authors guide the reader into the cosmology and practice of necromancy, and more specifically, sciomancy—which aims to provide relief to the living and the dead through occult action. Wife and husband team Rob and Nonie Douglas have put in the time—both in the library and in the field—to create a densely packed and invaluable look at the work of interacting with spirits of the dead, and occasionally spirits of other kinds, as well. The book is thoroughly researched with an emphasis on classical texts like Agrippa and medieval grimoires, and it breaks down the necromantic worldview into something empirical but alive—an Ars Scientia … This is not a simplistic book about ghost-hunting, but instead a deeply rooted and incredibly painstaking examination of a widely misunderstood occult practice."

—**CORY HUTCHESON**, author of *Llewellyn's Complete Book of North American Folk Magic*

UNQUIET
VOICES

About the Authors

Rob Douglas has been committed to the study and practice of magic and occultism for more than thirty years. Learning at his mother's knee, Rob grew up amid rich cultural practices from rural Scotland that included laying ghosts and a legacy of regional magical traditions. His love of esoterica led him to become a dedicated ritualist and independent researcher with specialist knowledge in medieval ceremonial magic and British initiatory traditions. Together with Nonie, he has provided spiritual counsel, resolved many hauntings, and advised paranormal investigators on difficult cases.

Nonie Douglas is an artist, writer, and esotericist who is drawn to the practice and preservation of mystery traditions from the British Isles, which she shares with her partner, Rob. Impelled by her pursuit of ancestral spirituality, she teaches about the soul's journey and brings peace to the dead through traditional cultural rites. Her artwork focuses on reviving magical arcana and philosophy through imagery and symbolism. As part of the Scottish diaspora, Nonie helps others who are seeking a genuine spiritual path to reconnect to their origins and respectfully embrace living traditions.

Visit Rob and Nonie at arcaneborders.com.

THE MAGICAL ART OF

LAYING GHOSTS

UNQUIET VOICES

ROB AND NONIE DOUGLAS

Llewellyn Publications | Woodbury, Minnesota

First Edition
First Printing, 2024

Book design by R. Brasington
Cover design by Shannon McKuhen
Interior illustrations
    Nonie Douglas: 29, 31, 43, 83
    Llewellyn Art Department: 6, 33, 64, 65, 66, 67, 68, 70, 132, 133, 135, 165

Photography is used for illustrative purposes only. The persons depicted may not endorse or represent the book's subject.

Llewellyn Publications is a registered trademark of Llewellyn Worldwide Ltd.

Library of Congress Cataloging-in-Publication Data (Pending)
ISBN: 978-0-7387-6555-6

Llewellyn Worldwide Ltd. does not participate in, endorse, or have any authority or responsibility concerning private business transactions between our authors and the public.

All mail addressed to the author is forwarded but the publisher cannot, unless specifically instructed by the author, give out an address or phone number.

Any internet references contained in this work are current at publication time, but the publisher cannot guarantee that a specific location will continue to be maintained. Please refer to the publisher's website for links to authors' websites and other sources.

Llewellyn Publications
A Division of Llewellyn Worldwide Ltd.
2143 Wooddale Drive
Woodbury, MN 55125-2989
www.llewellyn.com

Printed in the United States of America

To Rob's indomitable mother, a beacon of support and encouragement in our practice, who will be reading this book in the afterlife with a contented smile.

ACKNOWLEDGMENTS

This book would be incomplete without a tribute to Dorian and the impromptu conversation about necromancy that led to this project. Also, to our sons and daughter, without whom this book would not be possible, especially our eldest, Hunter, who threw himself into a support role from the day he left active military service.

And we must say a special thank you to our ever-patient editor, Heather Greene, whose encouragement was unwavering, and to all the team at Llewelyn. Thank you also to our dear friends Brianna, Jay, David, and John for your endless support—you inspire and enrich our lives.

And lastly, thank you also to those living and deceased who remain unnamed, whose communication and love has helped us better understand the realm of the magic and the mysteries of the beyond.

CONTENTS

TABLES AND FIGURES

INTRODUCTION

As custodians of living tradition, we have been fortunate to inherit a rich legacy of surviving British esoterica. Like many, we share in the hunger of all who long to rediscover its secrets. When we decided to write a book about restoring these practices, it was brought to our attention that there was one corpus of material that needed to be prioritized, that being the care and protection of the spirit realm.

Among many magic and spirit workers is a growing awareness of the footprint our mode of life is making on the unseen worlds. Those initiatory practices charged with maintaining the borderland between life and death are dwindling in numbers, and meanwhile its mistreatment is ever growing, whether by ignorance or design. The same disregard shown in history for the natural environment is repeating itself in the subtle realm of spirits.

There is an urgency for our and future generations to become educated in the responsible use of magic, to preserve the balance of subtle forces and facilitate our fellow humans in their voyage beyond the veil. For any individual who has ever wanted to make a real difference in the world, this is the most imminent and powerful cause that a magician can undertake.

In our own Scottish culture, the practice of resolving a haunting or spirit incursion is known as laying ghosts. This practice is still there today in the seemingly sleepy villages and local communities across the United Kingdom. Children are taught about laying ghosts and informed as to who in the village can be approached if the spirit world comes into collision with our own.

In these regional communities, such spiritual matters are taught "at the mother's knee" or "by the hearth," which is to say that they are transmitted generationally. It is taught that the world is not only what we see—much more remains unseen. There is a multiplicity of spirits (not just the deceased), and they are always present and active. No matter where you are, you can feel a sense that you are never truly alone even in the most remote locations. When it comes to the subject of ghosts, speculation about their existence is never really a topic, rather an expectation that if you have not experienced them yet, you soon will.

Our Background

When Rob was eight years old, his grandfather told him that the only true remedy for the fear of the unknown is to understand it. He also made it clear that the spirits of the dead are just people. Some are good while a few are not, but most are very ordinary, sharing all our human hopes, fears, and flaws. They can be generous and give guidance or ask for our help, and only a few desire to bring harm. The takeaway was that if you don't fear meeting a living person, then why would you fear the presence of a dead one?

Fear-driven denial is not native to the mind of a child; it is a behavior that is taught and reinforced. Just like Rob's grandfather, when our own children shared their interactions with spirits, we expressed that we were not only supportive but interested. Consequently, they naturally accepted what they had seen and did not attempt to irrationally justify it. To them, it was simply a reality. When they came of a reasonable age, we taught them about laying ghosts and, later, the intricacies of the art that they continue to pursue to this day.

When we first met thirty years ago, Rob was already involved in multiple initiatory traditions. Nonie did not know anything about the path she was stepping onto, only that it was nameless and felt true. She was awakened into a world of magic which was deeply cultural and authentic, and whose secrets burrow like a network of tunnels beneath the surface of daily life.

Laying ghosts is one of the many esoteric practices Nonie came to embrace as a part of the family. She was honored to be present when Rob's grandmother, a remarkable woman who, as a WWII veteran, consoled the dead and laid many souls to rest in her time. Nonie was also humbled to perform the service of sin-eating alongside Rob's mother and had the privilege of keening at her funeral.

Since the early days of our vocation in magic, people suffering from spirit activity have sought us out, an experience common to many magicians. It is assumed that because we engage in occultism, we are more likely to have the solution and tools to settle these problems. To deepen our understanding of laying ghosts, we turned to the study of medieval ceremonial magic, which is at the heart of many surviving British esoteric systems as well as the discipline of traditional necromancy specifically.

THE NECROMANTIC ARTS

The art of working with the dead, or necromancy (Gr. *nekromanteia*) has been documented for more than two thousand years. It is one of the most ancient and natural esoteric practices known to human society, but it is also one of the most maligned.

The medieval art of necromancy renewed these traditions, bringing together the strings of pre-Christian practices with the structure and nomenclature of ceremonial magic to create an integral system that would inspire the generations that follow. Its influence can be found in later magical practices including laying ghosts, but over the centuries, it would itself become fragmented and scattered.

Our passion to restore the fundamental wisdom of necromancy has led us into figurative dark corners with dusty manuscripts, putting together pieces of a puzzle to revive a corpus of knowledge which has been suppressed for more than seven centuries. Our direct experience of the Scottish custom of laying ghosts and other initiatory practices has given context and meaning to our research. The result is a cohesive system of identifying, classifying, and working with unquiet spirits rooted in authentic historical traditions which we have modernized for contemporary use.

Over the years, we have engaged in numerous investigations, resolved far more cases than not, and helped both the living and the dead in difficult circumstances. Using the methods described in this book, we have been able to competently diagnose the cause even in locations that had been the subject of months of disturbance or previously inconclusive investigation. We have been discreetly called upon by paranormal investigators, psychologists, spiritual leaders, and other professionals for assistance and advice. However, our most rewarding experiences are those where we have personally brought peace to lost souls, alleviated fear of the unknown, and restored balance to lives that were in turmoil.

The information presented in this book is a representation of the wisdom that augments our familial art of laying ghosts adjusted for a broader audience. It has been tried, tested, and trusted, based on decades of in-depth research and personal practice, and centuries of wisdom. It is the foundation upon which we base our own investigations and that we have taught to others.

It is our humble hope that in sharing this knowledge, we can inspire and empower you to protect and preserve the realm between life and death with compassion for those souls who journey through it.

How to Use This Book

Unquiet Voices is a practical resource for magicians, Pagans, and spirit workers interested in navigating unseen realms. Combining the principles of classical necromancy and modern investigative methods, the information will enable you to confidently recognize and identify the spirits of the dead, to know when they are present and how to diagnose their effects.

Rather than providing ceremony or rituals, this guide focuses on sciomancy, the art of necromantic investigation or communicating with the dead wherever they may be encountered.

Sciomancy is ultimately a practical magical art and not a standalone initiatory system, as there are no degrees, titles, or certificates. Its logical and practical approach does not take years to master and allows the practitioner to respond at a level they feel comfortable with. If you are called upon to do this work and are willing to dedicate yourself to its practice, you can learn the art of sciomancy.

Format

This book is divided into three sections. Part one is a discourse that explains the magical arcana of necromancy. The knowledge is presented in a sequential order to build on and clarify what appears before it, starting with a broad understanding of the invisible universe and drilling down into the specifics of how to identify types of deceased human spirits.

Part two focuses on the practical components of conducting a necromantic investigation, concluding with methods to lay an unquiet spirit. The information relies heavily on an understanding of the arcana presented in part one.

At the end is a lexicon of important terms used throughout this book and relevant to the study of necromancy.

Developing a Lingua Franca

Specificity and consistency in technical language is vital. Throughout this guide, we share the magical terminology we employ so that it may serve as a comprehensive lingua franca to describe important esoteric principles and classifications of spirits, many of which are Graeco-Latin words. The benefit of using the lexicon will become apparent in the development of a reliable frame of reference for sharing knowledge and understanding the technical aspects of necromancy.

A Different Approach

Some of the concepts found in this book are likely to be new to the reader or different from information previously encountered in the public domain. In preparation for this guide, we reviewed more than a thousand hours of amateur and professional investigations and hauntings to identify the most common errors and encounters. Rather than ruminate too heavily on the mistakes of others, we have aimed to arm the reader with a fuller understanding of the subject so that these errors can be avoided. The goal is to provide a workable system that can be used and understood. It is not meant to replace personal experience or the traditional wisdom of other esoteric systems.

A Universalist Approach

To understand the realms of the dead requires a thorough grasp of how the invisible universe functions. In this book, we have relied mostly upon teachings of early medieval arcana from the period before the revival of Jewish Qabalistic and Christian Renaissance magic in Europe. This less-studied style has a universalist approach and was very influential in preserving localized pre-Christian traditions. It also offers a three-world view that will make sense to many modern esotericists.

Spiritual Doctrines

Throughout this book are references to polytheism, reincarnation, and other principles of magical tradition that may not accord with your own religious experience or spiritual understanding. We ask only that you appreciate them in the context of historical European magic meanwhile remaining true to your own spiritual integrity. We each have pieces of a grand puzzle, and every perspective should not only be tolerated but respected as teachers of the singular truth to which all spiritualities ascend. If your convictions are authentic, they can never be threatened by innovative information, only confirmed and the depth of your understanding increased.

Cultural Application

Except for an occasional reference to the Scottish practice of laying ghosts, we have tried to take a common approach to the subject matter and suggest formulas rather than ascribe to the proclivities of any one practice or culture. We have also deliberately omitted or only hinted at material that should not be performed without a mentor. We anticipate that you will be able to embrace the principles being imparted and hope you will furnish your own practice and ability. For those individuals who, like ourselves, are custodians of traditions, we sincerely hope that this information is of benefit and will help your system flourish.

In this book, we provide you with the knowledge, understanding, and tools to inspire you to become a true sciomancer. You can become a stalwart guardian of the veil who takes the magic of necromancy from the smoky, dim seclusion of the temple and out into the dynamism of the real world, where spirits dance in the shadows and things that go bump in the night are terrifyingly real. The beauty and mystery of a new world awaits you, if you have the courage and compassion to answer the words whispered by unquiet voices.

PART I
THE ARCANA
OF UNSEEN

CHAPTER ONE

THE ARTS
OF NECROMANCY

Unquiet voices haunt us. They whisper to us, guide us, and beguile us. They tease us with their presence beyond the veil and at the fringes of our vision. Are they ancestors trying to help us, or monsters hoping to deceive us?

For centuries, we have tried to perceive the spirits of the dead, to classify them and know how to interact with them. Firsthand accounts verify that spiritual entities can be heard, seen, sensed, and conversed with, yet actual knowledge about the realm between death and beyond remains an unspoken mystery.

It is undeniable that ghosts are popular subjects not only for entertainment but as a genuine pursuit of understanding. But when people are faced with a serious dilemma that involves the spirit world, they often do not know whom to turn to. Those who try to remedy a situation may do more harm than good, despite their best intentions.

This book approaches the subject of laying unquiet spirits to rest from the magical art of necromancy, the medieval art of communicating with the dead from Europe. Deeply rooted in Pagan mystical traditions, medieval necromancy has for centuries pursued knowledge pertaining to the realms of the dead and the motivations of its shadowy inhabitants. Known for its sophisticated system of communicating with spirits of the deceased, its practice was vilified in history as the most diabolical of arts and remains largely misunderstood to this day.

The accumulation of magical understanding and experience associated with necromancy is eminently practical and therefore as relevant today as it was in the distant past. Meanwhile, the traditions that preserve this hidden wisdom are dwindling, and access to authentic information has become obscured.

TRADITIONS OF NECROMANCY

Communication with the dead has always been an important part of religious and spiritual thought, ever since the day when that first person lost loved ones and sought to share one more moment with them. The spirits of the deceased have simply crossed that bridge which leads to our next great adventure. Unlike other types of spirits contacted through magic, the dead have endured similar experiences and share our essential character. It is only natural that our curiosity would be directed toward understanding them.

Contrary to the sensational and popular image of the art, necromancy has always been an integral part of the evolving human story, abiding in every age and ethnicity. Regardless of what it is called or what name is used culturally, necromancy as a general concept and practice exists in all spiritual beliefs—from ancestor rites among indigenous peoples to the Roman Catholic cult of saints. We human beings have always sought to benefit from communication with the souls of those who have passed into the great mystery. Such communion inspires us to understand the mysteries of death and thus it inflames our philosophical minds.

Transmission of Knowledge

Necromancy is historically a discipline within the medieval magical tradition. Magic in that time was learned in a formal apprenticeship and still is among some living traditions. This education can be quite complex, forming the fundamental understanding necessary to effectively embrace a full magical vocation. During a period of up to seven years, the apprentice gains habitual discipline, cultivates pertinent skills, and learns the intricacies of ritual along with the multifaceted philosophy and magical theory of their line.

Conventionally, students learned the art under a teacher until they had achieved a level of competence that justified their own practice, when they too could take apprentices. Like trade vocations of the period, this system was usually organized in three levels or degrees: apprentice, companion, and master. Each master was responsible for the education of apprentices and the guidance of companions who would aid them in their rites. When the students completed their learning, they would be raised to the degree of master and recognized by their teachers as peers in the art.

Following the suppression of the twelfth-century Enlightenment in Europe, education was viewed as a threat to religion. The institutions of the Catholic Church attempted to curtail potentially dangerous ideas by controlling the doctrine of education itself. Contrary to that worldview, magicians felt that education should encourage the liberation of the mind and empower the will. They offered an independent stream of literati, often finding themselves philosophically in conflict with orthodoxy.

This contention led the medieval church into an open war of propaganda and ultimately the Inquisition, releasing countless polemics wielding the weapons of bigotry, ridicule, and denigration against proponents of intellectual freedom, especially magicians.

Unfortunately, as time passed, these same ecclesiastical opinions influenced the literature of magic so that the art appeared to degenerate in practice. Late ritual texts employ necromancy only occasionally, and its use is reserved for very base motives such as discovering hidden treasure. Where it does appear, it is often in increasingly corrupted formulae, sometimes deteriorated entirely into absurdity. The compassion, purpose, and wisdom of original necromancy appeared to be all but lost, and with it, the noble ideal of connecting the living with their loved ones beyond death and helping souls who may be suffering a traumatic experience following physical demise.

In the Renaissance and Enlightenment periods (sixteenth through nineteenth centuries) the emerging rationalists continued to denigrate magic and necromancy through mockery and ridicule. Whether propaganda of fear or parody, these misrepresentations have been inculcated within the academic establishment and are still with us today. They founded the context through which most people view the subject.

The word "necromancy" is now loaded with preconceived imagery, a singularly disturbing depiction that plays on collective primal fears of the unknown. No matter how reasonably we approach the subject or how sympathetically we try to comprehend it, this imagery lingers in the shadows of our minds. Drawn from the repulsion imposed historically by religious condemnation, today's sensational portrayal of necromancy has saturated a popular media that makes a trade of fear and horror as marketable commodities, insidiously reaffirming the dark image of the art.

Laying Ghosts

As necromancy became denigrated and persecuted, the opportunities to find a trained necromancer dwindled, yet the frequency and urgency of spirit incursions remained. In Scotland during the Reformation (ca. 1525–1560) and the rise of radical Protestantism, harsh religious suppression meant that people did not have recourse to a priest or magician who could administer rites to aid the deceased. The reformed church, which had led a bitter persecution against magicians, witches, and Catholics, further curtailed prayers and services to the dead by an act of Parliament stating "praying, reading, and singing, both in going to and at the grave, have been grossly abused, are no way beneficial to the dead, and have proved many ways hurtful to the living; therefore let all such things be laid aside."[1] It was not until the 1800s that funerary prayers were again allowed to be said in public and church burials were permitted.

Without the means to seek out a person skilled in the art of necromancy, communities began to deal with the problem themselves by applying ritualized and investigative methods often modeled on previous magical traditions.

The localized methods known to our family in Scotland were called laying ghosts (ghaists). Similar practices were known across Ireland, the United Kingdom, and where immigration occurred, such as the Appalachian and Ozark mountains where laying haunts or "haints" is recorded. While they varied from region to region, these practices shared many common magical elements born out of the more organized necromancy from which they descended. A description of a Scottish method:

> … When ghaists showed their pale faces in the days of yore, the
> ministers of the word laid them by praying; that is to say, they
> described circles, stood within them (for over the circumfer-
> ence of a circle no ghaist durst pass), and there they addressed

---

1   Westminster Assembly, *A Directory for the publique worship of God, throughout the three king-
    doms of England, Scotland, and Ireland together with an ordinance of Parliament for the taking
    away of the Book of common-prayer … .* Printed for Evan Tyler, Alexander Fifield, Ralph Smith,
    and John Field, 1644, 73. https://quod.lib.umich.edu/e/eebo2/A36061.0001.001?view=toc.

the foul spirit until it sank into the earth; they then crossed the
place with lines, which hindered them from rising anymore.[2]

This quote embodies three essential practices consistent with necromancy
that will be explored in later chapters: the use of protective magical circles in
which the magician stands, the belief that unquiet spirits rise from the ground,
and the use of crossed lines to prevent them from reentering a space.

While these regional practices of laying ghosts may not be strictly considered necromancy in its classical or medieval sense, they certainly may be perceived
as such in a broader context. It shared a comparable knowledge, ritualism, and
function, including magical methods of protection, conjuration, adjuration, abjuration, and various other elements consistent with traditional methods.

Laying ghosts was always practiced in private or secret and by someone who
was considered to represent a spiritual authority either through the integrity of
their character or their secret knowledge. Ironically, despite the strict imposition
of the reformed church to avoid contact with spirits, a community often expected
certain church elders to not only communicate with spirits but to discreetly bring
them to rest.

Often the means of resolution of an unquiet spirit lay in discovering what the
spirit needs and helping them to achieve those ends, as Rev. Walter Gregor has
recorded of a Scottish practice:

> …and there glided in noiselessly a lady sheeted in white, with
> a face of woe and told her story to the man on his asking her in
> the name of God what she wanted. What she wanted was done
> in the morning, and the spirit rested ever after.[3]

Paranormal Studies

In the postindustrial world of cold rationalism, the human need to understand
and communicate with the spirits of the departed exploded in the social consciousness of Victorian modernity with the formation of Spiritualism. Yet even

. . . .

2   John MacTaggart, *The Scottish Gallovidian Encyclopedia* (Glasgow, UK: Thomas D. Morison,
    1824), 313.

3   William Henderson, *Notes on the Folk-Lore of the Northern Counties of England and the Borders*
    (London: W. Satchell, Peyton and Co., 1879), 337.

in that nascent scientific age, Spiritualists were accused of being nefarious necromancers. Spiritualists themselves balked at the accusation and sought to distance themselves from what was considered such a distasteful term.

Of course, what they were doing was filling the position that the ancient necromancers had once maintained, namely being conduits between the realms of the dead and living, effecting the same work under a different moniker. Unfortunately, societal pressure based on the erroneous dark image of necromancy caused them to disavow a potential source of wisdom that could have brought accuracy to their own philosophy.

In our own digital age, the same impulse to understand the interaction between the living and the spirits of the dead has fueled an exponential rise in paranormal investigation. These researchers generally seek to prove the existence of the paranormal through scientific means and often attempt to understand why a spirit may be haunting a person, place, or object. Like their Spiritualist predecessors, paranormal investigators have been accused of engaging in a type of necromancy, and many similarly renounce the accusation, emphasizing that their methodology is scientific and not magical.

ORIGINS OF NECROMANCY

Necromancy as an organized practice has been a part of the documented history of ancient Greece from the eighth century BCE. It was this revered form of necromancy that laid the foundation for the philosophy and practices of the subsequent medieval art, although the practice is likely to be much older.

That necromancy is an ancient classical practice is confirmed by the erection of an oracle called the Nekromanteion, located among the Greek Epriot tribe known as the Thesprotians. This site is said to be located near the Acheron River, believed to be one of the five chthonic rivers of the classical underworld. Homer (ca. 800 BCE) refers to the Acheron as the location where Odysseus must make an offering to the dead and speak with the spirit of the prophet Tiresias.[4]

It is probable that like many of their Western descendants, the ancient Indo-Europeans believed that the entrance to the lands of the dead was found in the West, and the Nekromanteion may have alluded to this ideal. Interest-

· · · · · · · · · · · · · · · ·

4 Homer, *The Odyssey, with an English Translation by A. T. Murray, PhD, in two volumes,* trans. A. T. Murray. Originally published in 1919 by W. Heinemann (London) and G. P. Putnam's Sons (New York), 381, lines 510–513. https://archive.org/details/odyssey11home_.

ingly, the original homeland of the Indo-Europeans consisted in part of the area around the north of the Black Sea, and the waters that lay to the west would have included the Mediterranean region in which the Nekromanteion was located. In later historical periods, the Western European people would locate the land of the dead beneath or beyond the Atlantic, but the Atlantic was unknown to their archaic predecessors.

The rite that Odysseus undertook to communicate with the spirit of Tiresias was known as *Nekyia*. It involved physically descending into the depths of the Nekromanteion as a ritualized enactment of the journey into the realm of the dead to perform the rites of communication. When a magician seeks to descend into the dominions of the dead in a spiritual body and receive visions of communication, the process is called *katabasis*.

Medieval Necromancy

Medieval necromancy is a vast and multifaceted art that encompasses a specialized knowledge base and set of skills that enable us to communicate and work with the spirits of the deceased. The traditional arts of necromancy are divided into two methodologies. The first is called necyomancy. It is the direct evocation of the spirits of the dead, in which the necromancer attempts to call the spirit of the deceased into a space which is magically prepared for communication, usually for the purpose of acquiring knowledge or to procure a magical effect.

The second branch is called sciomancy and may be described as investigative necromancy, which involves finding and communicating with a spirit within the specific location where they are active. Agrippa speaks of these methods in his *Third Book of Occult Philosophy*, although somewhat obtusely:

> But there are two kinds of necromancy, the one called necyomancy, raising the carcasses, which may not be done without blood; the other sciomancy, in which the calling up of the shadow sufficeth.[5]

. . . .
5   Heinrich Cornelius Agrippa, *Three Books of Occult Philosophy* (Llewellyn's Sourcebook Series), ed. Donald Tyson (St. Paul, MN: Llewellyn Publications, 1992), 606.

Necyomancy

Necyomancy is named after the Greek process of Nekyia. It is most often performed in a dedicated temple, which emblematically represents the liminal space between the world of the living and that of the dead.

Medieval magicians continued to use the name of the original Greek oracle as the correct term for a necromancer's personal temple, the necromantium. As a permanent temple was often difficult to maintain, the means of communication, usually a specific consecrated mirror, was also often called a necromantium. The triangle of art in the famous grimoire, the *Goetia*, is a prime example of a necromantium as a mirror.

By employing necyomancy and drawing the spirit to the relative safety of a necromantium, the magician may then pursue the questioning of the spirit no matter where it ordinarily resides. To achieve this, a tangible link to the spirit of the deceased is obtained, allowing for specificity in engaging the identified spirit. These links are known as relics, and historically included not only the grave or tomb, but portions of the carnal remains of the individual. The theory is that spirits remain attached to the form which they had once inhabited and therefore the use of relics can induce the spirit, through their natural attachment, to return to their relic and it is to this practice that Agrippa is referring when he misleadingly states that necyomancy is the raising of carcasses and cannot be performed without blood. In truth, a relic need not be human remains nor require the use of blood; it can be any object that has a physical connection to the life of the deceased.

To date, modern authors who have ventured into the subject of necromancy have focused exclusively on necyomantic practices of evocation, all too often concentrating on the ethically questionable records of very late historical ritual manuals. Such practices are beyond the scope of this book and are, in our opinion, better suited to the instruction and guidance of an experienced mentor. Experience being the only true teacher, a written text is simply a tacit source of knowledge that can never provide the subtle nuances necessary for a safe, responsible, and successful practice.

Sciomancy

The second method of traditional necromancy, sciomancy, is all but forgotten yet eminently more practical. It requires the skill to detect human spirits in the place where they frequent and provides a means to diagnose the cause of unwanted spirit activity. It is this knowledge that can be applied to quell a disturbance or "haunting" caused by an unquiet spirit. It is more immediate and practical than the pursuit of necyomancy and has relevance to a variety of contemporary magicians and spirit workers. While necyomancy is generally a private pursuit for necromancers, sciomancy is a service that may be provided to help others, both living and dead.

Observations and Experiments

These historical necromancers employed what we might call an empirical process: forming a hypothesis, testing, observing, and recording. Their experiments informed them of the spirit world in ways that lay outside the established religious doctrine. They proceeded to adjust their understanding at a time when doctrine was considered infallible, falling further and further from the church's teachings. They had the courage to embrace the verity of their observations over the imposition of religious edicts, even though these truths were ultimately founded on disavowed Pagan philosophies.

From this long history of recorded observation and experiences, necromancers developed a system of classification to recognize and identify the presence of a spirit. This information was handed down from one generation of magicians to another but became fragmented as necromancy declined. Although elements of its wisdom were retained, the value of its purpose was misnamed in grimoires and obscured under other practices. These may have been deliberate attempts to redirect attention away from the forbidden art of necromancy, but over the years it has led to misunderstanding and misinformation.

DAEMONOLOGY

In both of its forms, necromancy is a complete and significant branch of the magical discipline devoted to the study of special classes of spirits of the lower, or sublunary, realms. These entities, which include human spirits, are defined as being immortal but subject to reincarnation. Possessing free will, they are neither inherently good nor bad but play a role in choosing their own destinies. Traditionally they are called daemones, (L. from Gr. *daimones*) and their study is called Daemonology.

Native European faiths embrace a universe of diverse entities with which they maintain strong cultural relationships. The Pagan practice of forming magical alliances with these spirits depends upon a mutual arrangement wherein the spirits perform a service or services in return for something they desire. An example might be gaining favor from a daemon to grow crops in exchange for an offering of their first fruits. Usually the method of reciprocity a magician would employ is to make an offering of incense.

When contracting a spirit, the magician has the control to refuse any unacceptable or unreasonable transaction. Although historically there is some indication that animal sacrifices were offered to some spirits, they are not considered necessary in ceremonial magic and are considered unethical in most countries today. Often perfumes or other innocuous methods are more than acceptable.

Demonizing Daemones

The debate about whether the human soul is daemonic continued among Christian theologians for more than a millennium. By the twelfth century, the powers of the church identified daemones as nonhuman evil entities and denounced any practice that would seek to contract or otherwise respectfully engage with them. This view is reflected in the warning given in the grimoire *Liber Juratus Honorii* (*The Sworn Book of Honorius*) regarding the conjuration of certain spirits:

> And concerning these, a Christian should seldom or never let himself enter into dealings with them, nor should their advice be believed…And it is especially the pagans who operate with these, and very rarely should Christians.[6]

Just prior to the advent of the Inquisition and its subsequent tortures and executions, the practice of magic was infested by the religious politics of the day, and the rituals of evocation transformed from a respectful congress with daemones to a coercive methodology which sought to dominate and enslave spirits in the name of God.

The medieval church declared that offerings to any spirits other than God were a sin. They defamed the Pagan methods of spirit evocation, calling it *nigro-*

. . . .
6   Honorius of Thebes, *The Sworn Book of Honorius: Liber Juratus Honorii (illustrated edition)*, ed. Joseph Peterson (Lake Worth, FL: Ibis Press, 2016), 283.

mancy, Latin for the "black art" or "dark art," implying it was a disreputable practice of nefarious origin.

Daemonology in Law

At a later period, the term "nigromancy" was used to differentiate between what the church declared to be a licit form of magical practice and that which they deemed illicit. The licit practice was dominating the daemon in the name of God and forcing them to comply with the magician's intentions. The Pagan practice of making reciprocal commerce with a spirit was considered the work of evil and was forbidden, forming part of the rationale for the suppression of remaining vestiges of the old religions. Simply put, those magicians who did not fear and enslave spirits were not only malefic, they were also unlawful.

Protestant King James VI of Scotland and I of England, an ardent and cruel advocate for witch-hunting, emphasizes this differentiation in his 1597 three-part magnum opus *Daemonologie*. Written in the form of a dialogue, his character Epistemon expounds:

> "...for they say that the witches are servants only, and slaves, to the devil, but the necromancers are his masters and commanders."[7]

The fact that he misnames the conjurers as necromancers and the nigromancers as the witches is indicative of the indiscriminate confusion in magical terminology common at the time. Part of his argument asserts that both forms of magic should be illegal, but in doing so he maintains the opinion that one form is more tolerable.

DECLINE OF NECROMANCY

After the inception of the name nigromancy, its relationship and similarity to the older name of necromancy became so confused that the two became interchangeable terms. By the seventeenth century, ritual texts reputed to be necromantic primarily contained ceremonies for the evocation of nonhuman daemones. They seldom included rites for raising the spirits of the dead but when they did, they were corrupted and morally ambiguous.

. . . .

7   Donald Tyson, ed., *The Demonology of King James I* (Woodbury, MN: Llewellyn Publications, 2011), 68.

During this period, as "necromancy" replaced "nigromancy" in many texts, its translation ("the black arts") became a blanket term for any magic considered to be illicit. It created the impression of a shadowy cult that served the whims of devilish fiends. This view supported the suppression of alternative spiritualities and fueled the tragedy of the witch craze.

Disambiguation

In more recent centuries, historians and ethnologists have made clear efforts to address the confusion between the practices of necromancy and nigromancy made by proponents such as James VI and I as well as to educate the populace about their cultural history. As an example, this definition from a secondary school book from 1915: "Necromancy, the art of questioning the spirits of the dead; not to be confused with nigromancy or black magic, i.e., magic wrought by the agency of evil or heathen spirits."[8]

Despite these efforts, some modern scholars continue to perpetuate the confusion between the terms. To disentangle the Gordian knot of magical practices and literary confusion requires precision in our use of language to express a simple and clear set of definitions consistent with the meaning of the words themselves and sensitive to the original sense of these practices.

Daemonology refers to the study of those entities called daemones and includes the practice of spirit evocation. When the evocation is in accordance with ancient Pagan ideals of civil commerce with these spirits, the practice has come to be called nigromancy.

Necromancy is those arts that deal with communication with the spirits of the dead. As the human soul is classified as daemonic, necromancy is a specialized branch of daemonology. When communication with the dead is pursued with a sense of compassion and seeks to resolve the cause of a spirit disturbance, it may justifiably be considered a subbranch of nigromancy.

THE ROLE OF THE MAGICIAN

Ultimately, this is a book about magic. There is no lack of fascination for magic in the modern world or for embracing and exploring the wisdom of our mystical ancestors. While magic is a spiritual path, it also serves as a practical response to

---

8   E. P. Roberts, *The Isle of Gramarye Or Tales Of Old Britain Part I* (London: MacMillan Company Ltd, 1915), 114.

real life events yet is in no way a shortcut—after all, magicians refer to their operations as "workings" for a reason. It offers alternative tools to navigate through the storms of this world.

Magic is an exciting adventure of revelation and experience. While some think of the practice of magic as an artifact of bygone days, the continuing evolution of the art in today's world of information, technology, and curiosity is both an incredibly relevant and exhilarating quest.

In fact, the practice of magic has become wildly popular, which places us in a thrilling historical period in the art's development. Communities have grown exponentially in the past few decades, and enthusiasm for magic resonates with more people today than throughout its long and storied history. Unfortunately, a conscientious and disciplined effort to recover or even compile arcana and to experiment and test them has yet to be as fully embraced.

As a sciomancer, it is important to hone your abilities and knowledge of magic so you can effectively respond to a spirit disturbance as and when needed. In addition, you must also cultivate key personal strengths and spiritual fortitude.

Calm Reason

Magic is first and foremost a practical application of enigmatic and subtle forces. In your attempts to construct a thorough appreciation of the nuances in your magical practice, you must be cautious of imposing your preconceptions and biases upon the knowledge and symbols you employ. Exercising self-examination with a disciplined mind and questioning your thoughts and behaviors is no easy task, but you must cultivate introspection to truly comprehend the wisdom inherent in the arts of magic.

Reason is also the rule and guide when acquiring new esoteric knowledge, assembling its symbolic language, and understanding its methodology and philosophies. The same is true of the investigative process. When you are working with real people, real trauma, and real spirit crises, there is no place for self-delusion, reactionary emotions, misinformation, or shortcuts. Reason and logic in your methodology is essential to offer straightforward explanations and efficacious solutions.

Compassion for the Living and the Dead

The word "compassion" literally means to share the suffering of others. In the context of an unquiet spirit, care should drive you to resolve the event with a view to the best outcome for all those involved, living and dead. Poignantly, compassion is achieved when an event is approached with a balance of dispassion and mindful consideration.

Fundamentally, the magician must maintain an inherent compassion but remain guarded against sympathy becoming a deleterious distraction. An overtly sympathetic position toward the living can engender subtle misrepresentations founded upon the desire to believe wholeheartedly or emotionally identify with the sufferer's distress. We must remember that although the trauma may be real, it may not have a spiritual cause.

Concerning the spirits involved, compassion demands that we also consider their spiritual needs. Ghosts are temporary residents between life and what comes after, and remaining in this state too long is ultimately harmful to them. We can aid them to resolve the issues that prevent them from moving on, but it may be necessary at times to mitigate predatory or dangerous effects. In these circumstances, the conviction to take action when needed is equally as compassionate.

Willingness to Learn

One of the defining characteristics of a magician is to seek truth. This requires the faculty to shift your perception at will rather than rely on the accidents of external stimuli to change your point of view. You must be willing to overcome conditioning and face the imagined terrors that might still dance in your mind. Anyone who works candidly in magic understands that the more you learn, the less you know. The questions will always be greater than the answers. Like the necromancers of the past, you must find the courage to approach this body of knowledge and the invisible world of spirits from a healthy perspective with an open mind to value it as a truly noble endeavor.

Knowledge of the Arcana

In the practice of sciomancy, it is essential to have a comprehension of the unseen world and how and why spirits manifest. It behooves us to educate ourselves as much as possible when it comes to comprehending spiritual causes and the nature of the mysterious wonders that interpenetrate all reality. To serve the role of a magician as "one who knows" is a difficult but worthy aspiration. To the world at large, you will be the person others will engage when the mysterious rises to challenge their mundane certainty. People will seek you out, desperate and confused, and they will expect you to have answers that will bring them clarity and security.

Practical Skills

Necromancy has adopted expedient applications based on practical experimentation and observation. What remains after centuries of pragmatic utilization may be considered authoritative. Obviously you should explore the viability of any technique intended for potential use, but you can have reasonable confidence in time-tested methods.

An effective investigative methodology is integral to the practice of necromancy when applied in the field. The modern necromancer must understand observation techniques and develop a skilled interview process and an efficient procedural model. Therefore, there are some superficial similarities between sciomancy and paranormal investigation, though they are quite distinct in their intent. Beyond these investigative tools, it is essential that a necromancer develop the competent faculty to see and hear spirits, to facilitate communication with the dead. You must also be able to magically protect yourself and others, use language and words to magical effect, cleanse spaces, and perform magical rites.

Precommitment to a Resolution

Because sciomancy is taxing and at times tedious, it should be approached as a marathon, not as a sprint. While it can occasionally be dangerous, this work can more often be emotionally overpowering. Every investigation is unique and may need to be repeated until enough information can be gathered, allowing you to proceed to a suitable resolution. On the other hand, there are times when a lengthy investigation is rendered impossible. You must remain both flexible and well prepared for whatever conditions you may be asked to engage in. Anyone who decides to become a sciomancer should conscientiously cultivate the qualities of endurance and fortitude, humility, and professionalism.

CHAPTER TWO

ARCANA OF THE UNSEEN WORLDS

The study of magic is an ocean as wide as it is deep. Its pursuit entails much more than the manipulation of subtle universal forces; it demands an accumulated and consistent body of knowledge to affect conscientious change and avoid potentially adverse consequences.

Necromancy is a serious and comprehensive discipline within the art of magic, and as such can comprise a lifetime of study. It is essential to possess at least a rudimentary knowledge of the principles that influence the unseen world, including the manifestation of a spirit, whether an apparition is likely to be sentient, and to know with confidence whether danger is real or imagined.

In this and the following chapters, we will focus on building essential occult knowledge pertaining directly to the art of diagnosing and resolving spirit driven disturbances to help the modern practitioner thoughtfully implement their art. The universality and practicality of this information will become self-evident.

We encourage you to seek to understand the material presented and apply your own logic and experience to critically question this body of knowledge. It is not offered as a replacement for any living tradition or cultural spirituality, ancient or modern, but as a comparative collection of authentic principles that can enrich your own practice.

ARS ET SCIENTIA

In medieval European tradition, magic is considered both a science and an art, based on key principles dating to classical times. Embracing both accumulative knowledge and practical skills developed through experimentation and observation, it consists of both the *ars vetrus* and the *ars nova*, the old art and the new.

Ars vetrus refers to those tested and proven skills of magic, encompassing the accepted knowledge, rites, or magical philosophy derived from the application and exploration of magical principles. It is the corpus of wisdom refined over centuries of observation, experimentation, and confirmation of universal truths passed in a line from master to student. Complete secrecy protected it from profane influence, resulting in these teachings becoming known as arcana, occult or esoteric knowledge.

Ars nova describes the experiments that push the envelope of a magician's comprehension. Ars nova becomes ars vetrus when the understanding gleaned from those experiments has been tested against the principles of magic and successfully and seamlessly integrated into the system.

Arcana

Magic has never been considered an abrogation of the laws of nature; rather, it is a holistic approach of intentionally creating change in harmony with the processes of universal forces. These forces are described as secret laws or principles of magic—in a word, arcana. More than theoretical speculation, the arcana provides an understanding of the mechanics of how magic works which has been tested by generations of practitioners. This knowledge forms the basis of the ars vetrus, making medieval magic eminently suitable as a comparative methodology to understand the realm of the dead.

By understanding the arcana of magic, we can learn to grasp the complexities of realms beyond our temporal existence. These universal laws remain an objective and observable reality and naturally find their reflection in the various forms of esoteric thought that permeate nearly all cultures and religious spiritualities. The same forces and phenomena the medieval necromancer observed are witnessed by countless individuals all over the globe. It is only the societal perspective and symbolic language that gives the appearance of confusion and divergence, yet when analytically deconstructed, any apparent dissimilarity is revealed to be illusion.

Vocabulary

Most academics who study medieval and Renaissance magic see a relationship to philosophies that are described as Neoplatonism and assume that magic is founded on these ideals. However, Neoplatonism is a purely intellectual pursuit and therefore cannot be synonymous with magic, which is ultimately defined by its accrued practical observation. It would be more accurate to say that medieval magicians borrowed the language and some established concepts of neoclassical thought to explain and preserve the arcana of magic as it was known to them.

While the nomenclature of the arcana of medieval and Renaissance magic is primarily rooted in the classical languages, its pragmatic character affords us a useful lexicon that can be employed universally regardless of the origins of our own independent traditions. When you are called to a spirit disturbance, it is likely that you will need to engage with others who do not share your personal mysticism. Precision in language is even more urgent in cases of spirit events that bring together witnesses and participants from diverse backgrounds and beliefs in a single location. Historically, the terminology and philosophical explanations of arcana vary slightly between lines of traditions. The version presented here is what we find to be the clearest and use in our own practice of ceremonial magic, including sciomantic investigations.

A UNIVERSE IN EVERY ATOM

Primarily, magical philosophy is pantheistic, meaning the divine source and the manifest universe are essentially one body. This theory postulates that when matter is reduced to its finest or smallest part, the fullness of divinity is represented in every individuated primeval particle. This is the principle behind ancient Greek atomic theories as contemplated by Leucippus, Democritus, and Epicurus. The Greek word *atomos* means indivisible or the smallest possible division of matter, conceived in magical speculation as a spark of the divine light. Modern scientific atomic theories differ in their concept of indivisibility and should not be confused with the original philosophy referred to here.

In many magical texts, these fundamental points of divine light are also referred to as philosophical fire. This fire is neither natural flame nor the archetypal fire described in esoteric elemental theory; rather, it is the very essence of being.

Prime Material

In the ancient understanding, these sparks or atoms are described as existing in the void and are gathered together or scattered apart, moving according to a divine pattern, ultimately creating and dissolving material forms. The atoms are eternal, but the forms created by this evolution are transient and temporary. Collectively, these atoms form the transformative substance of the universe, which Aristotle describes as *hyle* and is associated with the alchemical concept of the prime material.

Coagula

The gathering of atoms together is called coagula and ruled by agape, also known as the law of attraction. Various permutations and collations of atoms within the void are grouped first by idea and then as a temporary form. Coagula is often considered to be esoterically feminine in nature, symbolized by the divine mystery of pregnancy and birth. Just as the womb has the capacity to form life, so can the body of the universe manifest forms within its varied parts. The animated universe, with the facility to bring into due form disparate ideas, is sometimes known in magic as the Soul of the World.

Solve

Conversely, the action when atoms diffuse and separate is called solve, from the Latin *solvere*, meaning to dissipate or dissolve. Through the law of repulsion, atoms expand outward; forms and ideas break apart, allowing atoms to become available to attract together in new ways. Thus the process of separation is generative and therefore considered esoterically masculine. All manifest forms are in a process of *solve* due to the motion of their existence.

Conjunctio

The interplay of both *solve* and *coagula* creates what is known as *conjunctio*, or primordial mercury. In this way, conjunctio in its various manifestations is the foundational principle behind transformation and ideal form.

Together, these three primordial modalities describe a dynamic universe consistent with a medieval worldview in which matter does not disappear; it is renewed and transformed into a constant synergy of creation and destruction.

Solve

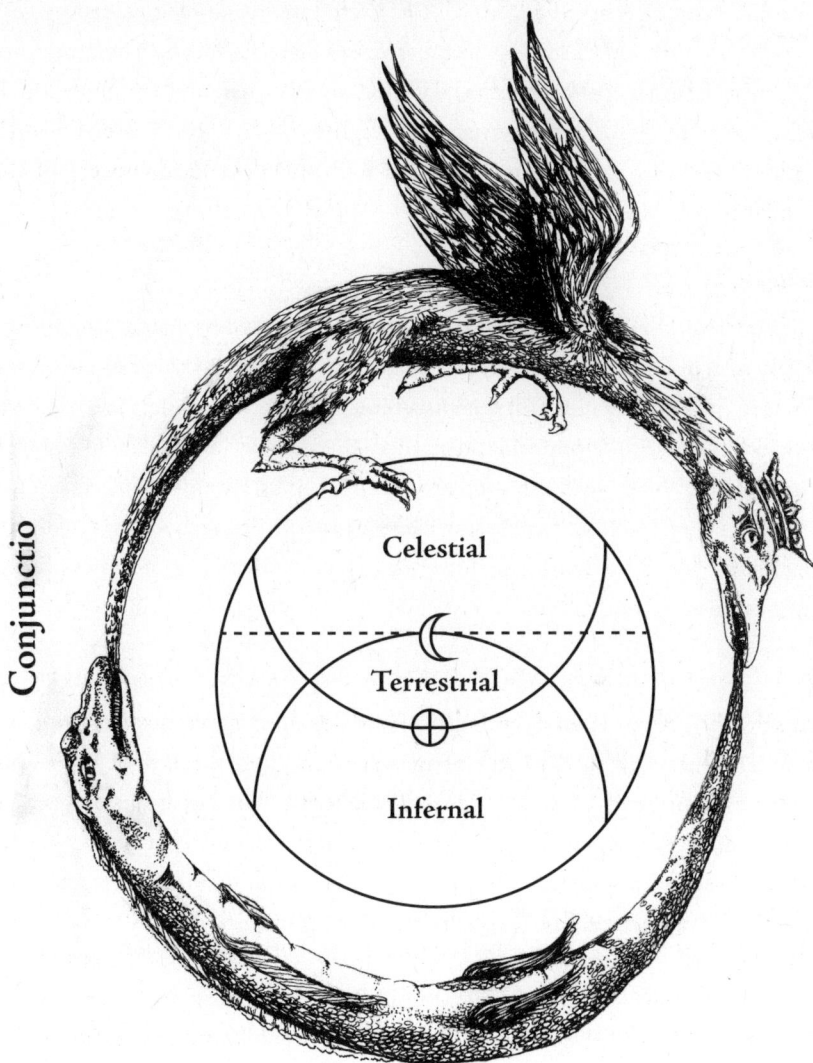

Conjunctio

Celestial

Terrestrial

Infernal

Coagula

The Three Realms and the Primordial Modalities

These same principles apply to all existence, from the formation of the cosmos to the reincarnation of souls and the manifestation of spirits.

Three States of Hyle

The constant motion of atoms, called kinesis or movere, is caused by the interplay of solve, coagula, and conjunctio that affects the density of hyle, which is loosely described in occultism as manifesting in one of three primary states or conditions: aether, pneuma, and phasma. An understanding of these three states of universal substance and how they transition from one to the other is critical to the practical art of sciomancy.

Magical doctrine teaches that potentiality and form are dependent upon the density of hyle. Phasma is a dense state of hyle, pregnant with potentiality while aether, as the lightest, is the most enduring, and pneuma is the balancing state between them. These three states are also representative of the quintessential nature of ancient Indo-European divisions of mythological spheres of existence; namely, the celestial realm, the terrestrial realm, and the infernal realm (also called the underworld or the chthonic realm).

Aether

The first state, aether, is the lightest gathering of hyle, where the space between the atomic particles is the greatest. It is considered the phenomenal reality of those worlds inhabited by celestial entities. It is also the essential nature of the numinous soul, which is eternal because of its aetheric substance.

Pneuma

As the hyle coalesces further, it forms the second state of density known in Greek as *pneuma* and in Latin as *spiramen*. Pneuma is the balanced state of equilibrium that permits independent physicality of form in accordance with the laws of nature. Among the realms abiding in this second or middle state of density is the world we inhabit as incarnate human beings.

Phasma

Finally, the densest coalescence of hyle is perceived as a viscous liquid light known as phasma, and the worlds existing in this state are conceived as infernal or chthonic realities. Phasma may be loosely translated as "moldable light," as it is dense enough to be sculpted to create an effect. As such, it is necessary for phasmic conditions to be coalesced enough for a disincarnate spirit to interact with our reality.

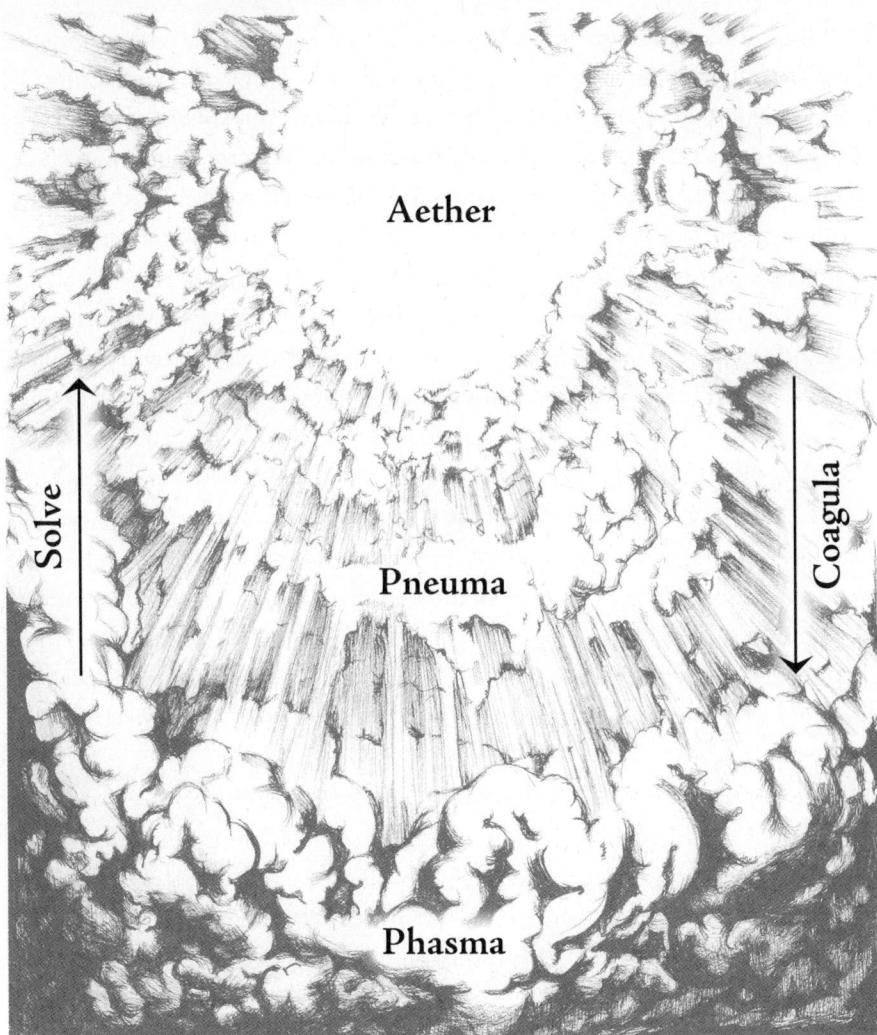

Three States of Hyle: Aether, Pneuma, and Phasma. Aether is the lightest and most celestial matter. It is the substance of souls. Phasma is a denser and more malleable substance of the spirit body that can be shaped into form.

THE SUBLUNARY REALM

The aetheric or celestial realities are described in astral terms; that is, representing the firmament or heavens. All worlds below the celestial realm are referred to as sublunary. In the ars vetrus of medieval Europe, the moon is perceived as a lens, receiving the powers of the firmament and casting the astrological influences into our reality.

This perspective is too often overlooked in the history of magical philosophy, but it is fundamental to understanding the rationale of the art. As described in a version of the *Picatrix* from the thirteenth century: "You should pay attention to the Moon in all workings…for she received the influences and impressions of all the stars and planets and pours them down onto the inferior things of this world."[9]

By the Renaissance, the focus in historical magic had shifted from the sublunary realm to the superlunary or celestial spheres. This meant there was a dissolution in the understanding of the arcana. Magic cannot alter the eternal influences of heaven, but it can bring potentiality into form through the changeability inherent in the sublunary admixture of elements.

The magician attempts to develop the faculty to willfully condense pneuma into phasma, implant that substance with a function or intelligence, and thence liberate it to create the desired change. According to magical theory, the coalescence of a phasmic form (*eidolon*) excites an internal motion according to the nature of its intelligence (*eides*). This motion is the actualized potential in the idea, which Aristotle named *energia*. When the energia is potent enough, the ideal form is projected into the phenomenal existence of an established world. In short, it becomes a "real" thing.

The process is natural, but understanding how it occurs reveals that it can be exploited according to will. When a magician works an operation, it is this process that they are consciously engaging in. Consequently, the practical work of magicians is primarily concerned with the nature of the sublunary realm through the manipulation of phasma. This is the root of the mechanics behind the emergence of spirits into our physical environment as well as the use of amulets, talismans, circles, and almost every aspect of functional magic.

9   John Michael Greer and Christopher Warnock, trans., *The Complete Picatrix: The Occult Classic of Astrological Magic Liber Atratus Edition* (n. l.: Renaissance Astrology Press, 2011), 70.

Table 1: Three Realms and Their Correspondences

Realm	Celestial	Terrestrial	Infernal
Alternate Names	Firmament Heavenly Astral	Earthly Middleworld	Chthonic Underworld
Lunar Influence	Superlunary	Sublunary	Sublunary
Quality	Endurance	Stability	Transformation
Density of Hyle	Aether	Pneuma	Phasma
Spirit	Soul	Mind	Spirit
Primordial Modality	Solve	Conjunctio	Coagula
Alchemical Symbol	Sulphur	Mercury	Salt

Cosmoi: Many Worlds

Due to an indefinite number of atoms in the sublunary realm, an indefinite number of worlds or cosmoi are considered to exist, formed through the influence of coagula to draw atoms together and conjunctio to hold them in place. Of these innumerable worlds, seven are closely associated or considered to be abutted against one another. Our sense of these worlds is that they share the same space but are out of phase with each other. The physical cosmos, that in which we as incarnated beings live our lives, is also one of these seven established worlds.

Medieval ceremonial magic was influenced not only by classical philosophy but also by both Hebrew and Christian mysticism of the time. It is from Hebrew that an allegory was borrowed to serve as a model to chart the relationship of these seven cosmoi. This is the concept of the Seven Earths, seven planes of sublunary existence separated by seas that exert a powerful influence on each of the others. There are a few lists bearing Hebrew names for these worlds; although they make a fascinating study in their entirety, only two are relevant in the art of necromancy. The first is our own living world, which is called *Cheled* in Hebrew according to Stephen Skinner.[10] The other is named *Arqa*.

Arqa: The Land of the Dead

Arqa is the Hebrew name for the world where the souls of the dead retire between lives, comparable to the Greek Hades. Within Arqa is a region euphemized as the "Little Eden" that can be equated with the classical Greek Elysium, a numinous domain void of tribulations. While the Little Eden is located within a sublunary and phasmic world, it is composed of the most rarefied hyle or aether, sharing the essential numinous nature of the soul itself.

Beyond the two realms human souls traverse, the other five worlds have their own phenomena, peoples, and cultures. The study of all seven worlds is known as daemonology. This study and the place necromancy holds in it will be the subject of chapter 4.

Metacosmos: The Sea Between Realms

The unformed space between worlds is depicted as seas and waters, which are collectively called the metacosmos by Epicurus (341–270 BC). The metacosmos is of the nature of solve, which causes the dissolution of form to occur constantly. In the Hebrew scheme, the metacosmos is called *Telom*, meaning "the deep," and any straits between worlds are referred to as *Bohu* and *Tohu*, meaning "seas" and "waters." One could imagine these seas (or metacosmoi) as interpenetrating zones, neither entirely of one world nor another but indiscriminately imbued with the nature of both.

Qarth Arqa

The metacosmic sea between the world of the living and that of the dead—that is, between Cheled and Arqa—was conceived as being a frigid and turbulent zone. The idea of coldness was a philosophical analogy to explain the peculiar phenomena indicating the presence of a bound human spirit, namely a distinct drop in temperature. This led them to name it Qarth Arqa, *qarth* translating as "cold."

A way to conceptualize this allegory is to imagine that our physical world is an island in a great sea. Across the sea is another island surrounded in mist,

10   Stephen Skinner, *The Complete Magician's Tables* (London: Golden Hoard Press, 2006), 149.

on which stands a walled palace with a gate where the souls of the dead go to rest after life. The palace is Little Eden, the distant island is Arqa, and the strait between the two islands is Qarth Arqa, dividing our worlds.

The Drowning Sea

The name "Qarth Arqa" was almost lost to the history of magic but for one single reference in the *Pseudomonarchia Daemonum* by the Dutch physician and occultist John Wierus (1515–1588). The text contains a long list of spirits and their influences, and under the description of the spirit named Gamigin, a supposed diabolical marquise, he reports the following:

> ...he brings also to pass, that the souls, which are drowned in the sea, or which dwell in purgatory (which is called Cartagra, that is, affliction of souls) shall take airy bodies, and evidently appear and answer to interrogatories at the conjuror's commandment...[11]

The term *Cartagra* is evidently a linguistic corruption based on an attempt to latinize the Hebrew *Qarth Arqa*, here said to thematically mean "the affliction of souls." The root of the word "affliction" originally carried the sense of self-imposed purging or an act of humility, implying the self-created act of purification or catharsis in which the soul needs to successfully pass through via this process.

The allegory of the tribulations experienced by spirits trapped in this region is depicted as human souls drowning in the sea, where the human spirits are bound in the metacosmos, submerged in the turbulence of Qarth Arqa.

All human spirits found inhabiting Qarth Arqa are in some form of distress, bound by their attachments to a life that should be resolved so that their soul may be liberated to proceed into the Little Eden. Yet, the divine plan does not forsake these spirits; the essential nature of all metacosmoi is dissolution, and ultimately every spirit in this shadowy borderland will face dissolution of their form whether they shed it willingly or by the erosion of time. In so doing, their souls will be liberated from their phasmic body and align once again to their eternal nature.

. . . .

11   John Wierus, *Pseudomonarchia Demonum* in Reginald Scott ed., *The Discoverie of Witchcraft, 1st edition*, book XV (New York: Dover, 1972), 223.

For the purposes of necromancy, the borderland or sea of Qarth Arqa is further broken into seven regions representing a symbolic geography of the experiences a spirit has following their earthly demise. Referred to as the Seven Hebrew Hells, they form a major theme of necromantic theory. We will return to fully explore the Hells in chapter 5.

Chapter Three

Cosmology
of the Soul

Like most esoteric traditions, the ars vetrus embraces the concept of an immortal soul and the process of reincarnation. The cosmology of the soul repeats the pattern of the multiverse being formed of the same divine substance. As recorded by astronomer and philosopher Giordano Bruno (1548–1600), "Since the soul is not found without the body, and yet is not body, it may be in one body or in another and pass from body to body."[12]

The word "soul" possibly derives from a Proto-Germanic word, *saiwalo*, thought to mean "belonging to the sea," capturing the essence of the journey of the soul across the metacosmic waters to the island of the dead, where a soul finds rest between lives.[13]

By experience and understanding gained through many lives, it is believed that every soul is engaged in a perpetual evolution, moving ever toward apotheosis or godhood. The numinous reality which lies between lives is the soul's natural state and integral to its eternal vocation.

Accumulated experiences of the soul throughout its many previous incarnations dictate the composition of the challenges or lessons for the next life. This

. . . .

12 *The Atlantic Monthly*, "The Trial Opinions, and Death of Giorano Bruno by William R Thayer, Vol LXV March 1890," 289. https://www.theatlantic.com/magazine /archive/1890/03/the-trial-opinions-and-death-of-giordano-bruno/633462/.

13 "Soul," Online Etymology Dictionary, https://www.etymonline.com/word /soul#etymonline_v_23918.

process is called *adrastia*, named after a lesser-known ancient Hellenic goddess of fate to whom even the great gods were said to adhere when they heard her goat-skinned drum. Thus, according to the rules of adrastia, the soul decides upon the qualities of the life they are to assume next and chooses the best time, place, and conditions to be born. The choices the soul makes as to the circumstances of birth are the logic that underpins natal astrology.

THE ENS

The nature of the eternal soul is the penultimate contemplation of all spiritualities. In magical philosophy, the soul (or ens) is both individuated and, at the same time, one with the entirety of the divine source. This is not a paradox—the divine is fully represented within each of its singular parts. The soul is immortal and divine, eternal and aetheric.

Numen

In magical arcana, the ens is described as a single spark of divine light. It draws around itself aether, forming a luminous cloud called a numen. When the ens is in a disincarnate form, the numen can sometimes be perceived with the naked eye as a bright orb or as light leaving the body at the time of death. The ancients called the numen the form of fire. French philosopher Jean Bodin (1529–1596) is reported to argue that the spheric appearance of the soul is proof of the disembodied existence of spirits:

> …and so likewise the souls of men departed, if corporeal (which he most easily contends) to be of some shape, and that absolutely round like Sun and Moon, because that is the most perfect form,…therefore all spirits are corporeal he concludes, and in their proper shapes round.[14]

. . . .

14 Democritus Junior, *The Anatomy of Melancholy: What It Is, with All the Kinds, Causes, Symptoms, Prognostics, and Several Cures of It* (London: William Tegg & Co., 1849), 117. Originally published 1621, from 1845 edition: https://archive.org/details /anatomyofmelanch00burtuoft/page/116/mode/2up.

Genius

The genius is the intellect of the soul, which is impressed upon the substance of the numen. It is this genius that individualizes the ens and grants it the means to pursue self-awareness, its core disposition that persists eternally throughout its immortal existence. The genius can be referred to as representative of the true self, as it is the consistent persona of the soul that is in a state of evolution.

Memorix

The immortal ens does not discriminate. It only understands its existence through experience and memory. This function is called memorix, and it alludes to the faculty of the soul to filter and assimilate the experiences of the soul in its various incarnations.

MENS

While essentially singular in nature, the soul becomes more complex when it incarnates. The immortal nature of the ens does not comprehend the illusions of time or place, nor does it have a sense of survival. To function in a sublunary incarnation, the soul creates a temporary interface to facilitate the accumulation of living experience. This interface is called the *mens*, or mind. The mens makes up the persona of an individual but is a temporary creation that relates to a single incarnation only. When that incarnation has reached its terminus, the mens is no longer required and the knowledge is assimilated into the memory and experience of the greater ens.

The mens is described as composed of two parts: the animus, which interfaces with the suprarational aetheric world, and the anima, which interacts with the emotive and instinctual phasmic realities.

The Animus

The animus functions as what we consider to be the intellect, or the *nous* in Greek. It is the processing faculty from which we derive logic. It relies on *ratiocinatio* (reasoning), and its purpose is to dispassionately filter and analyze a being's personal experience. It allows the soul to perceive linear existence and quantify and qualify knowledge, making sense of what would otherwise be senseless stimuli.

In some esoteric traditions that prioritize the virtue of the rational mind as superior, the animus is elevated in status and is referred to as the "higher self" or, in other more modern ceremonial practices, the Holy Guardian Angel. It is often erroneously thought of as the true self, a term that should be reserved for the ens alone. This tendency is echoed in modern psychology, in which the rational mind is mistaken for a sense of individuality, wherein referring to "I" indicates the ego. But in truth, the rational mind is not a personality—it is a powerful function of our human condition. Devoid of emotion, it filters and interprets our experience through which we perceive value and a sense of progression that helps us understand consequence and determine a reasonable course of action.

The Anima

The second adjunct, the anima, is created to sustain life through instinct and emotion. By activating the drive to overcome adversity, it initiates the creative imbalance that propels animation so the ens can extract virtue out of the experience.

The faculty of the anima is the imaginatrix (phantasia). The cultivation of imagination is an important faculty central to the practice of magic. It can be refined and matured, and when directed, incites innovation, art, and invention. In magic, it is harnessed to effect change and transformation, but when one's control is lax, it has the detrimental potential to create delusion. The magician must be diligent in applying reason to imagination; maintaining that careful balance unleashes the transformative power latent in all souls.

Due to its function as an interface with the phasmic realities, both a person's life force and magical power lie inherent in the anima. However, the instinctive nature of the anima means that it is obsessed with survival and thus can demand the recognition of its own personal character or identity.

TRIPARTITE SOUL

Together, the components of the ens, animus, and anima describe the tripartite soul. Using different terms, the Greek philosopher Plato (ca. 428–348 BCE) compares the relationship of the three parts of the incarnate soul to a charioteer driving two winged horses, one black and one white, each pulling in different directions:

> "... the human charioteer drives his [soul] in a pair; and one of
> them is noble and of noble breed, and the other is ignoble and

of ignoble breed; and the driving of them of necessity gives a great deal of trouble to him."[15]

The two horses can be compared to the animus and the anima, respectively. The animus is depicted as a noble, light-colored horse of celestial origins, equating the rational mind with the powers of heaven. The anima he depicts as a dark and unruly horse, its nature derived from chthonic powers. The charioteer is the immortal ens.

Like the charioteer who must learn to drive the two horses in harmony despite their propensity to strain against each other, the harmonic application of the functions of memory, reason, and imagination are the keys that unlock the secrets of magic and understanding the tripartite soul. If we are to better ourselves, we must align our natures to the divine purpose of the ens, discerning with reason, remembering past experiences, and imagining new vistas of innovation.

In European traditions, the three aspects of the soul are explained as being reflective of the threefold world. Where the eternal soul meets the celestial world, it manifests as the intellectual self, or reason. Where the divine soul meets with the underworld, it creates desire and imagination. But the immortal aspect of the soul (ens) that carries from life to life extends between the divine source and the world upon which it is incarnate; for this reason, in our traditions we consider the center of the world to be wherever our feet walk.

SIMULACRUM OR SPIRIT BODY

Though the words "soul" and "spirit" are vulgarly employed as synonymous terms, they are in fact very distinct. The soul, or ens, represents the eternal and aetheric aspect of a sentient being. The spirit is the phasmic, temporary form that has no sentience of its own. In the process of incarnation, an ens will clothe itself in a phasmic body, or spirit. The intelligence of the numen, or genius, is impressed onto the phasma to create a prototype upon which the incarnated corporal body is modeled. This prototype is the simulacrum, the image of what the body will become. In Plato's analogy, the spirit is equated with the vehicle pulled by the two horses.

. . . .

15   Plato, *The Dialogues of Plato Vol. I, Translated into English B. Jowett*, trans. Ben Jowett (New York: Random Press, 1892), 250–251, verse 246b. https://archive.org/details /dli.ernet.524833/page/249/mode/2up.

Disincarnate Spirit

After death, the phasmic simulacrum should begin to dissolve, much like the physical body. The dissipation of the simulacrum is essential to liberate the ens from the constraints of its recent incarnation and continue its journey.

Being merely a function of rational operation, the animus ceases to create new pathways of reason at the time of death, remaining only as a copy of what it was. Meanwhile the vital forces of the anima slowly erode and return to the elements.

Sometimes in the stages before death, the anima's survival instinct will try to cling to physical life well after the conscious faculties have departed, which can lead to a prolonged death. In the same way, the anima may also resist dissolution of the phasmic body after the point of death by holding on to emotional tethers. In effect, this binds the ens to the physical world and prevents it from returning to its natural aetheric state. When this happens, the soul of the deceased lingers in the metacosmos in the form of a spirit but, having lost the temporal powers of the mind, is often confused and emotional. These are the distressed souls we call unquiet spirits, subject to the attachments of their former life. The danger of this occurring is the reason for many of the rites and rituals around death.

Balance and Protection

When the ens creates the animus and anima, it does so by providing them with a certain flexibility to cope with the trauma of incarnation. This resilience is one of our greatest strengths and allows us to overcome the challenges and obstacles so necessary to our soul's progression. Consistent with the soul's symbolic connection to the sea, the ens learns to navigate a dynamic, jostling sea of potential and heartache—the very purpose of life is exploration and embracing the interwoven adventure of questing, discovery, and recovery.

When working with spirits, this plasticity can become a liability if reason is not set as a vigilant guard upon the imagination. Just as permission to act can come from a person's animus or anima, it can also occur due to the influence of an external intelligence. In preparing to work with spirits, you must be cognizant that they may attempt to subtly influence you. They may even try to elicit license for behavior that is destructive and toxic. You will also need to guard your phasmic or spirit body, which (due to a similarity in substance) can be affected by the entities with whom you will interact, should you allow it.

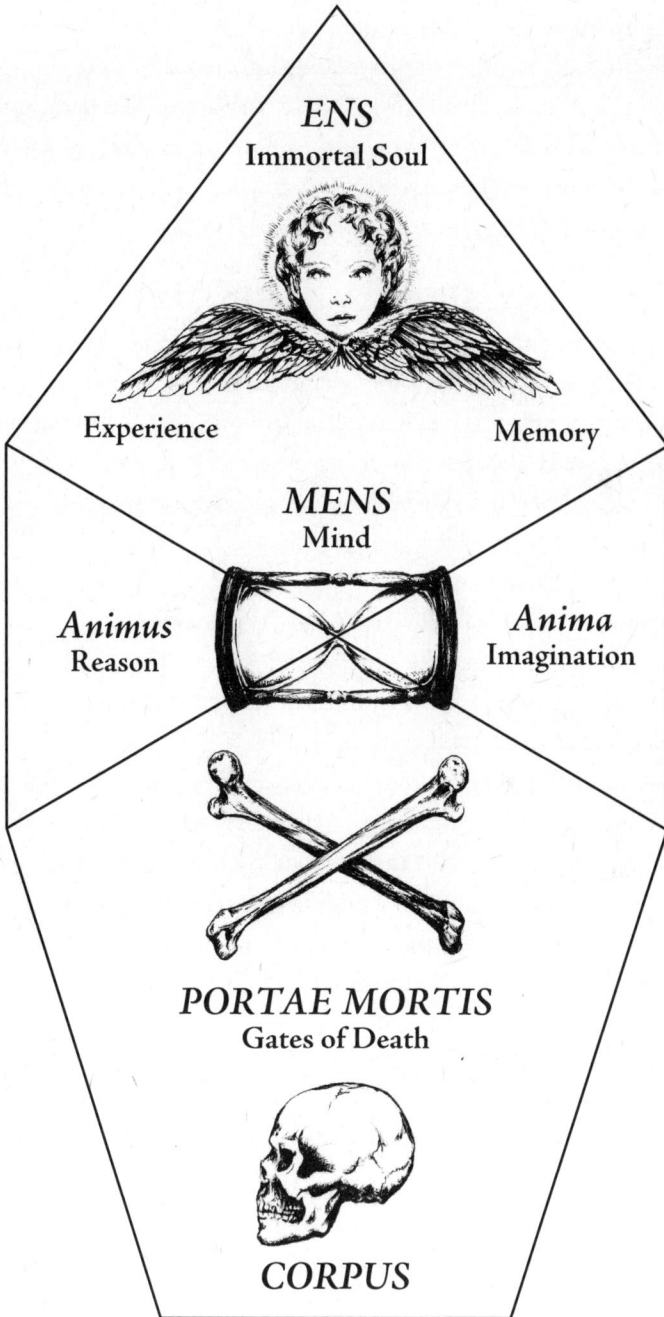

ENS
Immortal Soul

Experience   Memory

MENS
Mind

Animus   *Anima*
Reason   Imagination

PORTAE MORTIS
Gates of Death

CORPUS

This imagery depicting liberation of the winged soul after death is commonly found on eighteenth-century gravestones in the north of Britain. The hourglass depicts the release of the mens and the crossbones is the separation of the earthly body from its grave.

To combat these attempts, you can learn to develop skills in magical protection and fortitude in addition to undeviating adherence to a predetermined purpose that you do not waver from after contact with a spirit has been initiated. You must be armed with definitive knowledge, a determined will, courage, and professional detachment. With these skills in hand, you will be able to competently engage in the world of necromantic spirits.

SPIRIT MANIFESTATION

To physically manifest in our world, a disincarnate spirit requires certain environmental conditions. A spirit cannot manifest visually or audibly, nor can they manipulate objects unless the hyle is dense enough. A state of phasma is necessary for the boundary between the metacosmos or Qarth Arqa and our reality to blend into one another. If a spirit is present, such an environment will allow for an interaction upon our world or reality.

When investigating an enclosed location such as a house, the phasma will pool in the lowest points, usually basements. When entering these low points, a heavy feeling of darkness may be experienced. This feeling is not caused by the actions of a specific spirit but is due to the density of the phasma and the effects that pressure places on the local environment.

Likewise, at the height of the enclosed space (like an attic), the lighter phasma billows upward, reaches the limit, and begins to fall again. This activity produces a tense but frenetic energy and is therefore another likely place for manifestation. Along with the limits the physical building places on the flow, the natural tendency for phasma to settle and rise means that stairways are conduits of phasma. As such, manifestations are also often recorded on stairs.

Stages of Spirit Manifestation

When the conditions are right, spirits who wish to interact certainly will. It is a natural process, just as it will rain when atmospheric conditions are fitting. The relationship of human beings and spirits has always existed, and always will.

The way in which a spirit becomes visible follows a universal pattern of manifestation comprising progressive stages. This pattern applies regardless of whether it is a human spirit or one of the other sublunary entities. All these stages of manifestation occur at one simultaneous moment, but our perception and the environmental conditions dictate what we see. It is apparent the spirit does not have control of this process, nor are they affected by it. They do not choose at which stage of manifestation they will appear, and their perception of their own reality is not shifting. Our traditions identify four stages of visible manifestation, as follows:

1. Nube

   Often the first visible stage of manifestation will be a cloud or mist representing the the stirring of phasma around the spirit. This cloud, or nube, can sometimes be seen with the naked eye, but a person with the second sight can see it readily. It is often captured on film by paranormal researchers. The color of the mist can indicate the type of spirit manifesting. For a human spirit, the cloud or mist will be silvery gray, like tobacco smoke.

2. Numen

   The stage of manifestation following (and sometimes during) the appearance of the cloud or mist is the emergence of a dense sphere of luminous aether known to magicians as the spirit's form of fire and to paranormal enthusiasts as a spirit orb. The numen is the indication of the ens or soul and verifies that a spirit is sentient. Paranormal investigators consistently capture photographic and video evidence of orbs with differing density, shape, and color. True orbs are self-illuminating and of a distinct composition. A numen can often be seen with the naked eye. When a numen is in motion, it can appear as a white rod or streak.

3. Umbra

   If the spirit manifests further, it presents as a dark but recognizable silhouette known in magic as the umbra, or shadow, and it is the most common specter that you will encounter. When it is a humanoid umbra, it becomes what paranormal researchers call a shadow person; however, this term has unfortunately accrued the additional moralistic interpretation as an evil nonhuman spirit. This error has caused an irrational fear that has infected the subject of "shadow people" on the internet and within the paranormal community in general.

4. Apparition

Lastly, the form of the spirit presents as if it were composed of translucent light and, at times, transparent but of natural color. Infrequently, the apparition may appear as an opaque form indistinguishable from a living being.

Apparitions are sometimes more easily seen as a reflection, whether in a mirror or glass, or captured by a camera with a mirrored lens. When a spirit is seen from upstairs window, it is sometimes assumed they are hovering outside above the ground, but it is more likely the spirit is standing near you and you are actually seeing their reflection in the glass.

Another frequent sighting of apparitions occurs when people awaken from sleep to see a spirit on or around their bed. This is usually a sign they have tried to communicate with you while you are in a receptive dream or semiconscious state. Sometimes they may even appear to be floating horizontally above the bed, looking directly at you. People are often frightened by this, but it is simply the spirit trying to hold a conversation with you while you are lying down.

Depiction of the Stages of Visible Manifestation

Nube (Mist)

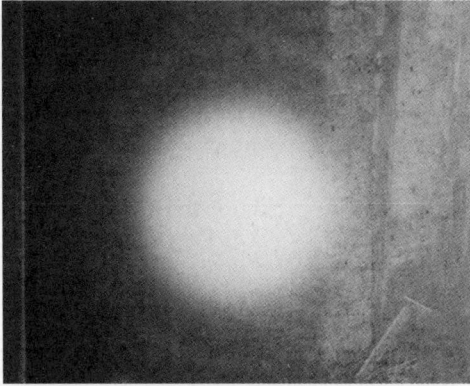

Numen (Orb)

Umbra (Shadow)

Apparition (Simulacrum)]

Nonsentient Spirits: Phantasms and Phasmata

Not all spirit activity is sentient. Some types of manifestations such as sounds or moving objects are caused by phasmic influences devoid of a numen or soul. Sciomancy recognizes two types of nonsentient spirit activity:

+ Phantasm: Phasmic activity without a sense of purpose
+ Phasmata: Phasmic activity that has a sense of purpose but is not conscious

Table 2: Two Types of Nonsentient Spirits

Type	Description	Examples
Phantasm	Residual echoes of an event impressed on the phasma	Vocal echoes or vision of past events Impressions on an object or place
Phasmata	Activity caused by a thoughtform or intelligence Communication if any, will be stilted and unresponsive	Illusion empowered by repetition, emotion, or popular belief Uncontrolled psychic intent Extreme emotion Thoughtform created by a magician

Phantasm

At the time of an event, a phantasm can impress itself on the phasmic environment. Under the right conditions, an echo of the event remains and continues to manifest. The manifestation does not have presence of consciousness. It appears as a replay of the same actions and behavior and will show no response to attempts at communication. Paranormal investigators have labeled this phenomenon a residual haunting, but to the magician it has always been known as a phantasm. Examples can include hearing echoes of voices, music, or other sounds; visual recordings of people and events; and ideas impressed on an object or place.

Phasmata

The second type of nonsentient spirit activity is called phasmata and is comparable to the modern understanding of thoughtforms. Fundamentally, phasmata are simulacra imbued with an intelligence according to a designated function. Phasmata can be unintentionally created, making them the kind you are most likely to encounter in an investigation.

Phasmata can occur when intense emotions impress an imagined form or intelligence upon a phasmic-rich environment that is then activated in some way. Once created, the phasmata has an independent existence and may be experienced by multiple unrelated witnesses. Phasmata can appear as full apparitions but may be perceived as other visual, kinetic, or audible anomalies.

Collective Belief

One type of well-known phasmata occurs when an illusion or story is empowered by repetition, emotion, or popular acceptance such as in a local ghost story, creatures, or "cursed" objects. Regarding paranormal interests, the practice of casting blame on inanimate objects is strangely quite widespread. A spirit board, doll, painting, or other object is often blamed as the cause of a supernatural event, when the true cause is likely to be much more complicated.

Uncontrolled Psychic Intent

When conducting a necromantic investigation, you will need to pay attention to the creation of phasmata that may result from your proceedings. Investigations can often take place in locations having heavy phasmic conditions conducive to the creation of momentary phasmata. You may experience events which appear to confirm exactly what you fear, or hope may be present. As an example, you can capture electronic voices confirming your preconceptions, whether that is the apparent words of the spirit you hope to contact or a seemingly inhuman growl. Other methods of communication can also be affected, such as spirit boards and flashlights. Any spirit communication should be cautiously tested without preconception to avoid the murky interference of phasmata.

Similarly (and much more commonly than most people would imagine), phasmata can be created by an individual with latent psychic gifts, especially if they repress their abilities or start to experience emotional extremes.

Magic Workers

Although phasmata can be deliberately created using magic, it is far less commonly the cause in the type of spirit disturbance you will come across. In these cases, the spirit can seem intelligent and purposeful, and it may even have limited communication but will soon be revealed to be not self-aware.

Differentiating Sentient and Nonsentient Behavior

Learning to tell the difference between phantasm, phasmata, and a sentient spirit is key in being able to identify the cause of a disturbance.

Table 3: Sentient and Nonsentient Spirits

	Repetitive	Purposeful	Responsive	Numen (orb)
Phantasm	Sometimes	Never	Never	Never
Phasmata	Always	Always	Sometimes	Never
Sentient	Sometimes	Always	Mostly	Always

MITIGATING SPIRIT INFLUENCE

So far in this chapter, we have explored the nature of the soul and the spirit and learned to recognize when a spirit is manifesting and how to tell if paranormal activity is sentient. We will now take a small detour to address the question most often asked: Can a spirit cause harm? As human beings, we are understandably wary of the dangers lurking in the shadows of the unknown. When we lack the knowledge of how spirits can adversely affect us, our fear can drive us to contemplate the worst evil that we can imagine. Conversely, some people refuse to believe that spirits can harm us at all, safely cocooned in their denial. The truth, of course, lies somewhere between these two views. Some spirits *can* intentionally cause harm, but only a few do. It is more likely any activity that results in harm is unintended, or involuntary. Sometimes the impact of these actions is obvious, but the most detrimental effects are likely to be subtle. You should always be aware of the potential for risk but do not assume acts are deliberately hostile.

The choice to investigate should include an examination of your willingness to enter a situation where danger is a possibility, however slight. You should endeavor to pursue mind-setting techniques and procure protection before beginning, and you should be resolute in the conviction of your authority. Courage is not the absence of fear but the ability to execute correct action despite fear. Knowledge can alleviate trepidation and provide the understanding of which actions are warranted. Luckily, our ancient magical brothers and sisters faced the same challenges and diligently ventured to catalog the dangers that can occur in working with spirits.

Physical Impact

The first and obvious concern is the risk of physical injury. Many people fear that if a spirit can move an object, clearly, they can harm a person. However, to put things in perspective, thousands of paranormal investigations take place across the globe without sustaining an injury that might be deemed severe. People are more likely to have objects thrown at them or be struck, pushed, or scratched, which to be frank, is not much worse than high school gym class. It is obvious that the potential for significant injury must be a solemn consideration and precautions taken, but such an extreme attack is isolated.

Mental Confusion

The true dangers associated with spirit interaction are much more subtle but no less grievous. As stated above, a spirit may cause confusion within a person's sense of reason, making irrational behavior seem warranted. This state can result in disproportionate hysteria, anger, grief, or other negative emotions. Such misdirection occurs through a process not unlike posthypnotic suggestion and may cause aberrant conduct entirely inconsistent with an individual's normal personality. At times, the sufferer may not even remember their reaction. Causing confusion may not be a pointed attack; it could simply occur due to the intensity of a spirit's desire to convey their message. It can also be accidental, in that the spirit is affecting a person through their own experience and without any malicious intent.

To guard against this negative impact, you must be certain of your own natural state and remove yourself from the location to regain your concentration when affected. The effects of this instability can be controlled through breathing and meditation. Once the mind has been settled and convictions reestablished, you may resume the investigation, mindful that this influence is a confirmed effect within the location.

Empathic Influence

Closely related to the above effect is the forming of an empathic relationship with a spirit or spirits. Some people are sensitive to the feelings of others to the point that they can vicariously experience an alien emotion. When interacting with spirits, such sensitives may feel overwhelming emotion or echoes of physical pain that can be debilitating. These emotions are transferred through the viscous medium of phasma, so the remedy is therefore similar to the one suggested for the previous malady. Cleansing the accrued phasma attached to the sufferer will eradicate the established link between the sufferer and the spirit.

Empathic reactions are almost certainly accidental; the sensitive naturally harmonizes with the traumatic emotions the spirit feels. These reactions can be used to understand the spirit's condition or define aspects of their history and can therefore serve a positive purpose in the investigation. However, if someone is susceptible to empathic relationships, constant care should be taken to protect them from forming such bonds while on location. The empathic experience can be traumatizing, and an investigative team should not capitalize on such a harmful effect to further their knowledge. Your first consideration should be the well-being of the living, and measures should be taken to protect any natural empath from the undue distress which may be imposed upon them during an investigation.

Deception

When a spirit with predatory tendencies realizes the plasticity of their phasmic body, they may choose to make themselves known in another form to further their own ends. Such spirits use their disguise to elicit sympathy or terror to gain the upper hand. These spirit impostors seldom have beneficial aims; if they can deceive, their purposes may be more likely to be carried out to effect. Be certain that the spirit you are in communication with is who and what you believe them to be. They should be tested, and any magical act that can reveal their true nature should be employed.

Daemoniacs

Finally, there is the extreme effect of visual or audible hallucinations caused by phasmata or spirit, such as an entity who is in a confused state or a spirit with nefarious intentions. These are not strictly true visions or communications; they are principally illusions and in magic are known as daemoniacs.[16]

. . . .

16 Don Karr and Stephen Skinner, *Sourceworks of Ceremonial Magic Series Volume VI, Sepher Raziel: Liber Salomonis* (Singapore: Golden Hoard Press, 2010), 176.

Within the Roman Catholic tradition, the word demoniac has been applied solely to a person possessed by "evil spirits." Prior to the adoption of the word by the Church, a daemoniac was often the name given to influences imposed on a person by a spirit, from the Greek *daimoniakos*, and so often referred to the hallucinations themselves, rather than specifically designating the sufferer. In magic, daemoniacs are considered relatively untrustworthy as they are accompanied by the imbalance within a person's emotional equilibrium.

If someone suffers a daemoniac event, remove them from the location immediately as this effect can create an elevated level of anxiety and poses potential health risks. Seek medical assistance if necessary. The entire investigative team should also suspend the investigation and reaffirm their control and protections. They should engage in an earnest risk assessment and develop a strategy before reentering the location.

Sciomantic investigations are solemn and critical endeavors and in a perfect world they would never be undertaken for the purposes of curiosity or adventure seeking. Some dangers are inherent in engaging with spirits, more so where they have the means to effectively manifest. Be aware of the risks and understand that they can be minimized through correct intention, meditations, and protections. Honor those with whom you share an investigation, be ever cognizant of their well-being, and never hesitate to seek medical advice where it is warranted.

If you decide to do this work, remember it is a choice that you have willingly made. Have courage and conviction in your purpose and pursue it with determination. The greatest tool you have at your disposal to ameliorate the potential dangers is knowledge. Know what you are dealing with and how to minimize and remedy negative effects, and seek to understand the conditions that precipitate a spirit crisis. Be guided by your own compassion and reason, and be sincere in your faith. Be open minded and surrender preconception, and like a true magician, embrace the faculty to shift your perception at will. This job is difficult, not only in its particulars but in the emotional toll it can take, so be certain you are resolute in your motivation to serve in the capacity of a sciomancer.

CHAPTER FOUR

SUBLUNARY SPIRITS

The sublunary domains are filled with an unfathomable multitude of diverse entities who are mostly preoccupied with their own forms of existence. Some of these are considered intelligent and humanlike, while others are beyond our comprehension. It is therefore not surprising that we might occasionally cross paths with spirits other than humans in our investigations. Innate fear and preconceived ideas lead people to invariably make false conclusions and take inappropriate actions in these situations. This chapter introduces a practical approach to distinguish whether a spirit is human or nonhuman based on centuries of accumulated knowledge and observation.

EARLY DAEMONOLOGY

The Pagan faiths of Europe recognize a variety of sublunary entities whom they lived alongside as neighbors and allies. These entities are recognized by many names in many cultures. To the magician, the art of working and communicating with these intelligent beings is the agency through which change can be affected and divine will enacted. To the established church, the study of these shadowy spirits has come to be declared evil. Yet to both, it has always been known by the same name—daemonology.

The word "daemonology" means the study or knowledge of those sublunary entities known to the ancients as daemones. In modern English, this word is rendered as "demon" and when spoken, immediately recalls the concept of an evil fiend of Hell dedicated to the temptation or spiritual annihilation of humanity. While almost universal, this interpretation is in fact a complete misunderstanding based upon the use of the word *daimon* in the Greek translations of the Bible to represent heathen gods and unclean spirits.

Defining Daemones

The Greek word daimon has barely changed from its origins in Proto Indo-European, wherein *dai-mon-* means a divider or provider, from the root *da-*, "to divide."[17] What the daimon divides or provides is fortunes or destinies.

To the ancient Greeks, daemones were a sort of divinity below the level of the gods but who are purposeful agents of universal change. In his *Symposium*, Plato describes the function of daemones as envoys or interpreters whose nature lay between the earthly and the heavenly, neither mortal nor immortal.[18] He also asserts that the person versed in the matter of daemones has spiritual powers compared against the more mundane powers of human beings who have no contact with these entities.

Lucius Apuleius Madaurensis (ca. 124–170) also reiterates in *The God of Socrates* the belief that daemones are divine middle powers and goes further to declare that human souls are also daemones.[19]

Divine Agents

Fundamentally, daemones are beings who are cocreators in executing divine communication. They are the source of the magic underlying the mundane and agents of change and transformation. They enact the vicissitudes of fortune or, as one may say, they divide the path of destiny. The ever-present existence of daemones underpinning and animating the sublunary realms is the spiritual mechanism of a magic animistic ideology.

Daemones are described as being of a middle nature, being both sparks of the divine yet inhabiting phenomenal realities. Their essential being or soul is eter-

. . . .

17   "Demon," Online Etymology Dictionary, last accessed 12/16/2023. https://www.etymonline .com/word/demon#etymonline_v_5575.

18   Plato, *Symposium*, verse 202d-e from *The Dialogues of Plato Vol. i, Translated into English B. Jowett M.A*, trans. Benjamin Jowett (New York: Random Press, 1892), 328. https://archive .org/details/dli.ernet.524833/page/327/mode/2up.

19   Apuleius, *The Works of Apuleius, Comprising the Metamorphoses, or Golden Ass, the God of Socrates, the Florida, and His Defence or A Discourse on Magic*, trans. George Bohn (London: George Bell, 1853), 367–373.

nal, yet they provisionally abide in an objective world. This temporary existence is naturally terminated at its completion, defining them as mortal. The human soul is also eternal yet abides in a temporary actuality, designating our own existence as somewhere between mortal and immortal, confirming the opinion of Apuleius that we too are daemones.

THE INFECTION OF EVIL

The medieval church held a significant political role in European society in addition to being an administration of faith. As such, they well understood the psychology of fear and employed it to turn people's minds away from Pagan practices the ecclesiastics considered contrary to their established doctrine.

Church doctrine ingrained the concept of evil in the population, describing it as an invisible power that has the inherent desire and potential for mortal destruction beyond our understanding with daemones as agents of evil. Being essentially flighty herd animals, humans have successfully evolved as a species by avoiding predators with sharper claws and gnashing teeth. In other words, our deep instinct for survival teaches us to avoid things that have the potential to bring us grievous injury. Thus the notion of evil ignites our innate and evolved flight response, and we are inclined to heed the warning on a deep subconscious level.

Over the course of centuries, the pernicious fallacy of evil evolved into a detailed superstition. It has served to disenfranchise people from spiritual entities with whom they have traditionally held commerce, and, worse, it has become deeply embedded into our evolutionary fear.

Fiendish Demons

During the late Middle Ages and the period of the early Renaissance (the fourteenth through sixteenth centuries), the ecclesiastical concept of demons as the inhabitants of Hell forming Satan's personal army and government had become fully developed. Besides religious mythology, this sensational imagery served a secondary purpose: continuing to encourage a fear-based disciplinary tool to force submission to religious authority.

Along with the development of this concept was a subversive curiosity that has inspired songs, poems, and artwork, evincing our natural fascination with the dark and disturbing corners of the human mind. So prevalent was this imagery that by the sixteenth century, when writers began again to look to the ancient wisdom of Greek traditions, they found it necessary to employ the use of the Latin *daemon* in English literature to differentiate the original Greek definition from the ecclesiastically endorsed evil demon.

Sadly, the history of magic suffers from the same aberrations. Many practitioners influenced by popular ideas adopted the concept of a hierarchy of hell and the evocation of its citizens into their works. This idea became so pervasive that the later ritual manuals and grimoires become synonymous with diabolical ceremonial practices containing lists of hellish hierarchies, inclusive of descriptions, and seals of their ministers. Manuscripts surviving from this period remain popular today. The curiosity regarding the origin of evil and its lurid imagery still elicits a visceral magnetism, and modern literature on the magical arts often revel in this attraction.

The fear that surrounds the class of spirits called daemones is of course as illogical as it is artificial. As necromancers, the presence of spirits both human and nonhuman is unavoidable. To fully embrace the sublunary worlds, we must consciously reevaluate for ourselves any type of mental conditioning we may have about the word "demon" (and all it entails) and liberate our minds to explore the truth of spirits and their essential natures.

Sovereignty of Choice

As previously described, daemones are functional agents of transformation animating the various sublunary realms. This animation occurs because of a certain intellectual liberty or free will all sentient sublunary souls possess. Choices have consequences, and those resulting effects create motion or change.

Nonhuman daemones cannot be grouped together as either good or bad based on their species any more than humans can. They make creative and positive choices and poor and negative ones. While some daemones embrace the accountability of personal liberty, others rebel against the yoke of that responsibility.

Since ancient times, magicians have sought to work with daemones by making a contract with terms that they consent to. Whether it is to do good or cause harm, the nature of the work is dependent on the magician's choices and should not be ascribed solely to the spirit who has been engaged. That is not to say that working with nonhuman entities is without risk, but any dangers are mostly incidental to magical practice and not specifically inherent in the disposition of any class of spirits.

Eudaemones and Cacodaemones

In ancient classical cosmology and later medieval arcana, daemones are grouped into two arbitrary divisions: eudaemones and cacodaemones, or good and bad spirits, respectively. These terms simply describe whether the actions of the entity are beneficial or harmful as perceived from a purely human point of view and should not be interpreted as a moral judgment of the intrinsic nature of any individual entity.

The only exception to this rule is in discerning the intent of disincarnate human spirits according to the dictates of human ethics, as their essential natures were originally cultivated during their living existence. As we will see in the next chapter, assessing whether a necromantic spirit is acting in a way that is beneficial or harmful is useful in evaluating their condition.

METHODS OF CLASSIFICATION

The many realms and sublunary worlds do not exist independently of one another. They rely on interchange for constancy and remain fractions of a divine whole. Like our own world, the various sublunary realms these beings inhabit are complex with many diverse spirits.

To effectively work with daemones, magicians discovered the need to classify a selection of these entities as representatives of a variety of existing worlds. From these classifications, ritual procedures were then able to be constructed and ceremonial methods refined.

Whereas later grimoires recognized a set number of entities which they attempted to catalog by rank and name, early daemonology comprised a more general taxonomy according to the type of daemon, their realm, and the phenomena by which they could be recognized. Magicians were trained in the traditional knowledge of the sublunary worlds in which these daemones originated and a comprehension of their essential natures. Further details and specification came from the individual experience communicating and contracting the specific spirits personally.

Psellus's Classifications

An ancient classification of daemones that survived into the eleventh century is attributed to the pen of Michael Psellus (1018–ca. 1078). As professor of philosophy at the newly founded academy of Constantinople, he revived the cult of Plato and admired Hellenic paganism, which aroused suspicions as to his orthodoxy.

In his work *De Operatione Dæmonum* (*On the Operation of Demons*), the author relates information received from a former member of a Thracian sect known as the Euchites.[20] Although the tenure of the work is to diminish beliefs considered heretical, Psellus goes to lengths to give information on the survival of their practices and is ironically responsible for preserving this lost Graeco-Thracian and pre-Christian knowledge to the present day.

Psellus presented a classification of six types of daemones. Curiously, he omitted the seventh group, the souls of the dead, from his list, possibly because it did not conform to then-current Christian dogma. The contested daemonic nature of the human soul and its redemption had become a contemporary theme of debate in the Orthodox Church, where the consensus favored a nondaemonic origin.

The groupings are based on the worlds the daemones inhabited and arranged by the properties of lightness and density of hyle, typical of the early medieval period. Psellus begins with igneous or fiery spirits that he designates as *leluric*, something his source informs him is the Thracian word for "fiery." The list proceeds in descending order of density through *aerial, terrestrial, aqueous,* and *subterranean* and ends in an aggressive class of spirits known as *Lucifugii*, or "those who flee the light."

Judaic Classifications

Another influence on the medieval classification of daemons came from the models of the sublunary realms from Hebrew tradition. As briefly described in chapter 2, these spiritual geographies are known as the Seven Earths and are equated closely with classical concepts.

After the twelfth century, the systemization of literary Qabalah heavily influenced European magic. Each of the earths and their entities became attributed with seven planetary correspondences, the mercurial world being associated with necromantic spirits.

Astrological Associations

Coupled with the adoption of astrology to consolidate occult correspondences, the influence of the Qabalah meant that the use of planetary associations was to

. . . .

20   *Michael Psellus' Dialogue on the Operation of Daemons*, trans. Stephen Skinner and Marcus Collisson (Singapore: Golden Hoard Press, 2010), 51–82.

predominate in later European magic to classify sublunary spirits. These planetary relationships were originally understood to be a sublunary reflection of the celestial power and should be considered symbolic rather than literal.

In manuscripts such as the *Fourth Book of Occult Philosophy* attributed to Cornelius Agrippa (1486–1535) or *The Sworn Book of Honorius of Thebes*, potentially dated to the twelfth century, information about the phenomena that accompany each realm is recorded and handed down from earlier magicians. Like the Hebrew model, mercurial spirits were attributed with the signs of deceased human spirits.

By the early Renaissance in the sixteenth century, the list of correspondences had lost its original import, leading to an interpretation whereby these beings were deemed to be actual officiants of these planets and their powers. The knowledge that mercurial spirits were referring to necromantic spirits began to fade. This confusion persists to this day among modern practitioners of magic who rely on the information found in such early grimoires, but often lack the historical context.

Registers of Daemones

Over the course of history, some magicians recorded the names and offices of the daemones with whom they had personal communication. Such a book was known as a *liber spirituum* or book of spirits, according to Agrippa.[21]

As institutionalized magic degenerated, omissions in training crept in. During the late Middle Ages and the Renaissance, the liber spirituum of past magicians were collated together to create a register of known daemones. These lists were further reworked and eventually reimagined into a Christian hierarchy of demons that were attributed ranks and offices accordingly. This information became the basis of subsequent grimoires familiar to modern magicians such as the *Grimoirium Verum* and the *Goetia*; although of questionable origin, they are typical of this era.

. . . .

21   Henry Cornelius Agrippa, *Fourth Book of Occult Philosophy* (Whitefish, MT: Kessinger Publishing, 1992), 57–59. Originally published 1559.

Aristotelian	Pre-900	Magicians classified sublunary spirits according to the phasmic density of their elemental world.
Alchemic	1100s	Daemones compared to planetary virtues, later confusion led to the idea that entities inhabit the seven planets.
Christian Ceremonial	1200–1500	Daemonology increasingly constrained into practices consistent with Christian ideology. Registers of known daemones were collated.
Late Renaissance	1600–1700	Misrepresentation of sublunary spirits as either celestial spirits or Christian demons.
Modern	Post-1800	Modern revivals misappropriate lists of daemones from previous centuries.

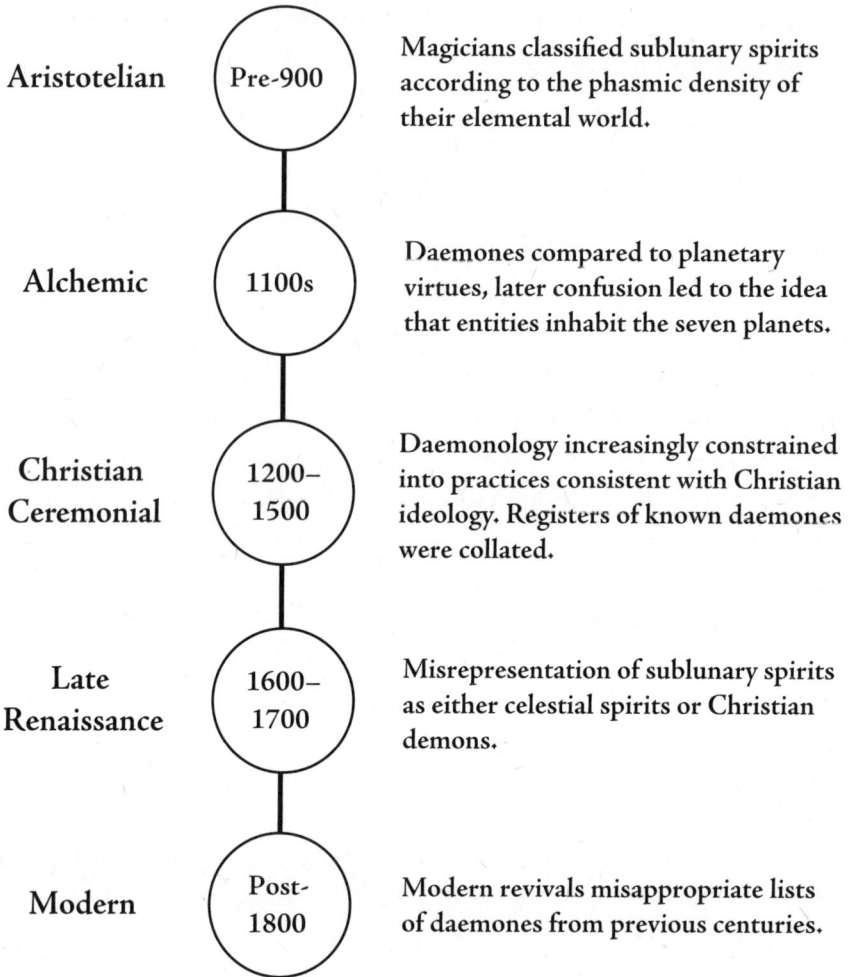

Timeline of European Classifications of Sublunary Spirits

IDENTIFYING DAEMONES

Learning to identify the activity associated with the different realms and types of entities is essential to sciomancy. The distinctive color of mist or orbs associated with spirit manifestation can clearly signify the type of daemon. Sounds, demeanor, and visible apparitions are also indicative. Some of the phenomena, being more subjective, are described in grimoires in the poetic metaphor of medieval language. Once experienced, however, they are easily recognizable and will prove useful to confirm an observation. Practical exposure and experience are the only true test.

Movements and Signs

Prior to any visible manifestation, the very first indication that a spirit is present is often their unique *movement* and *sign*.

Movements are brief but perceptible atmospheric conditions that reveal the realm temporarily interfacing with our own, usually described by the quality of light or air. The description of the movement indicates something about the nature of the daemon's habitation, and therefore the type that is emerging.

Signs signify the proximity of the spirit. They are usually described as sensations that can be experienced when the entity is present in a space and announces the possibility of direct communication. These observable movements and signs are not subtle but can occur very quickly, so operational awareness is a necessity when investigating.

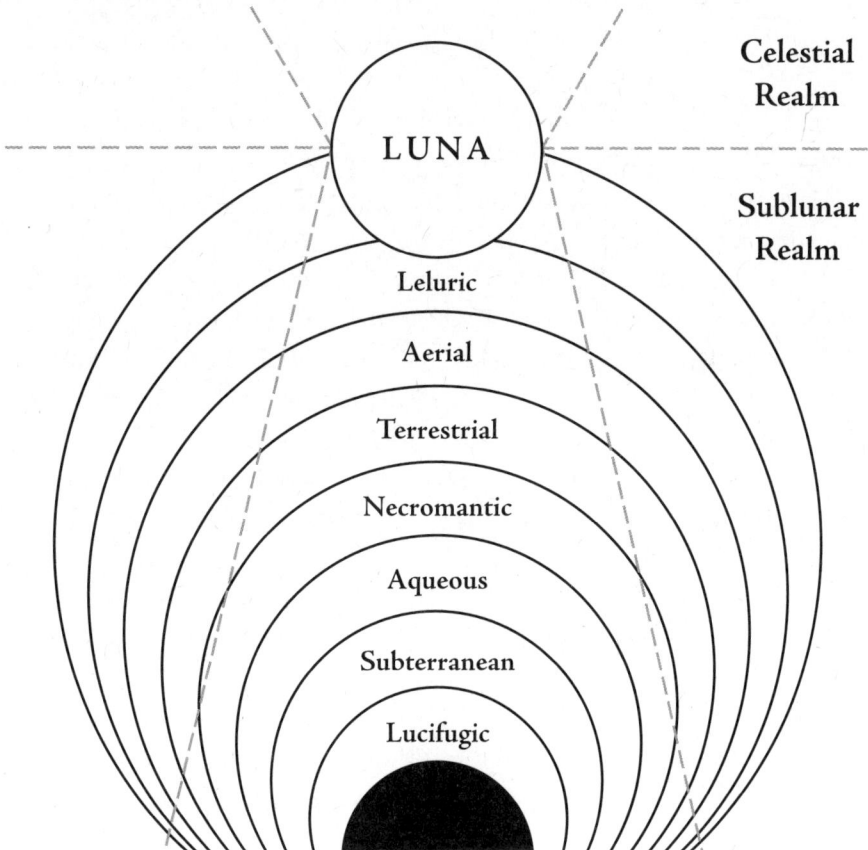

Seven sublunary realms and their inhabitants with increasing density

The Seven Daemonic Classifications

The following list of classifications is based on the traditional understanding of the nature of daemones, bringing together fragments from medieval texts. The name given is consistent with Psellus's classifications, followed by the planetary correspondence according to the grimoires. We have modified some descriptions for clarity based on our knowledge distilled from personal experiences.

Leluric Daemones

Leluric or igneous daemones are powerful spirits identified with the phenomenal supremacies of the upper firmament—that is, spirits of storms, strong winds, and similar atmospheric conditions—and therefore came to be associated with the virtues of Jupiter.

Jupiter

They are said to appear with a middle stature, healthy and ruddy, of human dimensions, and seem quick-tempered or agitated. In the grimoires their nature is described as sanguine and choleric, which means they are cheerful or approachable, though easily angered, or hot-tempered. They maintain a mild countenance and speak gently but with perceptible anger.

When they materialize as a mist or nube, it is a russet color, sometimes with a lighter hue toward the exterior of the cloud. This nube may be accompanied by a feeling of increasing atmospheric pressure. Any movement, which is the first perceptible indication of their immediate presence, is seen as flashes of light accompanied by an intermittent rumbling, like thunder. When they are more fully present the sign is a sense of agitation in the space, like an erratic motion. This is colorfully described by the magicians of old as "lions will be seen devouring men."[22]

Interaction between human beings and leluric spirits is uncommon, for as agents of atmospheric phenomena they are mostly indifferent to the habitations and occupations of humanity. When they are encountered, their perceptible agitation and anger coupled with the ruddy coloring of their manifestation can appear terrifying but does not indicate ill intention. Despite appearances, the

· · · · · · · · · · · · · · · ·

22   Honorius of Thebes, *The Sworn Book of Honorius: Liber Iuratus Honorii*, trans. Joseph Peterson (Lake Worth, FL: Ibis Press, 2016), 235.

nature of leluric spirits disposes them to offer people beneficial effects, such as joy, gladness, or aiding in reconciliations.

Aerial Daemones

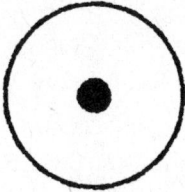

Aerial spirits are more willing to interact with humans but can behave aloof and haughty. Care should be taken when contacting them as they will take full advantage of any loopholes to further their own interests.

They resemble human beings, though larger and taller than most people, and they are extremely handsome. They often appear dignified and gentle, with an aura of golden light tinged with red, like rose gold, and so are described as being of a solar quality. If they show themselves, you may experience a sense that you are in the presence of a noble and benevolent being.

Solar

When they manifest as a nube, it is a citrus color, amber, or golden. Their movement or motion is like twinkling blue-white lights, but if you are not looking directly at them, you may see a momentary flash of light like that of sheet lightning, illuminating things brightly and then dissipating just as quickly. The notable sign that they are present is a perceptible rise in temperature, and you may begin to perspire.

Terrestrial Daemones

These are the most familiar of all daemones, given various names in folkloric traditions according to their form; for example, satyrs, pixies, and imps. Regardless of the diversity, their general nature, motion, and sign will be the same.

Their nube is described as appearing at first as a large swelling cloud, soft and phlegmatic, which is dark or black in color, like smoky quartz crystal or burnished iron. Their movement is a rushing sound like a waterfall or stormy sea. Their sign is expressed as resembling the appearance of rainfall—an extremely large number of orbs issuing from the aforesaid dark cloud with a liquid quality. Magicians classified them under the nature of the moon.

Lunar

Terrestrial spirits are intensely curious and will be drawn to unusual events, such as sciomantic or paranormal investigations. While on odd occasions they may be the cause of a spirit event, they are more likely to be drawn to the peculiarity of the investigation. They are very common, being the spirits of nature and the environment, and gather in great numbers.

They often behave like mischievous children reveling in pranks and jests, which can become a distraction and annoyance when engaged in an investigation. Frequently, they will interact with technology, creating false readings or vocal mimicry to confuse the reception of disembodied verbal messages or electronic voice recordings. If their incidental appearance is detected during an investigation, you must be cautious of their potential interference regarding recorded evidence.

At times they may appear individually. They can be of various forms, from inhuman impish images to semihuman appearances. One of their manifestations recorded by our ancient magicians is the apparition possessing glowing red eyes, described as watery, fluid, or blurry. Paranormal investigators have captured evidence of these red staring eyes and usually assume them to be malevolent or evil. However, glowing red eyes are a sign of terrestrial daemones specifically, and while like other classes of spirits they can occasionally be dangerous, these spirits are usually innocuous and curious.

Aqueous Daemones

Aqueous or marine spirits are usually associated with bodies of water, wells, springs, lakes, and rivers. Tradition asserts that these spirits are most akin to human beings and had formerly been amicable and friendly with humanity, but today are mostly fearful and suspicious of us due to developing religious condemnation.

These spirits often appear in a very human form, usually with a fair or attractive countenance and of a happy disposition, though when moved to anger or sadness they appear consumed by the emotion. When their nube manifests, it is usually of a verdant hue that often lightens to a yellow or gold near the top. In humanlike form, they are usually clothed in white or green and sometimes have a mantle of gold. Importantly, these daemones are not disincarnate human spirits but a species unto themselves with their own essential nature. They are recognized by the intensity of their emotions, and while they can make wonderfully loyal friends, if angered they hold grudges and can become resolute and tenacious enemies.

Venus

Their movement is like a clear star, or a bright and defined point of light, some-times blinking in and out of existence or pulsating. Their sign, when witnessed, is a frenetic and joyful sensation, metaphorically depicted by medieval magicians as "a maiden or maidens dancing about the space." These spirits were likened to the nature of Venus for their ability to love humankind and their association with water.

Subterranean Daemones

Subterranean daemones are like the traditional northern European depiction of dwarves. Their subterranean nature is reflective of the volcanic powers of the deep earth. They are considered incredibly magical but suspicious and distrustful. They are inimical to human beings; making commerce with these daemones is potentially dangerous, and they should be engaged with caution. However, if the magician can succeed in earning their trust, they are wonderful magical artificers who excel in talismanic knowledge.

Mars

When their nube appears, the color is fiery orange-red like bright, hot coals, giving them a correspondence with Mars. Their form is much like that of a human but of smaller proportions (although Agrippa states they are tall), and they are described as being "unattractive." They appear with a ruddy countenance like copper, seared and blackened a little by a flame.

Subterranean spirits may appear with light emanating from their heads, rem-iniscent of a stag's antlers. Their voice sounds deep and resonant like the bellow of wild bulls. Their movement as they present themselves is like the appearance of light from flickering fire, and their sign is comparable to lightning and thunder disturbing the space.

Lucifugic Daemones

Lucifugii are extremely dangerous, but human interactions with them are exceedingly rare. Their realm is in the deepest, sluggish viscosity of phasma entirely alien to our world. If they manage to cross into the metacosmos and pierce the veil into our reality, it is assuredly accidental, but once here their nature and frus-tration is caustic. Psellus explains them as barely sentient and eminently malevolent, driven by an overwhelming destructive impulse. They are associated with dark Saturnine qualities.

Saturn

So improbable are manifestations of these spirits that the ancient magicians could only describe them using the most symbolic or allegorical images resembling medieval depictions of devils. When they begin to first reveal themselves, they appear as a unique black cloud that shines like an obsidian mirror, quite different from the dark cloud that attends the manifestation of terrestrial spirits. Their bodies are described as slender and of a pale or sickly yellow color. The movement associated with them is said to be a strong wind accompanied with the feeling of a disturbance like an earthquake. Their sign is that the ground will become white as if covered with snow.

Necromantic Daemones

Finally, we come to the spirits of deceased humans. Being mercurial in nature, they are recorded as having similar abilities to any other class of daemones but lacking in the same intensity of power.

Michael Psellus omitted these daemones from his classifications. We may simply call them necromantic spirits, as we can more easily understand and engage with them than we can the other classes of daemones. The numen or orb of a human spirit is distinct, described in grimoires as being changeable, appearing translucent like glass or as an intense white fire.

Mercury

Authentic orbs, regardless of the class of spirit, look remarkably similar when they are translucent, but when bright or fully formed, the human spirit can be identified by the intensity and coloring of their numen. An orb that is bright and opalescent, like a small white sun, self-illumined and with a soft corona, usually of a blue hue, is distinguishable as a human spirit.

Other phenomena associated with necromantic spirits who have passed entirely through the veil and entered the realm of the dead are different from unquiet spirits or revenants who have remained within the confusion of the metacosmos.

These revenants are described as being of "middle stature," which means of human dimensions, with a liquidity in appearance and producing a cold sensation. This drop in temperature is indicative of the manifestation of human spirits only, specifically those abiding in the metacosmos. No other class of daemones produces this cold sensation. The only other daemon that perceptibly affects the atmospheric temperature are aerial spirits, which cause a notable heat.

The spirits of the deceased have an affable speech; their voice is recognizably human but is also described as hoarse or in a whisper. In the grimoires, a necromantic spirit appears "like a knight armed, clear and bright," meaning that these spirits have a luminosity resembling the light reflecting on polished armor or metal.

Their movement or motion is also their nube—a gray or silvery cloud—and when they are present, there is a sensation of fear or that the witness's hair will bristle. Both their sign and movement are common documented experiences.

APPLICATION OF DAEMONOLOGY

The congruity of the sublunary realities and experiences from multiple sources indicates the commonality of the classifications of daemones across many cultures. The Graeco-Thracian model preserved by Psellus implies that this knowledge is from a pre-Christian era. That a second method of classification based on planetary correspondences has also survived among magicians of the grimoire period strengthens the argument that these methodologies are artifacts of early European religion and, as such, have Stone-Age roots in the cultures and languages of Indo-Europeans. Thus, daemonology is not only a survival of Paganism but a functioning model of the magic developed within the original creeds of ancient Europe. It is no surprise that magicians of medieval Europe found that these classifications resonated with the cultural understanding and experiences of the spirit world they were already accustomed to and naturally inculcated that understanding within their grimoires.

British magic is an excellent example of how magicians have continued to maintain their native esoteric practices by adopting Greek and ceremonial concepts and applying them to their own cultural understanding of nonhuman entities. In the works of Reginald Scott (1538–1599), as a part of his treatise *The Discoverie of Witchcraft*, written to dissuade the irrational fear of witchcraft typical of the time, he collects information from numerous grimoires, including evocations of sublunary entities, and magical symbols related to each of the seven types of spirits.[23] Outwardly these grimoires appear like other ceremonial works, but to British esotericists they echo regional traditions and relationships with human and nonhuman spirits still practiced today.

. . . .

23   Reginald Scott, *The Discoverie of Witchcraft* (London: William Brome,1587), 216.

Leluric

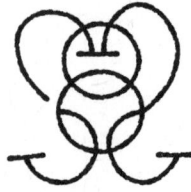

Aqueous

Aerial

Terrestrial

Subterranean

Lucifugic

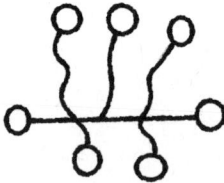

Subterranean and
Necromantic spirits
found in mines

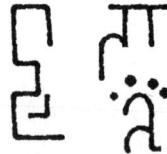

Necromantic

Symbols of Sublunary Spirits. Adapted from Reginald Scott,
The Discoverie of Witchcraft.

Cultural Classifications

The persistence of classifications of daemones hidden in magical practice are even more evident in culture and folklore where they can be clearly seen to have survived despite the efforts of incumbent puritanical faiths to suppress them. To give an example of how medieval arcana can supplement the understanding of sublunary entities in a cultural context, we will explore the traditions associated with the mysterious entities known as the Scottish fairies.

Local traditions assert that fairies are of two groups, the seelie and the unseelie. The anglicized "seelie" is from the Gaelic *sluagh* (Old Celtic *slougo-*), which means "a multitude," "people," or "host."

The seelie are aerial spirits. They are the trooping fairies in Scottish tradition, known in folklore for their pageantry as they travel across the landscape, moving from one destination to another in a royal tour. Their migrations mark the four festivals and the changing of the seasons, a process anciently attributed to passing the rulership from one wind to another. Seelie fairies are described as shining in appearance, fair-haired and tall, haughty, and self-interested.

The unseelie (Gael. *ansluagh*) are nontrooping or sedentary fairies who tend to remain in one location, usually near a body of water such as a spring, river, lake, or well. They are more likely to be sympathetic to humanity and have been said to marry into certain Scottish clans, according to legend. It is evident that these spirits closely align with the aqueous spirits described in the classifications who share in the qualities of Venus.

Tenacity of Low Religion

This approach of comparing local tradition to the classifications of daemones can help make sense of the confusion often involved in researching the various beings associated with cultural folklore. The tenacity of these cultural elements can be explained by the manifestations of high religion and low religion.

High religion is the understanding of the divine and the relationship of humanity with it, while low religion is more immediately related to the spiritual agencies that affect us daily. Because the expression of high religion ties to organized faith and rulership, it is historically more likely to be supplanted by an incoming creed or politic. Gods can be disavowed; mythologies can be denied and then replaced with new deities and mythologies. The distance of understanding between the divine and the human mind makes such a process effectively possible.

However, low religion is much harder to eradicate as it is bound to the everyday understanding and customs of a culture, an instinctual and tangible engagement. The spirits which inhabit the cultural landscape of a people walk the same paths, frequent the same forests, and interact with the same intensity as they have always done. Declaring these beliefs to be nothing but superstition is only effective when people are divorced from their cultural roots, such as in cities where the ivory towers of education can dictate what is true and real. These proclamations can only exist in the cultural vacuums of civilization and ring hollow to the rural person traversing the dark roads of the country, where history and otherworldliness swirl in a kaleidoscope of personal spiritual involvement.

These beliefs are more than folklore and legend. They are the spiritual heirlooms of systemized, pre-Christian faith. While the practices of low religion were threatened with the same focused extinction as the high religion, it survived due to the commitment and determination of esotericists to preserve and pass on this archaic knowledge which is the bedrock of magic, and to do so in secret without the scrutiny of others.

ENCOUNTERING NONHUMAN SPIRITS

Necromancy cannot be divorced from the study of demonology. It is not uncommon for a sciomantic investigation to reveal that a sentient spirit is not human or to be called to an investigation where the witness is certain they experienced something "demonic."

As a sciomancer, it is important to understand the nature of humans as daemones and be aware of the relationships humans have with these other types of spirits, both now and in the past. However, the main practical purpose of identifying a nonhuman entity is to eliminate their activities or presence from your investigation and focus on the symptoms particular to human spirits, including nubes, which appear as a silvery mist; numen, which manifests as bright round orbs; or a sudden sense of cold or dread that may cause shivering or bumps.

If you do happen to see a nonhuman entity, it should not be assumed that they are aware of you or mean you any harm. The best course of action is usually to ignore their presence. Nonhuman daemones are powerful in their own ways and have complex customs that can be difficult to understand and easily breached.

During an investigation, you should be careful with your words to only call upon human spirits and do not make any offerings or do anything that might imply a contract that you do not fully comprehend. Under no circumstances should you try to banish or exorcise a nonhuman entity. In the unusual case that a nonhuman spirit is causing harm, you should seek advice from a trained expert who specializes in the bonds humans have with other daemones and shares a connection with them. Depending on the circumstances, this may be a person from a tradition with strong cultural ties or someone native to the area.

Common Encounters

Apart from necromantic spirits, there are in our experience three types of daemones more likely to be the cause of a disturbance. These are terrestrial, aqueous, and in rare circumstances, aerial.

Aerial spirits are usually only encountered in a location where they have been evoked for a purpose and remain there as per terms of a contract. Commonly, this occurs because an ill-trained magician or spirit worker has conjured an aerial spirit to resolve a haunting without understanding the necessities of defining an agreement or how to dismiss them and, more to the point, without understanding who and what an aerial spirit is.

Aqueous spirits are more prevalent, being closer to humankind and capable of forming lasting emotional relationships that endure generations, for better or worse.

One notable example of aqueous spirits are the phenomena referred to as "white ladies." These ethereal apparitions of a woman dressed in a white gown are commonly witnessed throughout the world in desolate places near water. Their presence is often associated with folk legends of tragedy and loss, sometimes giving rise to imaginative stories that warn of their wrathful vengeance. Seldom are these spirits the cause of a disturbance outside their domain.

Terrestrial spirits are a different matter. When they are the cause of persistent phenomena, it is best to refer to regional practices to find a solution, ideally the customs and methods embedded in the area that have been developed over centuries. Wherever possible, seek advice from indigenous adherents of the local traditions. In locations where there has been considerable immigration, it is common for the incoming culture to have brought spirits with them, or they may have established practices the indigenous spirits find agreeable, such as negotiations with terrestrial spirits to benefit agriculture as seen among the Germanic settlers in Pennsylvania.

Disturbances by terrestrial spirits are quite common where new development is infringing on areas of wilderness, but it also occurs in built-up areas where the new residents do not respect agreements that have been made in the past. One of the ways that Scottish custom retains peace with terrestrial spirits is to dedicate an area of yard called a "devil's patch" that is allowed to grow wild and never touched. If an unknowing occupant moves in and decides to tear up this patch in the name of landscaping, they are sure to hear about it from the nonhuman residents.

Daemonology provides a matrix for classifying the generative agencies that animate creation based upon observations and experimentation developed over thousands of years. However, it is not an isolated study; it must be understood in the greater context of magical philosophy and its arcana.

The recognition that the human soul is of a daemonic nature reminds the necromancer of their spiritual obligation to evince the transformational power latent in all daemones in accordance with the divine plan. It also reminds us that we are potent and self-aware agents of change, mercurial catalysts, and willing co-creators of worlds.

Contemplation of this humbling charge should inspire us to transform ourselves and persevere in the imperfect human quest for true wisdom. This is the deep mystery of necromancy, a vital reminder of the authentic consequences of free choice and the courage to embrace our inherent universal potency.

Chapter Five

Necromantic Classifications

In the previous chapter, we discussed how the spirit of a deceased human can be distinguished from other types of sublunary entities by the unique phenomena associated with their presence. In this section we will once again turn to traditional arcana to explore the journey of the human soul after death and uncover a method of observing and classifying the types of necromantic spirits, which holds the key to understanding their intention.

We will first examine the classifications of spirits based on their observable behavior, which is most useful in the field. For a deeper understanding of these behaviors, we will map out the spiritual passage of death and the choices a spirit makes on the way. Finally, we will consider the important role that ancestor rites can play to assist a spirit while navigating this journey.

Approach to Spirit Classification

Ancient magicians relied on a sophisticated system of classification to recognize different types of human spirits, a process refined over centuries of tradition. During the medieval period, necromancers adapted the nomenclature for their classifications of human spirits from the ancestor cult of the ancient Romans that had, in part, previously appropriated elements of Etruscan spirituality.

Augustine of Hippo (354–460), an early Christian theologian who would have been known to medieval scholars, records the early classification of human spirits when he reproaches pagan practices, summarizing the writings of Apuleius (ca. 124–170): "… that the souls of men are demons, and that men become Lares if they are good, Lemures or Larvae if they are bad, and Manes if it is uncertain whether they deserve well or ill."[24]

It would be incorrect to say that medieval necromancers simply adopted the Latin model; rather, they accepted the fundamental principles and incorporated them to serve as a universalist system. They also borrowed heavily from Greek and the literary translations of Arabic and Hebrew traditions made available in Christian Europe during the twelfth century Reconquista in Spain.

While appropriating the peculiarities of an ethnic religion could be considered culturally insensitive by modern standards, instruction in classical philosophy and Judeo-Christian ideas was the foundation of education for the medieval necromancer. To embrace the erudite understanding of the ancients and recognize the similarity in their own arcana validated the ars vetrus of their traditions and opened the way for the twelfth century enlightenment movement and the emerging role of medieval Christian mysticism into the new millennium.

There are seven classifications of human souls. They can be grouped into three distinct types based on their present state of existence:

+ Human spirits, who are physically incarnated.
+ Disincarnate humans called lares, who have released their phasmic form and successfully passed beyond the Gates of Death. There are two classifications of lares.
+ Revenants, who still dwell in the metacosmos after death in a spirit form, having retained their phasmic body. Of these, there are four types.

Lares: The Restful Dead

Lares are an example of eudaemones, or benign entities. They are human souls that have passed entirely through Qarth Arqa and returned to their natural state. Having attained an aetheric and numinous existence, they have no need to maintain their old and defunct phasmic bodies. In fact, they can return here willingly through the metacosmos and create for themselves a temporary phasmic form when needed, discarding it when they again return to their homeland.

· · · · · · · · · · · · · · · ·

24   Phillip Schaff, ed., "Of the End of This Life, Whether It Is Material That It Be Long Delayed," chapter 11 in St. Augustine's City of God and Christian Doctrine (New York: The Christian Literature Publishing Co., 1890), 102.

Unlike revenants, whose souls are bound in the metacosmos, the sign of fear or paranoia associated with the presence of a human spirit does not accompany the manifestation of lares. Their presence is natural and calm.

The two types of lares are as follows:

1. Lares (Eudaemon)

   The word *lar* was imported into Latin culture from the Etruscans and means "aristocrat" or "lord." This classification refers to those human souls who have no need to reincarnate and have secured a permanent place in the aetheric realm. Having achieved a state of apotheosis, they have acquired all the wisdom, experience, and virtue they can upon the earth. Regarded as honored guardians, wisdom providers, saints, and messengers, they are known as heroes in Hellenic philosophy and in some grimoires as the Holy Ones.

   Lares may return to visit those who have communion with them through spirit manifestation, or they may simply project their consciousness to affect communication. They may protect against harmful spirits and function as guides to spirit workers and magicians.

   The feeling associated with lares is of comfort, clarity, and a gentle shift in perception. A lar may present an emblem or feeling by which you can recognize them. Some cultures believe these souls may choose to be reborn in the body of a human being to impart a special knowledge and wisdom of spiritual things.

2. Familiar Lares (Eudaemon)

   Familiar lares are those who have passed through the Gates of Death and dwell in the realm of Arqa, where they can find rest and peace and prepare for their next incarnation. It is the state the living hope to achieve at their time of death and that encourages them to lead good lives, resolving conflicts and regrets before they pass and shedding the burdens that weigh down the soul. One of the true purposes of funerary rites is to prepare the soul and guide it safely to this condition of grace.

   Familiar or domestic lares are so named because they are the most common and natural state of the dead. Their presence is recognizable and comforting. They may make themselves known by symbols and tokens, a comforting touch, or a whisper. Very often they communicate through dreams and the projection of their consciousness. Familiar lares can and often do return to a temporary spiritual body for the benefit of their family or friends. They can offer guidance and comfort, share in special events, and guide the newly deceased.

Revenants: Unquiet Spirits

These are human spirits bound in the metacosmos between life and death. Trauma or unresolved attachment prevents them from releasing their phasmic form, so they remain fixated on whatever belonged to their former lives and draws them back to our world. Traditionally they may be referred to as ghosts and the undead, and they are also known as revenants, which literally means "those who remain."

In a revenant state, the memory is impaired and degenerates. This is different from a lar, where their full memory is regained upon returning to their aetheric existence. As the faculty to process linear time ceases to function at the point of carnal death, only the memory of time remains. The way in which a revenant experiences time in the metacosmos is mutable. Therefore, although hundreds of years can have elapsed between the death of a person and our interaction with that spirit, they may not be aware of the linear passage of those centuries.

There is a limit to how long a revenant can maintain their phasmic integrity in Qarth Arqa. The way in which a revenant experiences time in the metacosmos is mutable because the faculty to process linear thought ceases to function at the point of carnal death; only the fading memory of what time is remains. Therefore, although the source of phasma can strongly influence the self-awareness and ultimately the self-identity of a human spirit.

Revenants who are close to the point of physical death do not feel the damages of dissolution. However, if they remain too long in the metacosmos without the aid of a healthy source of phasma, they run the risk of forgetting their humanity and devolving into a state that is barely recognizable.

One of the important actuating principles of ancestor rites found in all cultures is to guard against this predicament by offering phasma impregnated with a recognition of the personality of a spirit that in turn empowers that spirit's recollection of their own identity.

When a human spirit becomes desperate for phasma and begins to seek any source regardless of the ideas impressed upon it, the faculty of memory becomes further corrupted. These spirits can transition into predators, hunting other spirits or even living beings to sate the urge to maintain their phasmic bodies.

There is an event horizon, a point at which the revenant is so corrupted that they become savage and irrational. Encountering this type of spirit, known as a larva, is exceedingly rare, but you should remember that no matter how fearful or threatening they may appear or behave, they are human on some level.

The following list shows the classifications of revenants based on behavior, intent to harm, and level of self-awareness exhibited. These traditional teachings are founded in recorded observation passed down by magicicans, which we have expounded upon.

1. Manes (Eudaemon)

    Manes are benign spirits, named from the archaic Latin adjective *manus*, which may be translated as "good." While manes have yet to pass through the Gates of Death and therefore remain within Qarth Arqa, they have usually done so by choice. Their refusal to leave is due to an attachment to something they have left incomplete or cannot resolve. They are generally rational and understand their predicament, and oftentimes can be beneficial to anyone interacting with them. They are classed as eudaemones since they have no intention to harm. When people experience the presence of an active revenant spirit, it is most likely a manes, as this class is the most common by far.

2. Immanes (Cacodaemon)

    The name *immanes* is the negative form of manes, plainly meaning "nonbenign spirits," however the Latin is often misinterpreted as "monstrous." Immanes are distressed spirits, either traumatized by the events of their life or lost in confusion, they may act out unaware, sometimes resulting in harm, many times incorrectly thought to be directed aggression.

    Immanes are usually unresponsive to communication or respond unpredictably and bewilderedly as they are suffering a continuous emotional imbalance. They will usually appear in the way they remember themselves, which may be indicative of their trauma, whether it is their moment of death or a powerful memory to which they are attached.

    You should have a cautious compassion for immanes, just as you would have sympathy for someone suffering emotional or mental health issues. They are categorized as cacodaemones primarily because they cause harm to themselves by surrendering to their distress and delusions, and also due to their potential for erratic, harmful effects.

3. Lemur (Cacodaemon)

The name *lemures* has uncertain roots. It may be Etruscan or Anatolian in origin, but its use is confined to hungry or rapacious revenants in Roman culture. These predatory spirits desire empowerment either through the creation of terror or deceiving their victims to receive reverence. The reason for their nefarious machinations is the accumulation of phasma, which can be absorbed to maintain their spiritual body in addition to increasing their personal power. Although lemures possess the ability to interact and communicate, they tend to be deceitful and become aggressive or evasive if confronted.

Lemures are essentially afraid to move beyond the metacosmos, dreading that they will lose something of themselves in the transition or that they are unworthy to pass through the Gates of Death and will be punished. In this fear, they find the motivation to embrace rapacious behavior to sustain their spiritual bodies. Reveling in the new power and knowledge they have discovered after physical death, they have a means to fulfill their aberrant desires.

4. Larva (Cacodaemon)

Larva is the Latin word for "mask," and just as a physical mask obscures the identity of the wearer, the larvae have masked their humanity due to their devolved condition. These spirits have entirely forgotten their original human personality and remain merely savage and aggressive predators surrendered to the urge for survival, the accumulation of phasma by any means. Their spiritual bodies reflect this state as they visually resemble the sense of their spirit's inner drive, appearing in a form between an abnormal humanoid and the bestial.

When a spirit has devolved to this state, it is impossible to reason with them. Thankfully interaction with larvae is very uncommon. Larvae are more likely to hunt other lost spirits deep in the metacosmos. They are incapable of intentionally planning an excursion into our world and only find themselves interacting with it accidentally.

Table 4: Classification of Necromantic Spirits

Spirit	Stage	Communication	Form	Resource
Lares	No longer need to reincarnate	Dreams, symbols, and direct thoughts	Choose how and when they will appear	Do not require sustenance
Familiar Lares	Are on the path of reincarnation	Dreams, symbols, and direct thoughts	Usually appear in a way that can be recognized by loved ones	Do not require sustenance
Manes	Attending unresolved matters	Can be reasonable and communicative	Appearance reflects memories of themselves	Rely on ancestor rites or available phasma
Immanes	Trapped in delusion. May be unaware of death	Emotional and erratic, oblivious of their actions	Appear as the image they are fixated on	Dependent on available phasma
Lemures	Attempt to to stay in Qarth Arqa indefinitely	Deceptive; incite emotion to gain phasma	Can learn to manipulate their appearance	Predators and scavengers of phasma
Larvae	Losing their sense of humanity	No rational communication	Involuntarily bestial qualities and features	Instinctual predators that feed on each other

REGIONS OF QARTH ARQA

The classifications of necromantic spirits are largely derived from an understanding of the stages of catharsis a human soul experiences after death. Modeled on the Hebrew hells, these stages are conceived as a map of seven regions within the passage of death that explain the psycho-spiritual condition of the deceased. Each region represents a phase in a journey of redemption, an opportunity to purge the bindings that restrain them. These stages are not a hierarchy in which a spirit passes from one to the next sequentially, nor are they imposed by any punitive divine wrath. Rather, it is a dreamscape unique to each spirit who undergoes it, and the trials they endure are self-inflicted.

Models such as the Seven Hells are used as an intellectual map to explain the nature of attachments and the results of clinging to them. Although enigmatically named, it must be emphasized that this geography is symbolic and not physical. The hells occur in the mind and conditional reality of a spirit. The metacosmos is mutable, and any perceived place or location is a creation of the spirit's power of imagination which transforms the substance of the metacosmos into experiential landscapes.

The first three regions explain the First Death—that is, the pathway of the deceased from their point of physical demise to the emancipation of their soul at the Gates of Death. The remaining four relate to revenants and the Second Death.

Journey to the Underworld

To understand the metaphysical influences that accompany the soul on its journey, we can look to an analogy from Hellenic chthonic philosophy. These Pagan concepts were inherited by medieval necromancers and contextualized their understanding of Judeo-Christian mysticism such as the Seven Hells.

In the Greek chthonic mysteries, the metacosmos between life and death is named Erebos and personified by the god of that name. It is the passage of darkness the soul must traverse immediately after carnal death, which is comparable to Qarth Arqa.

Curiously, Erebos is believed to be the father of the three Moirai or Fates, Lachesis, Clotho, and Atropos. Most people familiar with Greek myths will know the Moirai as the goddesses who spin, weave, and cut the threads of a person's life. However, there is a chthonic aspect to these goddesses related to the process a spirit must pass through after physical death that leads to the resolution of the spirit's former life before the soul can pass from Erebos into the underworld and ultimately regain their place in Elysium.

Song of Death

The creatures known as sirens are said to sing songs that represent the harmonic necessities of the multiverse, maintaining divine intention in evolution and obviating the confusion of accident. These sirens are found in the upper, middle, and nether worlds, each dedicated to the harmony in each realm. In the choir of the

Cheled
Living Realm

First Death
Corporeal Transition
When the corporeal body
dies, the soul is temporarily
shrouded by the spirit.
Reason ceases.

Arqa
Realm of the Dead

Resolution
Spiritual Transition
Catharsis of the soul occurs
when the spirit releases its
phasmic form. The soul
returns to an aetheric state.

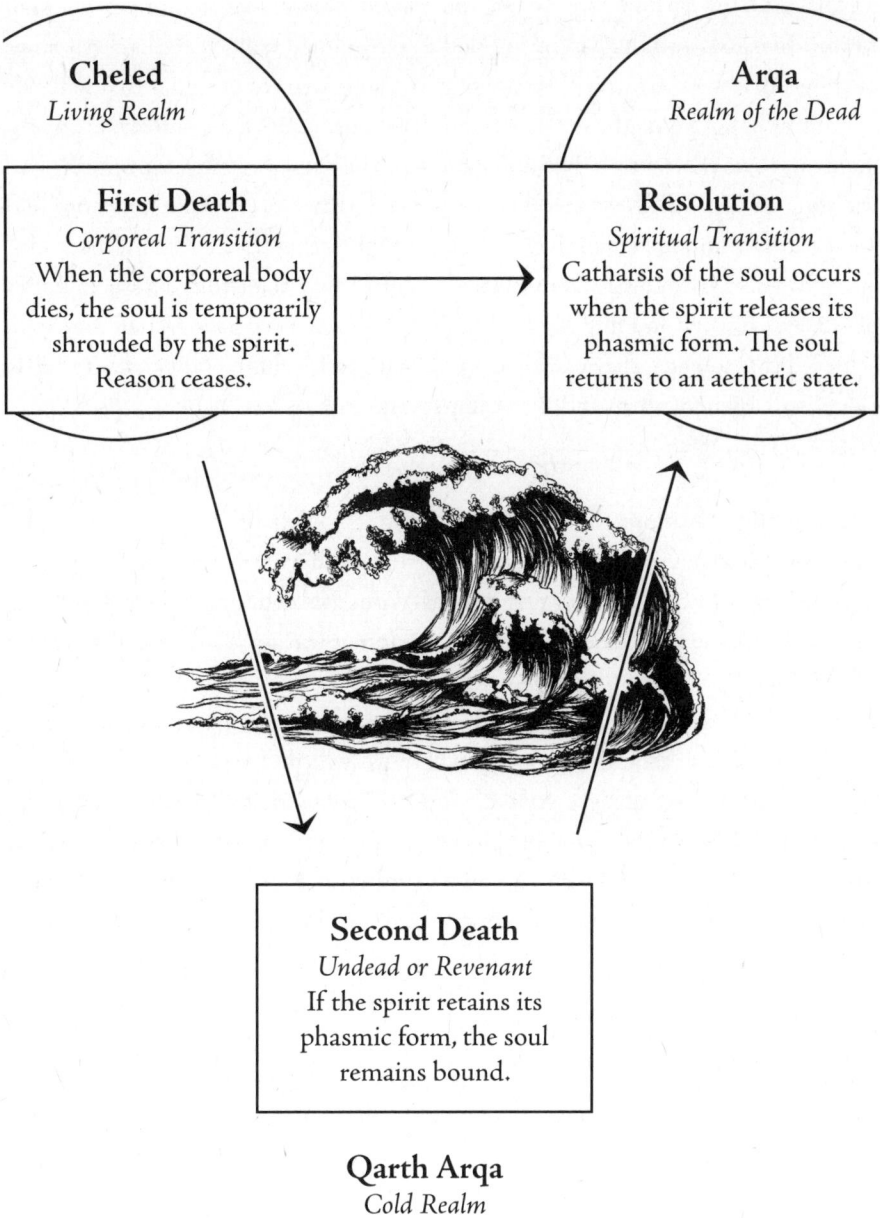

Second Death
Undead or Revenant
If the spirit retains its
phasmic form, the soul
remains bound.

Qarth Arqa
Cold Realm

Transition After First Death to Arqa or Qarth Arqa

underworld, the chthonic sirens sing the melody of catharsis that impels the soul toward Elysium, and the Moirai are said to harmonize with them. Lachesis sings of things that were, Clotho of things that are, and Atropos of things that will be.

These songs guide the deceased, who first must remove the emotional attachments to their mortal past, harmonizing with the song of Lachesis. According to the song of Clotho, they must also sever ties to their present circumstance and what was left undone when they passed through carnal death. Finally, the undulating tones of Atropos should inspire the spirit to lay aside their fears and hopes of what is to come and find the tranquility of the essential soul. When they have achieved this serenity, the veil revealing the path to Elysium (comparable to Little Eden) will open for them and they can pass through to rest.

Land of the Dead

In our family traditions, the passage to death is spoken about as one of adventure in which we will remove the persona that we have worn for our temporary incarnation to know ourselves and our loved ones more fully than we did in life. Though we do not speed death's coming, we do not fear its natural inevitability or what it holds for us.

Like the Greek sirens, the keening of our ancestral deities guide us homeward to a mystical land beneath the waves where we will find rest between lives. We view the Gates of Death as a welcome portal, knowing that we must be willing to judge ourselves and be accountable for our past life, and in doing so, we will return to our authentic state to be among our divinities and ancestors. For this reason, we are culturally encouraged to live a good life, so that we can have a good death without regret or remorse.

First Death

The passage of death depicted in these cultural examples is resonant with the condition referred to in necromancy as the First Death. When our physical form expires, our phasmic body must also separate from its earthly counterpart. Through the process of catharsis, we must then free ourselves of the burdens and attachments that bind us to our mortal existence, further liberating our soul from its phasmic constraints. It is only then that we may cross through the Gates of Death into that aetheric realm to which we are all destined. These three stages represent the first three regions of the seven hells, each of which is described in detail. Familiar lares are the classification of human souls that achieve the culmination of this innate process.

1. The Pains of Death
   (Latin: *Gehenna*, Hebrew: *Ge-Hinnom*)

   This region is named after the Valley of Hinnom in Jerusalem, where sacrificial offering fires took place according to tradition. These immolations metaphorically described a process known to magical philosophy as the fires of dissolution, wherein the spirit separates from its attachment to the physical remains of its former body. The discomfiture of this separation is described in Hebrew tradition as "the Pains of the Grave," and it is believed to generally take a minimum of three or four days to achieve independence from the carnal body.

   The period directly after death is a sacred time during which the transition of the soul can be greatly aided by the practices of vigil, protection, and anointing. In our own Scottish culture, preparing the body for burial also includes preparation of the soul-shrine, the numen or vessel that will carry the soul on its voyage, often attended by a joyous farewell or wake. If needed, practices to relieve the soul of its heavy burdens are also enacted, such as sin eating.

2. Shadow of Death
   (Latin: *Umbra Mortis*, Hebrew: *Tzal-Maveth*)

   The second stage of the journey is called the Shadow of Death but perhaps should rather be perceived as the "echo of life," as this is the time when the individual must resolve the things that call them back to their recent incarnation. Funerary rituals and guides lead the soul, but the soul also has an inherent attraction or impulse to seek resolution and advance toward their rest. In Greek traditions, this impulse is described as the function of sirens.

   Most souls pass through this stage of death easily, accepting the guidance they receive and shedding the encumberances of the life they have known. However, for some, the process of resolution consumes them as they review and settle the echoes of their earthly existence, thoroughly untangling all emotive attachments.

Traditionally, the passage through the Shadow of Death is believed to take a spirit up to a year to accomplish, according to our perception of time. During this period, the spirit should be aided by funerary practices but not expected to communicate until their transition is complete.

3. Gates of Death
(Latin: *Portae Mortis*, Hebrew: *Shaare-Maveth*)
Spirit: Familiar Lares

The Gates of Death represent the transition of the soul, the point where they leave their phasmic body behind and return to their natural numinous state in the Little Eden to await reincarnation, which in Hebrew is called *gilgul neshemoth* (the revolving of souls). Represented as the diaphanous veil through which we must all pass, it is likened to the shoreline of a distant land which separates the cold seas of Qarth Arqa from the land where souls find rest between lives.

When a soul enters the Gates of Death, it does so unencumbered by the emotive residue of its former life and all attachments to the world of the living. To those who have not found catharsis through the process of resolving the Shadow of Death, the gates remain temporarily obscured.

Second Death

To some spirits, the Gates of Death and what lies beyond present a terrifying prospect. They believe it is a place of wrath where they will be harshly judged for their iniquities. The fear of being condemned, of what is next, and leaving behind the life they have known causes them to stay in the metacosmos in a noncorporeal state rather than face what is ahead of them. Others are too lost to find their way or are simply not ready. In clinging on to these attachments, they deny themselves entrance into the Gates of Death, instead entering a state known as the Second Death. This self-imposed condition of catharsis within Qarth Arqa is what Wierus's *Pseudomonarchia Daemonum* refers to as purgatory or the "affliction of souls" (see chapter 2).

Gregory of Nyssa (335–395), an early Christian theologian, explains the process of catharsis in a dialogue to his sister Macrina:

"...those still living in the flesh must as much as ever they can separate and free themselves in a way from its attachments by virtuous conduct, in order that after death they may not need a second death to cleanse them from the remnants that are owing to this cement of the flesh, and once the bonds are loosed from around the soul, her soaring up to the Good may be swift and unimpeded, with no anguish of the body to distract her."[25]

The Second Death is the condition of existence of most interest to sciomancy—these are the human spirits bound within the metacosmos described as revenants, who are subjected to an ongoing dissolution of their phasmic bodies and experience a death comparable to the decomposition of their physical bodies.

This process is described in the biblical idiom "their worm dieth not and their fire is not extinguished," wherein the worm is symbolic of the maggot that feeds upon the putrefying carcass and the fire the passions and desires they refuse to release, a grotesque analogy about attachments to a life that can no longer be grasped or relived.[26]

1. The Region of Clay
   (Latin: *Lutem Fecis*, Hebrew: *Tit ha-Yavon*)
   Spirit: Manes

   The first state of the Second Death is described as a Region of Clay, a euphemistic reference to simple attachments in the spirit's earthly life. The seductive pull toward those things or people the deceased perceives as being left behind can be an intoxicating temptation.

   The truth is that if a spirit releases these attachments, the boundary between themselves and their loved ones is liberated. Ironically, it is the fear of losing their attachments that entraps the spirit, bogging them down in a place where that boundary appears almost impenetrable and the connection to the living world is all too often frustrated.

   The Region of Clay describes the condition of the manes, self-possessed spirits who have not yet heeded the metaphorical song of Clotho, who sings of things that are. Rather, they choose to adhere to

. . . .

25   Gregory of Nyssa, William Moore and Henry Austin Wilson, trans., "On the Soul and the Resurrection," in *Nicene and Post-Nicene Fathers, Second Series*, vol. 5 (New York: Charles Scribner's Sons, 1917), 448.

26   Mark 9:43, in which Jesus quotes Isaiah 66.24. Douay-Rheims Bible: https://www.drbo.org/.

the concerns and priorities important to them at the moment of death, temporarily delaying their progress. During this phase, the living can greatly assist the manes through prayers and offerings, allowing the latter to sustain themselves while they find resolution on their own terms and in their own time.

2. The Well of Dissolution
(Latin: *Puteus Interitus*, Hebrew: *Bar Shachath*)
Spirit: Immanes

   This state is called the Well of Dissolution because if the underlying attachment is not resolved, the immanes will ultimately devolve and lose their sense of humanity and, over a period, transition into the unfortunate condition of a larva. Immanes are distressed spirits who dwell in their trauma and come to define their existence by attaching their identity to the suffering they experienced in life.

   Lost in their internal turmoil, immanes have failed to hear the song of Lachesis, instead dwelling on attachments of things that were. The traumatic events of their living past overwhelm them and dictate their experience after carnal death, causing them to feel that they have little or no control. They essentially become their trauma, participating again and again in the suffering of the past. Over time, the nature of the metacosmos continually works its effect upon the immanes. Coupled with their lack of self-possession, their sense of identity is eroded and initiates a transition into the darkness of Sheol or Tartarus. Although they may not always be aware of the living, immanes can benefit from our compassion, prayers, and memorials that keep their identity intact until aid arrives that can lead them to find rest.

3. Perdition
(Latin: *Perditio*, Hebrew: *Abaddon*)
Spirit: Lemures

   Abaddon is the Hebrew word for "destruction" and is interpreted as "perdition." Theologically, perdition is a path of self-destruction caused by turning away from the divine. This is the state lemures inhabit either through fear of judgment or derision of authority, a choice to turn their face from the light of divinity and therefore the Gates of Death themselves.

Lemures conceitedly dismiss the implication of the song of Atropos, who sings of what will be. Attached to their dread of what is inevitably to come, they act adversely through denial, fear, or open rebellion. An illusion of exaggerated personal power feeds their sense of identity. They seek to enhance their phasmic body by either cannibalizing other spirits or exciting strong emotive responses among the living. Unlike manes and immanes, who can find peace from funerary offerings, lemures only find greater strength to fuel their predatory behavior.

Lemures are not beyond redemption; they can choose to turn toward the Gates of Death at any moment. However, the longer they maintain their attachment, the more predatory they become. Like immanes, they will in due course devolve to a larva and fall into the pit of lost souls.

4. Pit of Lost Souls
   (Latin: *Fovea*, Greek: *Tartarus*, Hebrew: *Sheol*)
   Spirit: Larvae

   Sheol (Hebrew) refers to a grave or pit. It is the ultimate state into which a spirit may devolve and thus forms the grave of the Second Death. Since biblical times, Sheol has been equated to the Greek Tartarus, such that the two terms became synonymous in medieval magic. Larva is the state in which a spirit dwells in predatory mutual destruction without intellect or reason, driven only by memories of the compulsion to survive. Eventually they will themselves fall victim to the cruel turmoil of their circumstances and consequently move through the Gates of Death, even if it is involuntary. In so doing, the soul returns to its native nature and the experience of having been a larva is integrated into the soul-memory without discrimination. The soul is then free to pursue their evolution once again and embark on the next stage of their journey.

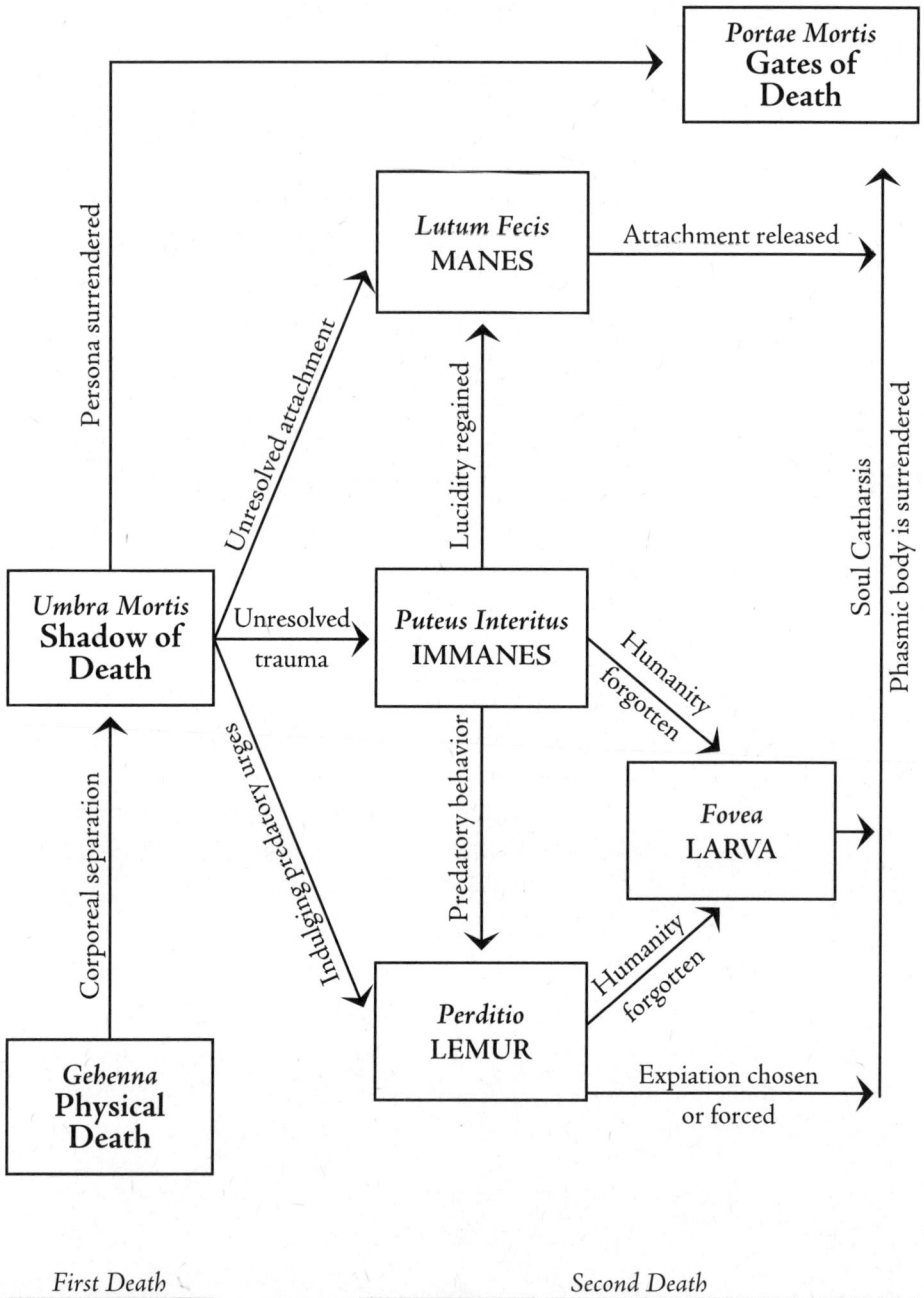

Portae Mortis
Gates of Death

Lutum Fecis
MANES

Attachment released

Persona surrendered

Unresolved attachment

Lucidity regained

Soul Catharsis

Phasmic body is surrendered

Umbra Mortis
Shadow of Death

Unresolved trauma

Puteus Interitus
IMMANES

Humanity forgotten

Corporeal separation

Indulging predatory urges

Predatory behavior

Fovea
LARVA

Gehenna
Physical Death

Perditio
LEMUR

Humanity forgotten

Expiation chosen or forced

First Death

Second Death

Seven Psycho-Spiritual Phases of Qarth Arqa, Also Called the Seven Hells

While the model of the seven regions of death or hells is described in culturally specific language (whether Graeco-Latin or Hebrew), its fundamental structure is universal and can be adapted as an understanding of a very real psycho-spiritual process.

Comprehension of Qarth Arqa and its phenomena can make sense of localized cultural or traditional metaphors by way of comparison. Clarity begets clarity, and by comparing our own individual traditions to a model such as this, we can enrich our understanding of other time-worn and beloved traditions.

THE ROLE OF FUNERARY AND ANCESTRAL RITES

There is much we can do to aid spirits in their journey. The ancient sages knew that ethical obligations to our fellow human family extended beyond their souls existing in a living state to also include those who have passed the point of death.

This sense of responsibility is the origin of all funerary and ancestor rites that can nourish, guide, and protect the disincarnating soul, as well as bring comfort to the living. More than mere customs, these are necromantic ceremonies and a natural extension of the social needs inherent in the human condition. By attending to these customs proactively, we can reduce the incidences of spirit disturbance.

Preparation

Preparation for death begins early in life. The relationships we form with what lies beyond our temporal existence are informed by our expectations, beliefs, and doubts. While there is a certain stability in the process of death, our subjective experience of it is malleable. Customs and rituals provide the waypoints to navigate the passage between life and death on a deep subliminal level. Having these spiritual pathways established prevents the newly deceased from becoming lost in the metacosmos or clinging to life. When we close our eyes for the last time, it is these familiar paths that greet us and show us the way forward.

Funerary Rites

Although it is often said that funerals serve to comfort the living, their ceremonies also render assistance to the deceased. When effectively employed, these rites foster a sense of solace in the transitioning soul; they provide purification to prompt the newly deceased release the tethers of their carnal body and its former life and accept protection and guidance as they embark on their journey.

Funerary customs may be as elaborate as they are simple, depending on the culture. For the grieving, rites should also proffer consolation and direction, encouraging them to loosen their grip on the deceased who should be allowed to freely depart.

Ancestral Rites

Like funerary ceremonials, ancestor rites are magical practices impregnated with transactional purposes. The first of these is to honor those people to whom we owe our very existence, as we are genetically the sum of all that has come before us.

Through communication with our forebears, we can attain the benefit of comfort and the garnered wisdom of accrued experience. When a soul becomes a lar, they enter a realm of understanding devoid of emotional attachment. The soul no longer has the opinions and character flaws they had in life.

It can be easy to judge those who have gone before us. Our ancestors may have made mistakes, but authentic wisdom is gained by the recognition of faults and overcoming obstacles. While we are not responsible for our ancestor's choices, we should attempt to evince acceptance and reverence for the tribulations in their lives and cultivate gratitude for what they can teach us. True spiritual and ethical progression is not a revolution; rather it is an evolution built upon both the successes and errors of the past. To that end, ancestor rites provide a two-way channel of transmission specifically with our familiar lares, exciting personal and communal spiritual progression. Traditionally, many cultures have ancestor shrines erected in their home where offerings and communion with the familial deceased take place. For example, in Roman houses, a place was marked for the commemoration of lares known as a Lararium.

Familial Duty

The familial responsibility of providing offerings for manes and immanes is anciently accepted and continues to this day. Driven in part by care for the souls of our forebears, there is also an element of self-preservation should you find that after physical death, you have become attached or lost.

The oldest known library, the Royal Library of Ashurbanipal in the kingdom of Assyria (685–631 BCE), contains cuneiform tablets describing the condition and causes of distressed human spirits. Called *ekimmu*, these are revenants who do not enter the afterlife but wander the earth.

Besides tragic or violent death, the Assyrians considered the cessation of ancestor offerings as one of the chief causes for the creation of an ekimmu. The following is an example extracted from an incantation against various types of spirits, wherein this cause of the ekimmu is clearly recited.[27]

> Or a ghost unburied.
> Or a ghost that none careth for.
> Or a ghost with none to make offerings.
> Or a ghost with none to pour libations.
> Or a ghost that hath no posterity.

Offerings to the Dead

Reestablishing offerings to the dead reduce the frequency of spirit activity and bring equilibrium where an unquiet manes or immanes is causing a disturbance. Often these gifts are in the form of prayers, libations, bread, fruit, or certain incenses. The evaporating alcohol of a libation or the essence of organic food-stuffs that have been dedicated as offerings releases a healthy source of phasma, as do acts and prayers of love and devotion.

Such repeated and regular offerings are intended to limit the dissolution of the spirits' phasmic bodies, allowing them to be sustained while they work to find resolution. More importantly they reinforce their sense of self-identity, to aid their healing through familial bonds and preventing them from devolving into a predatory condition.

Shrines and Memorials

Memorials serve as magical focal points for the continued relationship with the souls of the deceased, providing an anchor and a way by which devotions can be received. Granite was the traditional choice, especially for grave markers, for its ability to absorb phasma, allowing it to capture the person's essence as their remains decayed.

. . . .

27   R. Campbell Thompson, *The Devils and Evil Spirits of Babylonia*, vol. I (London: Luzac & Co, 1904), 41.

Many Scottish families visit the gravestone of loved ones during the day of All Souls (the day following Halloween), to commemorate the souls of the deceased. One tradition is to share or offer an apple, a fruit associated with the realm of the dead in Celtic and Germanic cultures. Another Scottish custom is to lay a stone on the grave marker that had been resting upon the hearth of the home during the previous year. This is a symbolic representation of sharing the family's experience directly with their loved ones. The hearth is the natural ancestor shrine in many homes where offerings and libations are made. As we say in our own family, "stone speaks to stone."

When founding new towns, ancient Romans would excavate a hole and lay a stone for the manes, called the *lapis manalis*. It was considered an entrance to the underworld and would also serve as a central memorial and sanctuary for all the town's potential manes and immanes where offerings could be made. The townsfolk would commemorate these spirits on the final day of the Parentalia, called the Feralia.

Magical Duty

In medieval necromancy, the duty to care for the souls of manes and immanes remained a central practice. In Catholic-influenced magic, the necromancer had a responsibility to liberate several spirits (usually three) from purgatory before they could proceed with the rituals of necyomancy. In other grimoire traditions more aligned to the pre-Christian mysteries of the goddess Hecate, incense or bread and wine were offered to wandering or lost spirits as a prerequisite before the magician could secure Hecate's authority to make conjurations. In one of the most well-known British necromantic procedures originally recorded in Reginald Scott's *Discoverie of Witchcraft*, the necromancer seeks to conjure the spirit of a suicide to discover the reason for their self-destruction and provide rest to the tragic immanes.

Restoring Understanding

The lack of spiritual understanding that has resulted after centuries of religious doctrinal denial followed by the secularism of postindustrial science has escalated the number of both manes and immanes. So too have the exponential rise in human population, and the subsequent deaths that follow flooded the metacosmos with distressed spirits. Under these conditions, it is apparent that the need for a conscientious restoration of ancestor rites is imperative.

It is always better when a magician can engage their ancestors within the context of their own tradition or through established cultural customs, but even a simple and renewed recognition of the souls of the deceased is a considerable advancement. In any event, we are the future ancestors with the wisdom and experience to impart to our descendants; with this knowledge, we should solemnly endeavor to establish enduring ancestor practices.

CHAPTER SIX

SIGNS OF UNQUIET SPIRITS

Sciomancy is an immediate art in which we need to use our skills of observation and experience to identify spirit behavior in real time. You must be able to assess threats and have a practical comprehension of how spirits influence their environment and how to alleviate any negative effects that may be experienced. In this chapter, we delve deeper into the movements and signs pertaining specifically to human spirits (introduced in chapter 4). We will also look at the nature of obsession and factors that can indicate a spirit infestation.

NECROMANTIC MOVEMENTS AND SIGNS

Every daemon creates a motion or movement as their presence approaches the liminal boundary of a metacosmos separating their world from our own. These movements differ as the phenomenal reality of our world overlaps with the unique corporeality of another sublunary realm.

With regard to Qarth Arqa, the phenomena that affect our physical environment are unique, reflecting the interaction between our realm and Arqa. The realm of Arqa is mercurial, and deep within it lies an eternal aetheric core, the Elysium or Little Eden in which souls find passage to their rest between lives. It interacts with our realm differently and may be conceived as a nexus between other sublunary worlds. Therefore, being an inhabitant of the border zone between the singular phenomena of Arqa and the habitation of the living, the movement associated with the presence of human spirits in Qarth Arqa exhibits slight shifts from the pattern of the phenomena attending the appearance of other nonhuman daemones.

Stages of Necromantic Manifestation

One of the stages of visible manifestation of any spirit is the appearance of a nube. This cloud of coalesced phasma is a necessary step before a spirit can manifest further.

Disincarnate human beings can be differentiated from other daemones by the color of the nube, a luminous gray mist. It is often the first visual event an observer witnesses and has been regularly captured in both video and still photographs.

According to the practice of necromancy, the appearance of a silvery mist is considered more than a phase of manifestation but also serves as the movement. Usually a movement presages manifestation, representing a shift in the environment. Given the unique nature of Qarth Arqa, there is no other movement associated with a human spirit; therefore the nube itself has historically served to represent the indication or movement of an approaching disincarnate human entity.

Oftentimes photographic evidence shows the appearance of a numen, or orb, emerging from or contained within the silvery nube. This numen is the essential center of the spirit body. It is said to be the original aetheric form of the soul and is ever present when a numinous spirit is encountered. A numen is never considered to be a sign proper, but a human soul can be identified by the composition of the orb itself. The numen of a human spirit is always of a regular spherical shape, self-illumined and opalescent, often displaying a thin blue corona. It is very distinguishable and recognizable, differing significantly from nonhuman spiritual orbs and entirely distinct from environmental detritus such as dust or water drops.

Identifying Revenants

Revenants can be further differentiated from lares by the sense of dread or paranoia and the cold that attends their presence that may cause shivering or raised hair. Due to their aetheric nature, lares do not affect our physical environment in the same way that revenants do. They neither maintain a phasmic body nor attempt to emerge into our world from the chaos of Qarth Arqa, as is the case with revenants.

The ancient magicians realized that the body of a revenant was uniquely cold. Today, unexplained cold spots are consistently recorded in paranormal investigations and universally recognized as evidence of a presenting spirit. This has been discovered to be an unexplainable and immediate drop in temperature of more than 5 degrees Fahrenheit or 2.8 degrees Celsius. Thus, the phenomenon of authentic cold spots can be considered a secondary sign of the immediate location of a revenant.

In paranormal circles, it is often hypothesized that the spirit draws the energy of heat to manifest and therefore creates a chill void; however, this idea implies an intentionality on the part of the revenant which lacks understanding. Centuries of observation and experience inform us that most spirits are unaware of their own manifestation and therefore do not consciously manipulate the environment to achieve that result. This cold void is in fact the actual form of the manifesting human spirit, heat being a phenomenon unknown within Qarth Arqa, a region defined by its cold character.

The two primary signs recorded by the ancient magicians indicating the presence of a revenant are a sensation of fear or paranoia and horripilation, or the hair follicles bristling. Apart from being a symptom of feeling cold, horripilation can be an effect of static electricity and provides a clue to the origin of both signs.

Table 5: Distinguishing Lares and Revenants

	Lares	Revenants
Sensation	Subtle sense of alertness Presence feels amiable	Paranoia and breathlessness Sense of dread
EMF	No discernable electromagnetic changes	Erratic electromagnetic or compass readings
Temperature	No symptoms; move naturally through the metacosmos	Hair bristling; isolated cold spot in location of manifestation (>5 F° / 2.8 C°)
Appearance	Choose the time and place they appear; may project an image of themselves	Reliant on a source of phasma to maintain their form; may learn to shape their appearance

	Lares	Revenants
Activity	Subtle and deliberate; may leave recognizable signs	Connected to a specific place, person, or object; may be erratic
Communication	Aware and intelligible. Often communicate in thoughts and dreams; know more than they knew in life	Varies depending on classification; knowledge is limited to former life and current state

Paranoia and EMF

One commonly recorded event in modern paranormal investigations is erratic spikes of electromagnetic frequencies (EMF) that are inconsistent with a previously established baseline. There is no evidence to suggest that human spirits directly or intentionally create electromagnetic anomalies. They are most likely caused by interaction between environmental conditions in our world and agitation from within Qarth Arqa itself. It is possibly a natural byproduct of the liminal veil thinning that allows for the emergence of a revenant.

Erratic EMF activity appears to accompany the coalescence of phasma and likely produces static charge in the apparition's immediate location. EMF effects appear to intensify in accordance with the process of the manifestation, peaking when the spirit appears as an umbra or shadow.

Electromagnetic Hypersensitivity

While there is no definitive medical evidence for the condition known as electromagnetic hypersensitivity (EHS), there are serious studies into the possible health risks of long-term exposure to electromagnetic fields. The reported symptoms of EMF exposure are largely anecdotal but there is a measure of commonality. When compared to the acute effects experienced during paranormal investigations, similarities again arise. It is possible that erratic EMF spikes may temporarily affect the sufferer and an awareness of this prospect should be a consideration when planning your investigation.

Paranoia and specifically sensations of unease or being watched are among the reported symptoms of EHS, showing a clear parallel with the signs traditionally associated with the appearance of revenants. Other effects such as a sense of emotional heaviness, headache, shortness of breath, and discomfort from a slight constriction in the muscles of the chest are also symptoms common to both EHS and experiences during an investigation.

While these effects are potentially caused by the environmental disturbance of EMF anomalies, they are in no way indicators of a spirit's intent. Whether caused by EMF or from more esoteric sources, it is worth noting that spaces in a home that are hot spots for the build-up of EMF from appliances are often cited as primary locations of disturbances assumed to be paranormal. These include enclosed settings such as kitchens, basement laundries, and, in more recent times, wherever the computer and Wi-Fi are located.

Symptoms of EMF Overexposure

Erratic EMF can accompany the appearance of temporary but debilitating symptoms in some people. When any of these effects appear chronic, or devolve into an anxiety or panic attack, medical attention should be sought for the sufferer immediately. In most cases, however, the effects are manageable and can often be assuaged by removing the person from the location and having them sit and breathe deeply. Of course, a second person should remain with them and monitor their condition until they have fully recovered. As dense or heavy phasma often accrues around a person suffering these effects, experience has provided another method of relief, which is relocating to a place near running water. For example, having a sufferer sit in a bathroom and engage in deep breathing while cold water is running from the faucet and shower may expedite recovery.

First Aid for Treating EMF Exposure

- Symptoms: Anxiety, headache, impaired cognitive function, nausea, overwhelming fear and dread, paranoia, shortness of breath, vomiting.
- Treatment: Move away from source of EMF. Breathe deeply into cupped hands to relieve hyperventilation. Sit next to running water. Use discarricare techniques (page 119) to restore balance.

Caution! Do not try to create artificial EMF fields for "better" results during an investigation. Call emergency services if the person shows signs of severe symptoms.

DEFINING TYPES OF ACTIVITY

As is common with all daemones, the primary necromantic classifications of spirits are divided between those which cause harm and those which do not share this effect, which is to say cacodaemones and eudaemones. While this division can be considered somewhat imprecise and subjective, it allows you the first opportunity to ascertain the level of precaution necessary when engaged in sciomantic investigation. Of the four classifications of revenants, manes are under the designation of eudaemones; the remaining three are under the label of cacodaemones—immanes, lemures, and larvae. This differentiation is important when you are trying to classify a revenant and determine the nature of a disturbance.

Table 6: Necromantic Eudaemones and Cacodaemones

	Behavior Type	Activity	Example
Eudaemon	Benevolent entity	Presence is beneficent	Lares and Familiar Lares
	Unresolved spirit	Activity pertains to their progress	Manes
Cacodaemon	Distressed spirit	Infestation and psychic influence	Immanes
	Predatory spirit	Deliberate infestation and oppression	Lemur or Larva

Spirit Disturbance

Experiencing the presence of a revenant or ghost is not indicative of a haunting. The word "haunt" comes from a nearly obsolete English word meaning "to frequent" and was originally used in the sense of location. It has since been applied more generically to include any activities of a spirit. For the purposes of sciomancy, this is too broad a description and is somewhat misleading, as an interaction with a spirit may not always be considered a disturbance.

A disturbance negatively affects a person or place, leading our magical predecessors to prefer the term "obsession," from the Latin obsidēre, "to besiege, occupy," or to "vex from without."[28] Obsessions are caused by a revenant's fixation on their attachments which binds it to individual people, objects, or locations.

. . . .

28   "Obsession," Etymological Dictionary, https://www.etymonline.com/search?q=obsession.

There are four divisions of a spirit disturbance: *infestation, obsession, oppression,* and *possession.* These divisions are described in terms analogous to the defenses of a fortification or castle. Infestation describes the confirmed indications of the activity of the foe's army swarming over the territory. Obsession is likened to that army besieging the castle, encircling it, and settling into a long-term occupation. Oppression is emblematic of a directed attack against the walls of the fortification seeking to make a breach. Possession is symbolic of when the castle falls to the foe: the defender's flag is lowered and replaced by the banner of the assaulting force.

While religious exorcists have traditionally employed these terms, they often consider them a progressive ladder of spirit activity whose ultimate goal is involuntary possession of a victim. This classification suggests an intentionality and uniformity in a spirit's activity that is frankly unrealistic and moralistic in its approach; it reinforces dogma rather than seeking a reasoned solution.

In fact, it is much more convoluted and complex than being simply degrees of a single intent. Infestation can be short-term, events that occur and then recede without any need of investigation. When infestation is prolonged and recurring, it can be indicative of an obsession. However, when an obsession is confirmed, it does not mean that the spirit is predatory or that oppression is assured or should be expected. Likewise, while involuntary possession does require oppression in order to take place, the vast majority of oppression cases never end in a possession.

Infestation

When a revenant is compelled by emotional or instinctual urges to act out regarding the subjects of their attachments, it can lead to paranormal phenomena, such as the manipulation of physical objects or the apparition of the spirit's form to living witnesses. When these manifestations reach a level of intensity or frequency to be a disturbance to our physical environment, this is known as infestation. The word *poltergeist* means "noisy ghost," and despite contemporary theories to the contrary, it is simply the German language descriptor for an infestation.

Measurable paranormal activities are the usual cause precipitating a necromantic investigation, and you should approach infestation as a source of information or a message that must be deciphered to determine the cause of the spirit disturbance. Infestation events should never be considered indicators of evil or malicious intent.

These phenomena are consequences of the spirit pursuing their attachments. They may not be deliberate actions and determining intentionality should be a consideration within an investigation. Moreover, attempting to discover attachments causing the infestation is an imperative for the sciomancer, as it is often the key to revealing the means to calculate an equitable solution to the disturbance.

Obsession

While the term "obsession" can generally refer to a spirit incursion or haunting, it is more specifically applied to a prolonged and enduring fixation of a revenant rooted in their attachments which impacts the physical environment and living people in a location.

An obsession demands an emotional compulsion. In sciomancy, revenant cacodaemones are most likely to be considered the cause of an obsession, though sometimes a manes may obsess if they are desperate to communicate their message. Lares and familiar lares never fall into fixated attachment. Their numinous condition, a state beyond the emotional urgency of a living being, provides them with the choice of action motivated only by a sense of well-being for their loved ones. Phantasms or residual hauntings are void of any sentience and therefore cannot become engaged in obsession. They are simply impressions left on the phasma at the scene of traumatic or important events. Phasmata can only appear to obsess when their intelligence is programmed to do so. Being artificial constructs, they are simply incapable of instinctual or emotional duress.

Manes Obsession

Manes obsess when they are fixated on their attachments, which can be many and varied. They are often incomplete tasks or concerns which may seem minor or strange to the observer. After the moment of physical death, the animus ceases activity, and a spirit must rely on the memory of reason to function. They are often unaware that their rational faculties are impaired and remain aberrantly attached to those things they have left unfinished, or to emotional connections they feel they cannot leave behind.

The most common attachment a manes has is refusing to leave a loved one and wishing to remain until that person or people join them in the afterlife. Sadly, when a living person is suffering intense grief at such a loss, they may also unintentionally hold a spirit back from pursuing their resolution. That spirit is then forced to remain a manes through the emotional attachment of grief imposed upon them, until their living loved one can find the peace to allow the spirit to move on.

Immanes Obsession

Immanes obsess though fixating on their own condition—that is, the attachments inherent in their own trauma. There are times when trauma and tragedy succeed in transcending the transition of death. A spirit who carries such emotional suffering into the metacosmos can become ensnared in their self-imposed confusion. These immanes are unfortunate spirits enduring a kind of existential psychosis with the absence of a rational faculty to forge pathways to recovery.

Often immanes are unaware of living witnesses to their unpredictable activities, and it is equally common for them to be entirely ignorant to the fact that they are deceased. As their disordered condition is self-focused, immanes are more likely to be attached to a location or an object rather than a person. When an immanes does implicitly fixate upon a living person, it is usually a case of identity transferal wherein the subject of their obsession reminds the spirit of someone involved in their previous life or connected to their original trauma.

Oppression

When obsession is targeted for the purpose of voracious satisfaction, it is called oppression. The indicators or symptoms consistent with a living person suffering oppression are dramatic shifts in personality with intense and unpredictable emotional outbursts. Often a victim becomes withdrawn and secretive, exhibiting seething anger or uncontrollable sadness and anxiety. Besides drastic personality changes, oppression will induce compulsive behaviors in a victim, such as extreme hunger or thirst; urge to constantly write, paint, or draw; and the repeated ritualization of trivial actions. Oppression is always preceded or accompanied by intense and protracted infestation; it never occurs independently of a chronic spirit driven crisis.

Lemur Oppression

A person who had urges to victimize people in life may reveal or maintain those proclivities following their demise and thus become lemures. When they enter the metacosmos, they may discover new knowledge and power, such as the ability to go where they choose in a moment or the mutability and plasticity of their phasmic form. These discoveries can lead them to attempt to satiate their compulsive desires through the agencies infestation and obsession grant them, targeting their preferred victim type.

The primary function of oppression is to excite emotional extremes in the victim. The reciprocity of intense emotion and the phasma created by it serves to not only reinforce the phasmic body of a revenant but in excess can make the spirit more powerful. Intoxication from increased empowerment coupled with the fulfillment of illicit desires can prove incredibly addictive to a lemur and serve to increase their commitment to frequently gratifying their urges.

Terror is a very instinctual emotion and an obvious vehicle of lemur oppression. However, love or reverence are also capable of producing a similar albeit more sustainable effect. By disguising their true nature and intention, a lemur may present an appealing and beneficial façade to engender trust and ultimately adoration. They may masquerade as deities, celestial beings, spirit guides, child spirits, and deceased family members, luring their victims into emotionally motivated reactions that provide the desired emissions of phasma. A magical method of revealing the true nature of a shapeshifting spirit should be a significant tool in the skill set of any necromantic investigator.

Larva Oppression

A revenant that has devolved into a larva is incapable of coherent communication, being simply a bestial shadow of human identity. Larvae do not have the intellectual capacity to be as creatively deceptive as lemures; for this reason, uncomplicated infestations that produce fear completely gratify their instinctual drive to appropriate phasma. While usually content to attack other spirits deep in Qarth Arqa in a mutually destructive frenzy, during the extraordinary circumstance that a larva oppresses a living human being, the consequences can be grave.

POSSESSION

An evaluation of spirit activity would be incomplete without a discussion of the phenomenon of possession. One may basically define possession as an event where a spirit sublimates the consciousness of a living person and imposes their own. It is not always a malefic affair; in fact, willing possession is often employed by skilled practitioners for beneficial spiritual purposes. Like any magical practice, possession is potentially dangerous, but the risks can be understood and mitigated by sincere and comprehensive training.

Voluntary Possession

Magical practitioners and spirit workers have often used the art of inducing voluntary possession for the beneficial purposes of otherworldly communication. Besides competence in the knowledge and skill sets necessary to successfully attain a state of possession, trust in the character of the entity and in the practitioner's own protection is critical.

This ability of permitting the personal consciousness to step aside and allow a spirit to engage with the living has come to be called trance mediumship in some circles. Trance mediumship is not a modern practice, despite the contemporary name or connections to the institution of Spiritualism. In fact, this practice spans the globe and is foundational in many cultural and tribal spiritual practices. It is an ancient form of magical transformation that is employed to facilitate human interaction directly with spiritual agencies. While voluntary possession by deities or celestial entities is also an ancient European magical practice, one may look to the example in today's Afro-Caribbean traditions where such divine possession is accorded a prominent religious role.

Possession as a concept is probably the most feared of spiritual phenomena, mainly because it is the most misunderstood. Accepting and respecting the usage of voluntary possession in so many faiths and spiritual traditions can lead you on the path to understanding. The good that can be achieved through practices like voluntary possession should balance the fear which so sorely taints the subject. Remember there are far more cases of voluntary possession willingly engaged in for the spiritual good of the practitioner's community than those very uncommon cases of violation caused through forced possession by a malicious spirit.

Involuntary Possession

When contemplating paranormal happenings, many people fear the threat of an imposed or involuntary possession. The root cause of this dread is that involuntary possession is, rightly, viewed as an intimate violation wherein the victim relinquishes personal control. Due to this fear crouching in the social conscience, it has become a popular subject for the entertainment media and the controlling moral doctrine of religionists.

The primary fear of involuntary possession that has formed the most enigmatic of Christian doctrine and practice is demonic possession, the Christian concept wherein a living person is invaded by a nonhuman fiend or devil. Culturally, this type of possession is the exception rather than the rule. Usually, it is not a nonhuman spirit that causes this imposition; rather, it is an angry, vengeful, or confused revenant.

Nonhuman spirits are not commonly driven to impose unwilling possession except in specific or extreme cases. The ideal of involuntary invasion by evil nonhuman entities engenders a terror that exacerbates the effects of any true possession, as does the fear that a spirit can spontaneously invade a living person's body. The truth is that a possession cannot occur without the permission or submission of the subject.

Lemur Possession

Despite media popularity, true involuntary possession is remarkably rare. Moreover, such violation is never spontaneous but follows an intense oppression designed to wear down the victim's resolve until they surrender to the spirit. Though an immanes may possess out of desperation, lemures are the usual perpetrators of involuntary possession in order to enhance the manufacture of fear and the phasma it produces.

Where the victim's personal or religious beliefs include the dread of the power of evil spirits, lemures will deceptively masquerade as evil nonhuman entities or devils to achieve their aims. For the most part, a lemur enjoys the power and freedom of their condition and imposing possession binds them to the victim, essentially ensnaring the lemur. For this reason, a lemur usually possesses only when other options seem wanting and they feel trapped. While it is not usual for a lemur to willingly seek to possess, there are a few who do so to revel in the drama of the interaction and fulfill their urges for recognition and power.

Possession Symptoms and Recovery

Regardless of the traditionally dramatic symptoms of involuntary possession, the primary presentation of a dominating spirit is the complete sublimation of the victim's identity and the display of a wholly differing personality. In addition to the symptoms of oppression, the victim will exhibit distinct signs that indicate knowledge or abilities that they could not know.

The usual method of resolving an involuntary possession is to perform certain rites for the exorcism of a person, ceremonials that are subject to the religion, tradition, or culture in which they were conceived. This type of exorcism may be justly deemed a ritualized battle between the violating spirit and the exorcist, but the power to free the sufferer from spiritual harm entirely depends upon the victim and whether they can make a concerted exertion of their own will. It is a common misconception that the purpose of exorcism is to effectively cast out a spirit—its actual function is to weaken the influence of the spirit until the victim can gather the resolve to reject the imposition.

To entirely push the intrusive spirit out, the victim must willfully reclaim their independence. Ultimately this can only be done when the sufferer takes responsibility for personal weaknesses that led to their submission. Following the ejection of a spirit, magical means to protect the victim should be undertaken. More importantly, the subject should be encouraged to get the help necessary to resolve underlying issues the spirit originally manipulated to gain entry.

Mistaken Possession

While involuntary possession is a potential reality, it must be recognized and accepted as incredibly uncommon; more earthly origins are far more likely. Hoaxes, fear-based excitement coupled with curious coincidences, and, more crucially, health issues have all been too often assumed to be possession. It is incredibly important that you are cognizant that many of the symptoms of oppression and possession resemble medical or mental health issues. Physical and mental ailments have been considered cases of possession by the ignorant throughout history, and the consequences have always been tragic.

Moreover, while true involuntary possession is an isolated phenomenon, it is often confused with other spiritual events. Oppression can induce personality changes in the living subject that may be misattributed to the imposed identity of a dominating spirit. Infestation events can also be generated by the living, especially in the case of repressed trauma, so it may appear to an outsider that the living person is the subject of a spirit oppression rather than the epicenter of the events. When personality changes occur alongside infestation emanating from such a living person, it is easy to mistake this as a case of involuntary possession.

Mediation

Another phenomenon often mistaken for possession is mediation. This is a term that describes certain trance states that can have an appearance like possession, especially when communication with a spirit occurs during the event. While mediation can be induced, it can occur spontaneously though intense spiritual empathy, which excites a symbiotic sympathy with a revenant and their attachments. The difference between mediation and possession is that while mediation creates a symbiotic union with a spirit, the mediator's consciousness is never truly sublimated under the spirit's personality. Mediation is more like a reflection, a window into the spirit's own experience. At times, the mediator speaks or acts as if they were the spirit due to this sympathetic bond. Rational investigative detachment and analysis are necessities in discerning the difference between authentic involuntary possession and similar spiritual conditions.

The remedies for possession are potentially dangerous and outside the scope of this book. Other causes for what appear to be a case of involuntary possession need to be fully explored in any investigation before assuming that a person has been violated by forced possession. Given the similarity of possession to emotional and mental illness, it is more important to investigate with a commitment to integrity and compassion that demands an obligation for the well-being of any sufferers. Unless there is incontrovertible evidence of spiritual causation in cases of involuntary possession, you should be responsible and encourage the subject to seek professional or medical advice.

A comprehensive understanding of infestation, obsession, oppression, and even the causes of possession are fundamental to sciomancy. Any effective solution to a spirit-induced crisis is contingent on unraveling the mystery behind the cause of the activity. You must be dedicated to unveiling the truth, and knowledge is the means to begin to look behind that mysterious curtain. Be intrepid, professionally detached, and committed to compassion. You are encouraged to expand your studies beyond this book and seek a general understanding of the human condition to reveal the intention of obsessive spirits.

PART II
WORKING IN THE FIELD

CHAPTER SEVEN

ESSENTIAL SKILLS

The success of necromantic investigation begins long before you are called to the scene of a spirit disturbance. It starts with the continuous cultivation and acquisition of knowledge reinforced by practical experience and spiritual work. While understanding the principles of necromancy is necessary, knowledge alone cannot prepare you for contending with the subtle factors inherent in confronting spirit world activities.

Sciomancy is a magical art demanding competency in the skills pertaining to the execution of its function. Natural talent may be an advantage, but it is unreliable without the proficiency to effect a consistent repetition of successes. Commitment to diligent practice is the only true method to foster personal magical ability; there are simply no shortcuts.

In this chapter, we will review the skills essential to become a better sciomancer, including techniques to build your spiritual fortitude and hone your subtle senses to hear, see, and feel spirits. Along with determination and a comprehensive understanding of the arcana, these skills are the cornerstones of success in sciomancy, necyomancy, and any other magical pursuit.

PERSONAL TRAITS OF A NECROMANCER
+ Compassion for the well-being of both the living and the dead
+ Respect for the arcana and philosophy of esoteric practices
+ Willingness and endurance to learn, study, and practice

+ Precommitment to achieve the best resolution for all concerned
+ A professional sense of internal calm and spiritual balance

SPIRITUAL FORTITUDE

Spiritual fortitude is more than having a sense of certainty in your beliefs or adherence to a particular faith. There is a practical component, and it behooves the sciomancer to implement methods to bolster their spiritual resolve to better deal with the spirit world. These should include mind-setting techniques, as well as spiritual exercises according to the religion or practice to which you may subscribe. Moreover, there is a fundamental sense of personal and practical authority that must be actively cultivated.

Attaining Dignification

The term "dignification" refers to a measure of magical authority or power invested in you as a magician. The ability to command respect through magical authority is imperative when interacting with spirits, especially when those entities are aggressive or contrary.

Rites of consecration and dignification can impress an authority upon you particular to the spheres of influence inherent in an individual esoteric system. This power resides and endures as a subtle artifact at an aetheric level.

Initiation, which is often confused with dignification, more specifically refers to the conferring of specialized or secret knowledge, usually through mentorship within an organized spiritual tradition. Although a much harder route, if you have not undergone a formal ritual of dignification or pursued training in an established system, you can still acquire and distill knowledge by your own effort and merit comparable to initiation. When such self-educated initiation reaches a certain understanding, it will naturally result in a level of dignification and personal magical authority over time.

Dignification is the single most essential element of your personal protection, and preserving it against corruption should be the constant concern of any practitioner. Magic requires humility and exists in subtlety; the smallest transgression can dismantle the best of magical endeavors, short-circuiting original intentions. Beyond being an act of disrespect, misappropriation of ceremonies and spiritualities for which you do not have permission severely undermines your genuine authority. For the modern magician who wishes to deconstruct the concepts and mechanics of a traditional rite or ceremony, you may do so by adapting and integrating that understanding into your own ritual usage without presumptuous wholesale appropriation. In fact, this practice of adaptation is a time-tested custom in magic to renew or revive systems, but it must be implemented mindfully with consciousness and respect.

Spiritualization

While dignification is the representation of magical authority impressed upon the soul of a magician, spiritualization is the temporary actualization of that authority. The technique of spiritualization occurs when you raise your consciousness to center it on the aetheric nature of your existence, inviting a juxtaposition between your own divinity and that of deity. This interpenetration activates a portion of divine authority that resonates within your phasmic body as a blazon perceivable on the most subtle level.

Spirits see these subtleties readily. They cannot but acknowledge your presence in a state of spiritualization, nor can they deny the divine authority radiating from your phasmic form. Of course, that does not mean that they will submit to your authority; they may resist or evade you if it interferes with their attachments or desires.

Revenants bound in Qarth Arqa are in some level of denial; they have turned their face from divinely apportioned laws and the progress of their spiritual path. When a sciomancer is in a state of spiritualization, they form a conduit to the universal intelligence governing the natural order of existence. To that end, when interacting with a spirit, you can learn to call upon an inherent deputization of divine law.

This authority is greater for a magician who has reached the state of dignification, but the repeated exercise of spiritualization can empower you and give you a distinct edge in dealing with spirits. It is an important practice you must not ignore, and it should become integrated in the preparations you naturally perform before undertaking any tasks. Spiritualization should occur just before you apply any protective procedures and be held in your consciousness throughout the execution of the work.

Compared to other mind-setting techniques or religious preparation, spiritualization appears easy, but it should not be underestimated. It is a commitment to spiritual work and a practical awareness that we are divine beings—in that realization lies not only authority but also responsibility.

EXERCISE
VISUALIZATION

. . . .

There are numerous methods to achieve this awareness, and they will be dependent upon what tradition an individual may adhere to. For completeness, what follows is a simple and efficient method for attaining a sense of spiritualization:

1. Find a comfortable location where you won't be disturbed.
2. You may wish to close your eyes until you become more practiced.
3. Visualize your body as damp clay, solid and mutable.
4. See your body transform from clay to water through dissolution.
5. When the body has become entirely water, visualize it heating and evaporating into steam and gases.
6. Once your form is gaseous, see it ignite into an incandescent azure fire.
7. Let the flames transition into brilliant golden light with an effulgent opalescent white sphere at the core or heart level.
8. Finally let the visualization fade but maintain an awareness that it remains in existence and that, for the time being at least, you dwell in a sense of spiritualization.
9. With practice, you will be able to call on this state of spiritualization quickly at any time.

Personal Protection

While some acts of magic do not need proactive protection, working with revenant spirits requires vigilant attention to shielding and defense, especially when entering an investigation where entities may be potentially hostile. However, spiritual protection should not be motivated by fear alone. Spiritual fortitude, dignification, and cleansing are important practices for removing chinks in your armor and ensuring the effectiveness of your protection.

Methods of magical protection must be practiced so they become natural and instantaneous. They should be considered as an obligatory procedural element in the preparation of any investigation both for yourself and others. The goal of protection should be to be spiritually impermeable and concealed. Never visualize a bright white light, as it will draw attention-seeking spirits.

EXERCISE
VISUALIZATION
· ·

Protective measures can take numerous forms. The following method is a simple measure that should be practiced daily. We recommend learning to make use of this skill whenever and wherever you may be while doing activities. You may need to start by sitting in a comfortable location and closing your eyes, but try to avoid becoming reliant on this.

1. Establish a calm, clear mind, becoming aware of your body.
2. Imagine a pillar of blue light surging from the earth to your groin, to your heart, and above your head.
3. Visualize the light cascading in a swirling opalescent mist around you.
4. Allow some mist to consolidate in an impermeable shell enclosing your entire being.
5. Empower the shell with conviction and a symbol of protection.
6. With practice, you can learn to think of this symbol to immediately reinforce your protection as needed.

Cleansing

Cleansing is the practice of purifying your subtle body from residual influences. The importance of spiritual cleansing in sciomancy cannot be overemphasized. Not only does it prevent you from attracting undesirable or negative influences, it also decreases the likelihood of being targeted by a predatory spirit. Without cleansing, exercises in protection and spiritualization will be ineffective. Spiritual cleansing also has the benefit of promoting inner clarity and restoring balance.

Cleansing should be a regular practice; however, the prescribed means and austerity of purification will differ between traditions. At the very least, spiritual cleansing should be practiced prior to and after interacting with spirits. Cleansing can be enhanced by practices of fasting, meditation, abstinence, and prayer.

Sanctified water is the simplest method of removing residual effects imposed upon your phasma. Methods can include asperging, bathing or ritualized washing of the body and rinsing of the mouth. Botanicals that rarefy phasma can also be used for cleansing and may be employed as incense, oils, or sprigs in a sweeping motion to cleanse the phasmic body and clothing. However, be aware of suffumigation that repels spirits before an investigation. A list of botanicals and their purposes is described in the following chapter.

Ars Remissionis, or the Art of Release

Ars remissionis is the conscious discipline of separating oneself from the influence of subtle forces, whether they be magical, emotional, intellectual, or environmental. Remission is a crucial skill in sciomancy that can help you to deflect and disengage from the influence of an entity, and to maintain a sense of professional detachment. It should be enacted in an investigation whenever you experience unexplained thoughts and urges or you are overwhelmed by fear and other emotions. It is also necessary after an interaction with a spirit to prevent unwanted connections.

The art of release also plays a vital role in magical workings that not only demand the ability to project charged intention but also the faculty of releasing that intent to do its work, as becoming fixated on an operation can negate the intended outcome and result in unexpected consequences. Furthermore, such mind-setting techniques solidify your determination and therefore provide confidence, buttressing your magical authority regarding the spiritual tasks at hand.

Ars remissionis is a knack or way of thinking that involves a level of precommitment, spiritual fortitude, and trust. To this end, esoteric systems have developed complex methods to engage this mindset and cleanse the subtle body of influences. Simple suggestions include meditation, breathing, and mind strengthening exercises; visualization techniques that simulate releasing ties; cleansing techniques involving water; and censing with a botanical such as white sandalwood for clarity.

Discarricare, or Grounding

Discarricare is the method of dispelling excess phasma to balance the subtle body. It also serves to bring mind, body, and spirit to the here and now. This important technique should be employed to attain the correct mindset prior to and during an investigation, following a psychic or magical event, or when a person is feeling overwhelmed or overexcited.

In sciomancy, you may need to assist others ground themselves and quickly steady their emotions or prevent panic. Grounding can also reduce the effect of intense or erratic EMF, or in cases when one feels overcome by empathic sensations or emotions. Should symptoms of anxiety occur, check for signs of shock or difficulty breathing. Do not hesitate to call for emergency assistance if required.

The following methods of discarricare can be employed in combination, for yourself or another.

+ Practice circular breathing, drawing from the base of the spine.
+ Place a covering over the crown of the head to dampen and draw down phasma.
+ Focus on your feet, as a representation of your roots to the earth.
+ Stand or lie on bare earth, allowing excess phasma to sink into the ground.
+ Embrace a stone against your chest while lying down, focusing on breathing.
+ Sit by running water, allowing it to carry away the excess phasma from around your body.

SEEING, HEARING, AND SENSING SPIRITS

There have always been talented people with the ability to communicate with spirits. They are called by many names, such as seers or mediums, and they often have a natural aptitude for seeing, hearing, or otherwise perceiving entities invisible to most people. Sometimes they seek to enhance these abilities through training and instruction. These gifted mediums and psychics are specialists who are finely attuned to their talents. Clearly, an accurate seer can be an incredible asset during a spirit investigation, especially regarding communicating with any active entities, but this is not always possible. Therefore, you should seek to develop a certain level of competency in these relevant abilities that will assist you if you are called upon for an emergent spirit disturbance.

Developing Your Subtle Senses

The most important capabilities in laying ghosts are whatever best facilitate communication with spirits to understand the causes of their obsession. Cultivating competency in the ability to see, hear, or feel spirits' emotive impressions are all pertinent to resolving a sciomantic investigation. People can be too ready to believe that these skills must be entirely innate or revealed due to the advent of extreme circumstances, such as loss or trauma. The truth is that while in some people an aptitude or talent may be inherent, it is possible for anyone to develop a working efficiency through the diligent and continuous practice of certain simple exercises.

Hearing

The first ability you should develop is hearing the voice of spirits. Sciomantic investigation demands a knowledge of the attachment underlying the obsession disturbing a location. The ability to hear spirits is an invaluable faculty in an investigation that is more immediate and dependable than capturing recorded electronic voice phenomena or using other voice tools. It opens a direct avenue of communication, therefore potentially expediting an explanation as to the cause of the spirit crisis.

Sensing

Cultivating the ability to sense a spirit's presence is the next faculty you should develop. A sciomantic incident is rarely static; the spirit may be constantly moving around, either unaware of the commotions of the living or in hope to either avoid or confront whomever is seeking them. The reliance on devices and instruments to capture spirit activity in modern paranormal investigation often means investigators learn of any phenomenon after it has already occurred. Developing the skill to confidently sense the presence of a spirit in real time allows you to act immediately and dynamically. Additionally, the ability to sense anomalies in a subtle environment is invaluable. Most people naturally have this sense, so it is only a matter of learning to discern the differences and know when a spirit is present or if there is another type of anomaly.

Psychism

Another useful skill is what has become known as psychism, the ability to receive impressions from a spirit, person, item, or environment. You may receive these impressions in any number of ways, such as through mental pictures, emotional empathy, touching relevant items (psychometry) or in dreams (oneiromancy). These extra sensory impressions can be incredibly pertinent during an investigation, providing connections in logic between disparate pieces of information. However, be mindful that psychic impressions very often need a level of interpretation and are therefore open to potential errors.

Seeing

We are not discussing the ability to see a spirit in a physical sense but rather to perceive it in detail in the mind and to be certain it is authentic. Pursuing the capacity to effectively see or perceive a spirit will allow you to access critical information that otherwise may remain undiscovered. The spirit's clothing or hairstyle can often indicate the period in which the entity lived, and a description of the facial features might lead to a confirmation of identity when compared to a photograph or video uncovered through research. The spirit may also attempt to communicate through gestures or behaviors once they realize you can see them.

A Technique to Build Subtle Senses

There are a variety of resources available for developing your subtle abilities. We have found the exercise included in this chapter to be the most reliable because it makes proper use of three fundamental skills—discrimination, the imaginatrix, and passive perception—all to teach you how to tell with certainty when an insight has been received from an external source.

Discrimination

The faculty fostered in this exercise and necessary for its skillful application is discrimination. The way we perceive the physical and the spiritual are permanently intertwined. Every preternatural aptitude is only an extension of a natural and familiar faculty. What we imagine seems real to our senses. Learning to differentiate with certainty whether a message or communication is truly external and not a creation of our own making is critical.

Imaginatrix

Those who train to develop magical skills will be familiar with the process of visualizing and projecting tangible conceptualizations. However, hearing, seeing, and feeling the presence of spirits are purely passive proficiencies, which is to say you must remain receptive to the influences and communications exerted by an outside source. This understanding is fundamental in cultivating these faculties, as it is counterintuitive to try to mentally project outward to make spiritual contact.

Part of the exercise focuses on recognizing the feeling of projecting an internally constructed idea. Through discrimination, knowing what the experience of projection feels like allows you to recognize when you are receiving an external stimulus that would otherwise be difficult to quantify. Essentially, if it feels like a projection, it is self-created; if it is an experience originating from outside of the magician's mind, it should feel foreign.

Passive Perception

Nurturing passive skills can be difficult because our minds want to work at filtering and arranging information, therefore trying to remain entirely receptive is all but impossible. One technique is to give the mind a task to concentrate on. Keeping the intellectual mind busy will allow passive acceptance of external communication. In the following exercise, we encourage you to intensively focus on the region of the body that will serve as the point of reception to occupy the mind—that is, your ears for hearing, eyes for seeing, and solar plexus for feeling spirits. This focus will activate your physical faculties and repurpose them to a more subtle function, creating a tangible experience out of a usually intangible stimulus.

Training yourself to trust that an external stimulus is working upon your passive faculties (sight, hearing, or feeling) is the fundamental goal of engaging in the exercises that develop these capabilities. It can be otherwise difficult to acquire these skills, as the intellect always wants to qualify and quantify an experience. Conversely, if the desire to achieve communication is too great, the imagination can express itself too freely. Prudent experimentation and earnest, healthy criticism are imperative in attempting to cultivate passive faculties. Seek to evolve trust in your own abilities through the experiences you accrue in a diligent and continuous application of relevant training.

EXERCISE
HONING YOUR SENSES

· ·

The method described here is to build subtle hearing (clairaudience), but you can apply the same principles to developing the ability to see and feel spirits. Practice is required to complete each step.

Step One: Imaginatrix

1. Verify what it feels like to project a sound from your own imagination.
2. Choose a distinct sound that is memorable and repetitive, such as a ringtone. Replay the sound in your head over and over until it is completely familiar.
3. Put all your focus on one inner ear, left or right. Replay the sound, imagining that you are hearing it with your chosen ear.
4. Continually practice until it is as if you are hearing the sound in your ear.
5. Commit the sensation to memory and practice regularly.

Step Two: Passive perception

6. Next, learn to open your mind to perceive sounds without prejudgment.
7. Relax in the quiet hours of night or while meditating. Lightly focus on the same inner ear and open your mind to receive sounds.
8. At first there may be nothing or you might experience ringing or discomfort. In time you may start to experience voices and sounds.
9. Simply observe, do not discern between real and imagined or ask questions. Try not to become overwhelmed or to pay attention to any particular voices.

Step Three: Discrimination

10. Finally, practice identifying voices and learn to listen at will.

11. Start trying to focus on a single trusted voice, such as an ancestor or guide. Experiment by asking a question and listening for a response.

12. Apply the skill learned in step 1 to eliminate projections of the mind. It may take many consistent attempts and practice to fine-tune this ability.

The perception of spirits should always be approached with an element of ars remissionis. By developing a formula for receiving communication from a spirit, we can extend a bridge that can be withdrawn when the interaction is complete. Without such a method, a person who has natural ability will suffer from intrusive thoughts and overwhelming emotion when a spirit tries to impress their message upon them.

SUMMARY OF FUNDAMENTAL PRACTICES
Table 7: Essential Skills for Sciomancy

Ars remissionis	Release attachments to spirits and the operation
Cleansing and purification	Remove residual influences
Discarricare	Remove surplus phasma and gain personal balance
Meditation and mind-setting	Achieve calm focus and balance
Personal protection	Guard against outer influences
See, hear, and feel spirits	Hone subtle senses
Spiritualization	Reinforce spiritual fortitude and authority
Study the arcana	Overcome fear of the unknown

CHAPTER EIGHT

SCIOMANCY
TOOL KIT

The popular vision of a spirit investigation would be incomplete without copious amounts of high-tech paraphernalia and innovative gadgets. However, the practice of laying ghosts demands more than a reliance on modern and often untested inventions. Long before the advent of electronics, when there were no EMF detectors, laser thermometers, or full-spectrum cameras, sciomancers analyzed an obsession through operational experience and an arcana-based systematic examination. That is not to say, however, that sciomancers did not use specialized tools to facilitate their practice—mirrors, bells, candles, and other magical paraphernalia have long been associated with necromancy and are as effective today as they were in the past.

Bearing in mind that sciomancy is always exercised on location, limitations pertaining to travel have always been a major factor in the selection of accoutrements; serious consideration should be given to accommodate the unexpected. Although the composition of a modern field kit may include electronics, it must also comprise low-tech alternatives, botanicals, and specialized magical equipment.

USING TECHNOLOGY

In our digitally driven world, it is impossible to avoid questions about the application of electronics and devices in a necromantic investigation. Many people think of spirit investigations as either a distinctly modern and technical activity or a source of entertainment. Stirring images of a ghost-hunter examining their bleeping devices while wandering in the eerie green light of a night-vision camera can draw viewers into the suspense, waiting for the apparition or noise that will make them jump and drop the popcorn. Naturally, audiences expect that the ghost-hunter will prevail, confident that eventually (if not already), we will apply the superior technology of our advanced civilization to the problem of the paranormal and prove once and for all the reality of the unseen.

Ars Nova

Modern paranormal investigation is still a nascent pursuit, emerging about a century ago in the earnest attempt of skeptical researchers to unmask fraudulent mediums and spirit photographers by employing scientific methods and contemporary techniques. Experimental technologies have advanced considerably over the years, and the consistent experiences of paranormal researchers have led to the continuous development of new and diverse devices. Today there are hundreds of ghost-hunting kits, digital applications, and electronics readily available. While some have proved to be effective, many are entirely theoretical or impractical.

There will always be some purists who would prefer that all new technologies be rejected in favor of relying entirely on their traditions to resolve a spirit crisis. While this opinion is perfectly valid and a matter of personal choice, it is worth remembering that the ultimate concern is to successfully resolve the event in the most effective way. If technology can aid you in achieving these goals, proven methodologies can be adapted to supplement your practice.

Experimenting

When choosing tools and devices, remember that the fundamental rationale of sciomancy differs from that of paranormal investigation. Sciomancy is about laying unquiet spirits to rest, not about collecting scientific evidence that proves the paranormal exists. Any technologies employed must be consistent with the purpose of attaining information to identify and classify the spirit, discover their attachment, and ultimately create a strategy to resolve the event. To be successful, you must be certain of what a device does, what it measures, and whether its potential function could propel your operation toward a successful outcome.

Some technologies have been proven over time, such as EMF meters, digital recorders, and cameras. Other instruments are more experimental; you may opt to test them during an investigation, having carefully considered their operation.

You should limit such experimentation so that it does not overtly interfere with the purpose of sciomancy, and you must evaluate the performance of the device with a reasoned detachment.

Embracing Low-Tech

A sciomantic investigation should not be defined by the technology you use. Ideally, you should be competent in using a variety of methods to gather information and complement your understanding of the arcana. Electronics can aid in the collection of data, but without the appropriate knowledge base, any analysis can only be subject to the technology itself and is therefore relatively limited.

Before spending too much of your hard-earned money on expensive equipment developed or adapted for paranormal research, become familiar with the use of various low-tech alternatives. In emergency circumstances, the low-tech sciomancer can employ their skill set immediately, while those who rely solely on technology will have to reschedule the investigation while they gather their gadgets.

The low-tech approach is the kernel of investigation, requiring lateral thinking and creativity. Although it may not have the same allure, becoming adept in its methods will not prevent you from also becoming skilled at using modern technology.

Nevertheless, despite all the tools and paraphernalia, it is important to remember that you are the ultimate paranormal multi-tool. The human body is well attuned to perceive the presence of the deceased. With practice, anyone can learn to ably detect and communicate with spirits.

Tools and Their Uses

Technology is not required, but a balanced approach can prove to be advantageous in gathering the information necessary to pursue a fit resolution.

Environmental Sensors

One of the characteristic signs of a revenant is an unexplainable drop in temperature in the immediate area where they manifest. This is experienced by the body as horripilation, or goosebumps, and is measured to be more than 5 degrees Fahrenheit (2.8 degrees Celsius). There are various instruments that can be used to aid in the discovery and verification of these cold spots. Remember, if you observe the presence of a spirit, detecting a cold spot is a sign that the entity is a revenant human spirit. If a spirit claims to be a nonhuman power, a cold feeling suggests a lemur trying to excite your fear or adoration. Examples of environmental sensors include the following:

+ Infrared thermometers allow you to determine surface temperature and emissivity from a distance. A cold spot can be detected by scanning an area to establish a baseline and locating anomalies.
+ Thermal imagers visually depict differences in heat to more accurately see where a cold spot is located. They can also clearly identify drafts that can be mistaken for paranormal phenomena.
+ Ambient temperature sensors are only useful to confirm general room temperature; they do not determine if the feeling of cold is localized to one place.
+ Low-tech methods, such as use of a feather or streamers, can be employed to indicate drafts that may explain a drop in temperature or other movement.
+ A small spirit level can be used to check the alignment of surfaces to discern if an object's movement is potentially due to physical conditions rather than spirit activity.

Electromagnetic Disruptions

Among the most relied-upon technologies in modern paranormal investigations are the EMF meter and any device that measures fluctuations in the electromagnetic field. It is often erroneously assumed that high EMF is indicative of a paranormal event. It would be more correct to say that when dense phasma is accompanied by wildly erratic EMF readings, it can indicate conditions in which a spirit manifestation is more likely. The body is very attuned to identify disruptions to the electromagnetic environment associated with spirit manifestation. The feeling can be described as eerie, unnerving, and nauseating. Examples include the following:

+ An EMF meter can be used to find irregularities which may indicate conditions favorable to revenant manifestation. However, it can also confirm high levels of artificial electromagnetic activity which may induce a sensation of paranoia, which is often confused for the presence of a spirit.

+ A handheld compass placed on a flat surface or magnetized needle floating in water provides a low-tech alternative to sensing disruptions to the magnetic field.
+ Dowsing rods can be used to identify disruptions caused in the place where a revenant is manifesting or from where they are rising.

Audio Equipment

Sound is the primary sense in the realm of the dead, just as vision is to the living. Electronic instruments that produce noise, whether digital or analog, can often have the potential to receive communications. Think carefully about the methods you intend to use, and avoid any that rely upon a yes or no answer—a deceitful spirit can easily abuse these, and they simply do not provide the means for intricate communication.

If you are using recording devices during an investigation, speak clearly so your presence can be easily discerned—do not whisper. Note that many spirits may try to be heard at one time, and devices can be ineffective if they are not exclusive to the spirit with whom you wish to speak. Examples include the following:

+ Electronic voice phenomena (EVP) and other audibles can be captured on recording devices. It is preferable to playback sounds in real time, so they are relevant to communication, but sometimes they only become discernible during analysis.
+ Voices can be heard with radio feed, white noise, and other transmitted sounds.
+ To broaden context and improve clarity of information, recording devices can be used in tandem with other communication activities (such as a spirit board) to capture EVP and log events.
+ Spirits may interfere with other noisemaking devices such as chimes and bells to draw your attention. Hang them in a place away from air currents to confirm activity.

Image Capture

Photographs have a special history in the study of ghosts and paranormal activity. When you are considering images, care should be taken to determine if they are truly paranormal. Mist, dust and image defects can be enthusiastically interpreted as supernatural events where in fact they should be identified and rejected. Here are some tips:

- Any reflective surface can be used for seeing spirits with the naked eye: a window, mirror, or some other flat surface in the space.
- Digital cameras can be very successful at capturing spirit manifestation at various stages, in particular numen and nubes. If a camera is mirrorless, it can be aimed at an oblique angle toward a glass or reflective surface for better results.
- Full spectrum cameras capture a broader range of light from infrared to some ultraviolet. Colored filters and lights may be required, especially for nighttime imaging.
- Analog photography and film, though now less frequently used, offers different results in capturing apparitions and the umbrae of spirits. This is due to a range of factors that affect the capture of light, including exposure rates and interior mirrors.
- The form of a spirit can be indicated when they interrupt a stream of light from a projector or handheld flashlight, causing a shadow. We have found a grid of laser lights surprisingly effective for this purpose.

TOOLS OF PROTECTION

Among the magical tools of a sciomancer, religious symbols, amulets, and talismans provide useful methods of spiritual protection that are both wearable and portable.

Symbols of Faith

A bulwark of conviction can create quiet confidence that aids in calming the chaotic tides of uncertainty that pervade a spirit disturbance. Many magicians and spirit workers adhere to a faith in something greater than themselves; while not always an organized religion, the belief is an abiding power in which they can put their trust. As a practitioner you are not required to be particularly pious or an advocate for any one religion—after all, faith is an internal and reciprocal revelation—but reliance upon a higher power can only be beneficial. Regardless of your spiritual creed, the protective power of any religious symbol lies in the fact that it is a physical representation of implicit trust and the sincerity of your relationship with supernal powers.

Symbols of faith can include laudatory or protective recitations or prayers but more often include physical items representative of an individual faith. While the form of the objects may have an emblematic imagery, it is the association of the items with the spirituality from which they originate that realizes their magical effect. This is the point of departure that differentiates a material icon of faith from other protective magical objects like amulets.

Amulets

An amulet is an object employed to repel a specific negative effect away from the user, such as ill luck, spirits, or accident. Amulets are always protective, and it is common for an amulet's form to depend on its culture of origin. They may be crafted or naturally occurring. Popular opinion dismisses amulets as simply good luck charms, but in truth they are valid magical accessories with deep ethnic roots. Their intrinsic link to the inherent spirituality enshrined in a culture and their continuous use over generations empower them with a genuine and natural magical potency.

The primary concerns regarding the use of an amulet are understanding exactly what the object is designed to repel within its original context and how it is activated. An amulet must be spiritually intentionalized like any magical tool, but it must be done according to the practices from which the amulet's form is derived. In short, amulets are extremely beneficial, but they must be employed thoughtfully with care and understanding.

Medieval ceremonial magic is itself a cultural practice in which amulets both simple and complex have been preserved in historic texts and grimoires, which can be a source of inspiration for a universalist approach to magical practice. Traditional necromancy makes use of two types of amulets that have proven to be incredibly effective protective measures when interacting with erratic or dangerous revenants: intentionalized iron and crossed lines.

Intentionalized Iron

The use of iron for protection is an ancient custom that has proven effective over time and is found in the magical traditions of multiple cultures. When magically actuated, iron has the unique effect of creating a barrier around itself that can repel or ensnare a human spirit depending upon their proximity to the item. Cauldrons, knives, chains, and nails have all been employed in necromantic operations for both protection and the binding of revenants.

Intentionalized iron affects any spirit with a dense phasmic body within a radius up to 4.5 feet (1.3 meters). It can be used to discourage a revenant from entering an area or worn as an amulet to prevent spirits from approaching a person. If you have one, a consecrated knife is useful as a symbol of power, as is a knife whose iron content has been intentionalized.

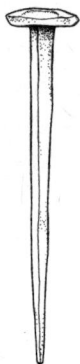

Farrier's Iron Nail

Crossed Lines

An often overlooked but extremely effective symbol of protection is the use of crossed lines that are magically empowered to restrain a spirit. In entertainment media, we have all seen the hero holding back the undead with a cross held up before them. This dramatic depiction is ultimately derived from the ancient magical use of crossed lines. This imagery is so indelibly engraved upon our minds that it is mundanely employed in signage to indicate that an action or location is unacceptable or forbidden. This meaning is the central idea behind the crossing of lines, and its use in necromancy is essentially to prevent a spirit from approaching the image or passing through a place where the lines have been crossed and magically intentionalized.

Crossed lines do not need to be physically visible to be effective. Symbols of binding and protection with crossed lines can be drawn with washes or oils on the body and clothing or above windows and doorways to prevent entry. Some symbols of faith have the quality of being composed of lines that intersect themselves, such as the crucifix, ankh, or pentagram, making them extremely valuable when employed as magical protection. Spirits often approach from behind, and curiously the stole of Catholic priests often has a Latin cross prominently placed at the back of the neck. Regardless of whether this design is intentional, it serves to protect the wearer from spirit influence while engaged in sacerdotal duties, which may include exorcism in some cases.

In necromancy, after a spirit has been removed from a location, the sciomancer will seal the place the spirit entered with magically activated crossed lines, usually coupled with the sprinkling of a confection of pasque flowers or violets and mugwort. The magical intention in this action is to prevent the spirit returning or rising through the same entry point. A similar method is echoed in funerary rights in which a cross is placed upon a coffin or at the grave site and flowers are laid to ensure a peaceful burial.

Traditional Scottish Amulet Made from Rowan and Bound in Red Cord

The practice of laying ghosts has developed a very effective amulet based on the concepts of magically intentionalized iron and crossed lines: two iron nails crossed diagonally and bound with either red thread or copper wire. A string or cord is attached to the head of each nail, and it is worn as a pendant. This process offers flexibility in protection and a means of controlling the immediate environment during the execution of an investigation.

WORKING WITH YOUR AMULET

Your article of protection must be properly prepared and imbued with power so that it can be activated through gesture or incantation. It is then through a similar process deactivated when the effect is deemed unnecessary. What follows is a general formula demonstrating magical intent, words, and actions you may wish to adapt.

Activating the Amulet
- Focus on the object and its innate qualities of protection. (Intent)
- Recite chosen words to empower the amulet. (Word)
- Use a specific gesture to touch the amulet with the right hand. (Action)

Deactivate the Amulet
- Touch the amulet with the same gesture using the left hand. (Action)
- Recite the chosen words to render the amulet dormant. (Word)
- Imagine the amulet returning to its former inert state. (Intent)

Talismans

Talismans are thematically related to the use of amulets, though the two methods should not be confused. Talismans are made for any number of purposes and always have an inscription of some kind, whereas amulets may be any object and serve the purpose of protection alone. The construction of a talisman is a distinct magical operation whose purpose is subject to the intent and design of the talisman itself. The thoughtful use of talismans can exponentially increase the possibility of resolving an active spirit event. They can be employed not only for protection but also to attract powers that can fortify the magician or affect the environment of a space, such as to absorb and contain phasma or repel against spirits or harm. The efficacy of a talisman depends on its presence; the modern

experiment to burn a talisman to release its magical intent is therefore counterintuitive. Traditionally, talismans are only burned to render them inert after
their purpose is complete. If incinerating a talisman results in success, it may be
because the act of burning a magical item is reserved for making offerings to a
higher power, and they have chosen to intervene.

The talismans presented here are examples of the type used for operations
such as sciomancy. A version of these talismans was recorded in Reginald Scott's
The Discoverie of Witchcraft (1597). As is typical of published work and grimoires
of the era, the symbols were corrupted through frequent copying or otherwise
deliberately misconstrued to thwart readers who tried to use them. The first is for
authority over spirits and would be worn by an individual, and the second is for
general protection. Our corrected version appears here:

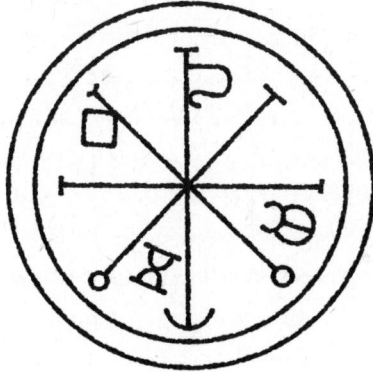

Talisman for Protection and Authority over Necromantic Spirits

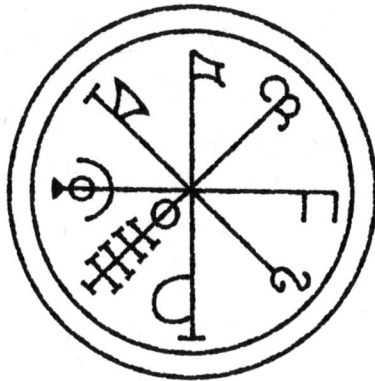

Talisman for General Protection Against Malicious Intent

TRADITIONAL TOOLS FOR SPIRIT COMMUNICATION

In Scotland, when the proponents of laying ghosts arrived on the scene of a disturbance, they carried with them a book, a bell, a candle, and a cross. The book from which they drew their prayers and orations would most likely be a King James Bible, at least in front of witnesses and depending on the persuasion of the practitioner.

The bell would be used to attract the attention of the spirit, its clear tone heard beyond the veil. In addition to providing a light source for the reader, the candle also offered the unquiet spirit a beacon—a single point of light in the darkness of death to draw them toward the practitioner and the shore of life. The cross, more than just a symbol of faith, was also an ancient amulet through which no revenant may pass.

These traditional tools comprised the basic kit for laying ghosts. Anything else could be acquired on location or was kept about their person, such as a flask of whiskey and a black knife known as a *skean-dhu* in Old Scots from the Gaelic *sgian dubh*. The person also likely had a few iron nails jingling in their pocket and some magical powders on hand.

It is better if your tools are handed down from previous generations, but they can also be acquired. New tools should be cleansed and dedicated to their purpose and empowered by ritual, though repetitive use alone will enhance their influence. If you feel you need to cleanse your tools after an interaction with a spirit, take care to only cleanse the surrounding phasma without stripping the tool's intelligence. You may do this with fresh running water or whatever your system of magic prescribes.

Communication with spirits is central to the success of sciomancy. The process to correctly and safely call upon and communicate with spirits is involved and will be more fully described in the following chapter. We will first focus on understanding and preparing the items that draw an entity for the purpose of communication and some traditional tools to facilitate your ability to see, hear, and sense spirits.

An interchange with an unquiet spirit is impossible without the ability to first attract their attention. In the practice of magic, the process of enticing spirits for the purpose of interaction consists of three well-established principles: sound, affinities, and relics. Choosing the appropriate accoutrements for convocation will be specific to the case at hand and will not become apparent until the identity of the spirit causing a disturbance is revealed.

The Principle of Sound

The idea that sound penetrates between worlds lies at the foundation of prayer, religious music, and other spiritual performances. The same belief underpins many ceremonial magical practices, including vocal recitations, orations, and incantations, as well as the use of simple instruments that are understood to draw the attention of specific classes of spirits.

Campana or Bell

When seeking to have conference with the spirits of the dead, we make use of a consecrated handbell, sometimes called the campana, to attract the attention of the spirit and draw them to our physical location. The clarity of the sound pierces through the confusion of the metacosmos, and a spirit will naturally turn to it. A central candle or lamp is also used to provide a visual focal point upon which the spirit can fix their concentration. To aid in this process orations may be recited between the pealing of the bell, adding and projecting intention into the veil, thereby vocally instructing the spirit as they approach.

Singing

Singing can have the same effect as the campana when it is delivered with strong, clear notes, and for this reason the keeners of Gaelic Scotland sing the dead to their final resting place. Whistling, however, does not serve the same purpose. Although it has become a common practice in modern paranormal investigation to excite a response from a possible spirit by whistling, there are two issues related to this: that there is no reason to believe that the responding spirit has any connection to the disturbance being investigated, and the fact that whistling, horns, and wind instruments have been used in magic for centuries as a means of gathering aerial spirits—for this reason alone, it should be avoided during necromantic operations.

Ambient Music

Whether meditational, spiritual, or cultural, ambient music can alter the phasma and render a space more special and attractive to a spirit. Any employed music should be appropriate to the situation, keeping in mind that the goal is to attract the obsessing spirit. Traditional music consistent with your system of practice can be very effective but use careful consideration on whether the music will be exclusively religious, as it can be difficult to predict if it will incite a positive or negative reaction from the obsessing revenant.

The Principle of Relics

Necromancy is popularly associated with the practice of employing human remains such as skulls and bones as relics. This use has been the source of many superstitions wherein necromancers were believed to reanimate corpses so that spirits could speak through them. While human remains can be and historically were used as relics, they are hardly necessary.

The principle of relics does not only refer to organic remains but also extends to any object directly connected to the former life of the spirit or what they possessed during their mortal existence. The best relics are objects impregnated with powerful emotion or defining experiences during the spirit's earthly life: a hairbrush, article of clothing, or jewelry are all valid, but printed photographic images also make excellent relics as they retain a true visage of the person in the fullness of their life.

The magical theory behind the application of relics is similar to the concept of a taglock or object link: a permanent phasmic connection exists between the subject and certain items, especially with organic material such as hair or fingernails. In a magical operation, a taglock or object link is used to direct the intention specifically to a chosen subject. In necromancy, a relic employs a similar connection to draw the entity to the item through the natural attraction all spirits have to the things of their former life.

In sciomancy, relics can only be effectively used when the identity of the obsessing spirit is confirmed and suitable items are easily accessible. Therefore, a relic would most likely be something you would attain from the site with the permission of the occupants partway into an investigation.

The Law of Affinities

In magic, the law of affinities refers to the sympathetic relationship that binds things of a like nature. In sciomancy, affinities are those things that specifically draw a spirit because of their likeness to something from the spirit's previous life.

Affinities differ from relics, which have a direct connection to the spirit's actual material existence.

As human beings, we tend to find comfort in the familiar, creating for ourselves a framework of who we are and how we understand our place in the world. When a person passes into Qarth Arqa, the residual memory of the familiar is an anchor of identity and contextualizes their sense of self to an even greater extent. Their new state renders them essentially incapable of directly processing new experiences, so adhering emotively to the things they knew in life provides their only true measure of the human condition. Well acquainted with this concept, necromancers discovered at an early date the value of exciting the memory of the familiar to allure and draw the attention of the human spirit that they hoped to commune with. Cornelius Agrippa (1486–1535) writes of drawing souls for communication by the things that are familiar to them:

> It is also to be understood, that those who are desirous to raise up any Souls of the dead, they ought to do it … for some kind of affection in times past, impressed in them in their life, drawing the said soul to certain places, things, or persons.[29]

As sciomancers, we must remember that the use of affinities is not rigid but rather an interpretive endeavor and demands a fluid and inspired creativity. An affinity can be anything that might evoke a memory and be alluring to the spirit—common examples include music, perfumes, objects, and activities.

Revealing information about the identity of the spirit in question can best indicate the types of affinities that may be employed. If the identity cannot be discovered with certainty, the era in which the spirit lived a mortal existence may be found through a description of the clothing they are wearing or other clues such as the diction and idioms recorded in EVPs or heard through clairaudience. Trying affinities from different eras can also allow you to discern the timeframe of the spirit's former life depending on which affinity generates more interest.

Modern paranormal investigators have developed a similar approach to affinities, using what they refer to as trigger objects to encourage a response from an entity. Though affinities and triggers are similar in essence, they differ in purpose and perception. Paranormal investigators usually employ triggers to excite a

29   Agrippa, *Fourth Book of Occult Philosophy*, 70.

response from an entity to gather evidence of the existence of spirits. The triggers they make use of are sometimes very contemporary or generic items that may be unfamiliar to the revenant, for example using a modern toy to attract the spirit of a child. The problem is that unless the item is within their framework of familiarity, the spirit may be unable to build a relationship with it. It is erroneous to think a revenant is fully cognizant of the living or our current era, or or they are capable of forging new concepts and cognitive experiences.

Sciomancy, on the other hand, teaches us to foster a perception from the spirit's point of view, as they may be somewhat divorced from the ability to properly analyze new experiences. Stimuli that appropriately comport to the time of the entity's former life have great value and are more successful at emotively attracting the spirit. The purpose in drawing the spirit to you, after all, is to create an environment that facilitates communication so that a resolution may be reached to ameliorate the effects of an obsession or settle it entirely.

Period Music

Once an era or genre can be discerned, music can be one of the most effective affinities because it also incorporates the principle of sound. Appropriate or specific music that stimulates emotional memories accords with the primary goal of employing any affinity. Reproducing the original sound of record players, gramophones, or other devices may provide a more authentic experience for the revenant. The music does not need to be loud; the spirit will resonate with recognizable music even at a distance, as their connection is dependent upon familiarity, not volume. When they arrive, you must still be able to attempt verbal communication.

Visual Affinities

Visual affinities—objects that would likely be memorable to the spirit—are the most common application of the law of affinities. These items could potentially be anything, so an inventive approach in choosing visual aids must be consistent with reasoned deductions from the data recovered during the investigation. The guide for selecting all relevant objects should be attempting to stimulate an emotional reaction in the spirit.

Even if they are from the same era in which the entity lived, innocuous items may not be enough to attract the revenant's interest. When objects have been conscientiously selected, they should be placed in close proximity to the candle or lamp to better present them to the spirit's perception.

Period-appropriate newspapers, magazines, or books are only useful if a direct connection with the spirit has previously been determined, in which case reading the pertinent text aloud may effectively elicit a response and eventually draw the spirit. If the investigation has shown indications that an entity may be unaware of their own death, however, reading their obituary can actually cause them to retract if they are not yet ready to confront the reality of their demise.

Activities

One excellent affinity is reproducing activities the reverent enjoyed in life, should they become uncovered during the investigation. Playing a hand of poker, a classic video game, dancing the Charleston, or whatever else can also add an element of levity in an otherwise somber investigation and encourage a spirit to recall their previous mortality. Life is a complex web of joy and tragedy, laughter and tears, and we cannot re-create the sense of life in the mind of a spirit unless we are willing to reflect that complexity in our application of affinities. At times, we must be willing to act silly and look a little foolish to serve a very serious objective.

Fundamentally, affinities serve to attract a spirit to what was familiar to them in their mortal existence. Appropriateness and creativity are the measure of effective application and are entirely dependent upon the conditions of the obsession and the spirit's attachment. Sincere thought must be given to each affinity selected and seen from the point of view experienced by the spirit themselves. You should remain respectful of the choice and treatment of any affinity and remember that once the spirit is roused, communication should follow with the aim of resolving the disturbance.

Other Traditional Tools of Spirit Communication

The ability to converse with spirits, to negotiate and discover what they want, is an invaluable skill when laying ghosts to rest. Dedicated magical tools can greatly augment your ability to see, hear, and sense spirits and focus your attention. Taking a formalized approach to spirit communication in an investigation will improve the quality of dialogue and allow you to share the results of your interactions with others more easily. The following are tools that we have used successfully and regularly.

Tools for Seeing Spirits

+ Scrying is the most useful method to enhance seeing. If you are using an obsidian or crystal ball, bowl of ink, or watch glass, you will need to exclude all external light from the surface. If you are using a glass mirror, you will need to turn it on an oblique angle so that you see neither yourself nor any external light with the mirror facing a blank wall or dark space.
+ An old method of speculomancy involves creating a viewer, such as a glass bead, hagstone, holey stone, or narrow cylinder. Hold the item close to your left eye so that your vision is obscured. Cup your hands around the object to prevent distracting light and gaze through the aperture.
+ A flickering candle, fireplace, or refracted light can be used to observe shadows. Do not focus on the flame, as it is easily influenced. A candle preternaturally snuffed out can be a sign from a spirit.
+ To see spirits in billowing steam or smoke is called capnomancy. Use a censer of incense, boiling cauldron, or pot of steaming liquid with appropriate botanicals. Allow smoke or steam to billow and create forms. Please ensure that all safety precautions have been taken if you attempt this.

Tools for Speaking with Spirits

+ Audiomancy can be enhanced using a seashell, animal horn, speaking trumpet, or cone as an amplifier to the ear, using subtle hearing to focus clairaudient ability.
+ Automatic writing or drawing is a useful skill to learn. Hold your writing implement lightly and allow the sensation to flow down the arm and let the pen move freely.
+ A spirit board can be as simple as cutout letters and a glass tumbler. You must know and trust the people you are using it with are sincere and not given to pushing the glass to create the answers they would prefer. It is better to have other people place their fingers on the planchette or glass while the questioner speaks. Always test a spirit to confirm their identity.

BOTANICALS FOR SCIOMANCY

It is valuable to have a supply of botanicals during an investigation, if you can bring them. Botanicals can be used in many forms and are the easiest and most reliable way to affect the phasmic environment at least temporarily, making them useful in managing spirit activity.

There are many forms in which botanicals can be applied. The methods listed here are only suggestions based on their traditional application and our experience. Each botanical has its own unique properties and occult virtues, so it is always wise to research and test them for yourself before employing them and be aware of any potential allergy risks or plant toxicity.

Consecrated Water

Consecrated water is one of the most important tools you have in sciomantic investigations. The occult virtue of water reflects the fluidity of phasma and its ability to retain an idea of purpose. For this reason, water easily holds intention and acts as a medium to conduct that intention to whatever it comes in contact with.

Luckily, water is something that can usually be procured and prepared on site and does not need to take up space in your kit. During a supernatural event, the use of holy water blessed by a priest is a common image in lore and media. If it is already in your practice to use holy water, it will work perfectly well. However, there are many other ways that water can be consecrated, and the method of your own tradition is obviously preferable. What we present here is a simple but effective method suitable for on-site investigations.

When on location, it is often more convenient to simply carry salt in your kit than bottles of preblessed water. The occult virtue of salt is spiritual purification in addition to preservation and cleansing. On site, you will most likely have access to tap water. While tap water cannot be considered as coming from a pure source such as a well or spring, the ritualized addition of salt will render the water magically pure and fit to carry the intention of your consecration.

EXERCISE
CONSECRATED SALT WATER

Uses: Cleanse and exorcise places, objects, and the phasma surrounding a person

Components: Water, salt

Method:
1. Fill a vessel with cold tap water.
2. Drop three pinches of salt into the water, three being the number of manifestation.
3. Stir with your right index finger while reciting an oration or prayer to intentionalize the water as a cleansing agent.

Washes

A wash is essentially an infusion—that is, botanicals that have been steeped in boiling water. Washes are incredibly versatile and serve many uses. For the purposes of sciomancy, washes are best prepared as concentrates that can be diluted on location with consecrated water. As water is a magical conduit, the occult virtues will be active regardless of how diluted the infusion is.

Creating concentrated washes is very practical for your travel kit. The method of making a concentrated wash is relatively simple; it is a matter of multiplication and reduction. Note that when creating your washes, it is more effective to use an earthenware or glass vessel than a metallic one.

Method:
1. Steep your chosen botanicals in hot boiled water.
2. After completing the first infusion, strain the material and reheat the liquid.
3. Add more botanicals and repeat this step numerous times for better results; this is called multiplication.
4. When you feel that the infusion is sufficiently potent, bring the liquid to a gentle simmer and reduce it.
5. Allow it to cool, strain through cheesecloth, and store in an airtight vessel safe for travel and use.

The following recipes are examples of appropriate washes for your sciomancy kit.

Savory Wash
Uses: Exorcise an intelligence or spirit's attachment to an object or place
Components: Infusion of summer savory (*Satureja hortensis*) that includes some feverfew (*Tanacetum parthenium*), and mugwort (*Artemisia vulgaris*)

Wash for Warding

    Uses: Apply to windows, doorways, and liminal spaces to protect from
        spirit entry

    Components: Infusion of centaury (*Centaurium erythraea*), rosemary (*Rose-*
        marinus officinalis), and marjoram (*Origanum majorana*)

Oils

Like washes, oils can serve numerous purposes. The most common form is macerated botanicals suspended in a light carrier oil. Maceration is a relatively easy
process but takes longer to produce than a wash. Grapeseed is a wonderful light
carrier oil used in maceration, where the grape is symbolic of spiritual agency.
Olive oil has historically been used to make magical oils and is an incredible carrier, however it is much heavier than grapeseed oil, limiting its potential uses.
Care must be taken when using oils to avoid staining; after all, you will be making
use of them on someone else's property.

Method 1

1. Place your botanicals in a light oil and seal the vessel so it is airtight.

2. Leave in a warm, dry place for about three weeks, shaking the oil daily.

Method 2

1. If time is of the essence, maceration can be accelerated by gently heating
   the mixture in a heatproof open container within a bain-marie (water
   bath) for an hour or two.

2. You can then apply multiplication (as in making washes) and reheat
   the oil as many times as necessary to achieve your preferred potency of
   scent.

Oils can be strained, bottled, and stored in a cool, dark place. The recipes that
follow are very useful for sciomancy:

Convocation Oil

    Uses: Anoint candle for gathering revenants

    Components: Oil with ground coriander seed (*Coriandrum sativum*),
        wormwood (*Artemisia absinthium*), and mugwort (*Artemisia vulgaris*)

Warding Oil
Uses: Apply on talismans of protection, or entryways to prevent spirits
  passing through
Components: Oil with centaury (*Centaurium erythraea*), rosemary (*Rose-marinus officinalis*), and marjoram (*Origanum majorana*)

Scrying Oil
Uses: Apply a dab to the forehead to improve subtle senses. Remove with
  rose water.
Components: Oil with cinnamon (*Cinnamomum cassia*), ground fennel
  seed (*Foeniculum vulgare*), and ground nutmeg (*Myristica fragrans*)

Suffumigation
The art of making incense is a major branch of historical European magic called *Ars Thymiamata* (from Gr. *Thumiama*, incense). This art studies the occult virtues of components and how they enhance, negate, or transform other parts in the same confection. It is a fascinating aspect of magic with a comprehensive theory that demands profound education and understanding in creating compounds or confections to become proficient. Thankfully, the use of incense for most magic does not demand such an education; you only need to have the necessary recipes or, if you are fortunate, know someone skilled in the art of making incenses.

Generally, incense is burned on charcoal blocks either in a thurible or a simple earthenware bowl. Historically, the bowl is partially filled with sanctified sand that has been sifted, washed, and heated to dry, after which it was blessed to the purpose. Sand can become very hot over time when burning the charcoal and does not always provide adequate airflow. A modern alternative is organic clay-based cat litter, which insulates against the heat very well. The larger size of the granules also allows air to flow more freely under the burning charcoal.

Using Incense
Incense is the preferable method when dealing with spirits because it has an immediate effect. As a practitioner, you should always ensure the space is adequately ventilated when using any type of fumes and be aware of any medical, allergic, or respiratory concerns.

If it is not possible to use incense, you may use an oil diffuser or make an infusion in water that can be gently heated to release an aroma as a milder alternative. Infusions can also be administered with an asperger or a sprig of hyssop, which is traditionally used for cleansing. The sprig is also appropriate for dispersing an infusion designed to rarefy phasma. For a practical albeit less traditional alternative, you may use a spray bottle to atomize the mixture.

Burning Sage

There is a popular belief in paranormal circles that burning sage cleanses a location of spirits. In truth, botanicals like sage, juniper, and cedar can have a rarefying effect on phasma, returning it to a state of pneuma that can prevent the physical manifestation of spirit activity; however, they do not encourage the entity to desist or to leave as is commonly thought. If the conditions causing hyle to coalesce remain, the state of phasma will return and the spirit activity may also resume, a process that usually occurs after two or three weeks. Burning sage regularly can keep spirits from interacting but it does not in and of itself expel them. If you use a botanical such as sage on yourself, do not reenter the investigation space, as the residue on your clothing can mitigate the potential for spirit interaction or manifestation.

Common sage (*Salvia officinalis*) has been used in European magical traditions to mitigate the effects of spirits for well over a millennium, for "…this breaketh or defendeth [against] evill shades & evill spirits from the place where it is."[30]

However, white sage (*Salvia apiana*) is a sacred botanical unique to certain Native American tribes. Unless you are a part of those cultures and practices, the use of white sage should be strictly avoided—it is problematic and a clear misappropriation of culture. Likewise, the use of feathers, wing fans, and abalone shells to burn sage are specifically Native American traditions. There are plenty of alternatives to distribute sage smoke and catch the ash without co-opting these traditions if they do not belong to you. It is important to remember that along with ethical considerations, the misuse of the sanctity that naturally resides in culture and tradition can have a profoundly negative influence on a magician's magical authority.

. . . .
30   Sepher Raziel, *Liber Salomonis*, British Library Sloane MS 3826 Folio 19.

Incense Pearls

Incense pearls are small, oval-shaped granules of incense (about the size of a pomegranate seed) that can be easily applied to burning charcoal in a controlled manner. The actual method of making incense pearls is not overly complex, but it does take some dexterity to make them with finesse. Most historical incense recipes do not give proportions, because the source components vary in their potency based on how they were cultivated, the effects of weather and other conditions. Therefore, only by producing the incense yourself can you control the potency of the final product.

The method of making incense pearls is both ancient and a very satisfying hands-on activity. Only three things are necessary: the dried leaves, woods, or gums from which the incense will be made, a macerated light oil, and beeswax (called "virgin wax" in the grimoires). In the following recipes, components are listed in decreasing order, the first component being primary. Assess and adjust as you go to find the harmonious balance of proportions that will meet your needs.

Method:

1. Grind and prepare your dry components with a mortar and pestle.

2. Move the mixture to a separate bowl and moisten with a few drops of the oil. Rub between your fingers to make sure the oil is evenly distributed.

3. Grate a small amount of beeswax into the mixture, just enough to bind it but not overwhelm it. The goal is to bind the mixture with wax, not create a wax product that contains botanicals.

4. Massage the wax into the mixture, warming it with your fingers as you do so.

5. When the proportions seem right to you, pinch a little of the mixture into your palm and roll it into a ball. Press it gently in the middle to flatten it slightly so it will sit on the charcoal block without rolling off.

6. Set the pearl on a tray and repeat the process with a little more mixture.

7. When you have finished creating your pearls, place the tray in the refrigerator to set them before moving them into a container for storage.

Convocation Incense

Uses: Coalesce pneuma to make a phasma rich environment

Components: Coriander (*Coriandrum sativum*) mixed with cardamom (*Elettaria cardamomum*) and mugwort (*Artemisia vulgaris*). Bind with beeswax and coriander oil.

Calling the Dead

Uses: To attract revenants and enhance communication

Components: Wormwood (*Artemisia absinthium*) mixed with mugwort (*Artemisia vulgaris*), mullein (*Verbascum thapsus*), and centaury (*Centaurium erythraea*). Bind with beeswax and wormwood oil.

Funerary Offering

Uses: Grant an offering to a revenant to nourish their spirit body or confirm a contract

Components: Thyme (*Thymus vulgaris*), wormwood (*Artemisia absinthium*), with mugwort (*Artemisia vulgaris*). Bind with beeswax and thyme oil.

Spiritualizing Incense

Uses: To elevate the spiritual atmosphere, sanctify or align with divine purposes

Components: Frankincense (also called olibanum, *Boswellia sacra*), mixed with myrrh (*Commiphora myrrha*). Bind with beeswax and lightly scented rose oil.

Expiation Incense

Uses: Give spiritual strength and courage to manes and immanes

Components: Parsley (*Petroselinum* spp.), thyme (*Thymus vulgaris*), with basil (*Ocimum basilicum*). Bind with beeswax and parsley oil.

Ligation Incense

Uses: Rarefy phasma into pneuma. Mitigate spirit activity for up to three weeks.

Components: Sage (*Salvia officinalis*) mixed with juniper (*Juniperus communis*) or pine (*Pinus sylvestris*). Bind with beeswax and sage oil.

Affective Incense

Uses: Increase an individual's focus and reduce emotional imbalance

Components: Frankincense (also called olibanum, *Boswellia sacra*), mint (*Mentha* spp.), and rosemary (*Rosmarinus officinalis*). Bind with beeswax and frankincense oil.

Spirit Expulsion

Uses: Incense to repel predatory revenants

Components: Peony root (*Paeonia officinalis*) with pennyroyal (*Mentha pulegium*) and chicory (*Cichorium intybus*). Bind with beeswax and pennyroyal oil.

Other Botanicals

Historically, a mixture of asafetida (*Ferula foetida*), black peppercorn (*Piper nigrum*), and a small amount of sulfur was used to expel spirits. This noxious powder is potentially hazardous and has an unpleasant smell. Interestingly, it is the origin of folklore about demons disappearing in the smoke of brimstone, although we do not recommend its usage.

Beyond this historical curiosity, here are some other useful botanical recipes for sciomancy.

Red Protection Salt

Uses: Create a barrier of salt to prevent revenant entry. Activate with orations.

Components: Mix salt and powdered ferric oxide (rust) with a mortar and pestle.

Cleansing Asperger

Uses: Cleanse residual influence from a person, place, or object

Components: Stem of hyssop (*Hyssopus officinalis*) and consecrated water

St. John's Wort
> **Uses:** Leaves of the plant are presented to immanes to bring clarity or indicate it is time to pass over
>
> **Components:** Sprig of fresh St. John's wort (*Hypericum perforatum*)

Pasque Flowers or Violets
> **Uses:** Lay on a grave at a funeral, when a spirit has been expiated or over crossed lines when a spirit has been exorcised at the place of rising to indicate a peaceful passing
>
> **Components:** Whole bud or petals of pasque flower (*Pulsatilla vulgaris*) or violets (*Viola odorata*)

SUGGESTED TOOL KIT

Not all items listed here are essential. In order of priority is your safety, magical tools, and botanicals, then low-tech, and finally electronic technology.

Basics

- First aid and supplies
- Backup communication, basic power and lighting
- Notebook, writing implements, chalk

Magic Tools

- Symbols of dignification or faith
- Printed or memorized versions of orations or prayers
- Amulets and talismans
- Intentionalized iron
- Bell and candle to draw spirits
- Affinities or relics connected to a specific spirit
- Mirror for scrying
- Preferred method of divination

Botanicals

- Consecrated water, salt, and asperger
- Botanicals for controlling phasma, and various purposes
- Burner, diffuser, or atomizer

Low Technology

- Divining rods to find spirits and their place of rising
- Compass to measure magnetic interruptions
- Flashlight or lamp to cast shadows
- Tape, string, etc. for emergent solutions

Technology

- Mirrored digital camera to capture visual manifestation
- Voice recorder or other tested equipment for EVPs
- Infrared thermometer to confirm cold spots
- Gauss or EMF meter to detect electromagnetic conditions

Chapter Nine

Rites for Working On-Site

Ritual is one element that plays a significant role in the skill set of a sciomancer, providing a means for spirit communication, protection, and resolution. Unlike necyomancy, which relies heavily on ritual form, the rites of sciomancy tend to be simple but are no less important.

Ceremonies that have been performed for generations, such as those in established esoteric systems or traditional cultures are trusted means of bringing about change, yet any rite is essentially defunct without the ability to actuate it. Regardless of the ritual employed, the power to bring an intention into reality lies in the competence of the person performing the ceremony.

The Importance of Magical Discipline

The ease of acquiring information today is opening minds and increasing a general interest in spirituality. Unfortunately, the instant gratification of information in the digital age has also fostered a sense of entitlement in the pursuit of magic. Modern seekers are encouraged to believe that simply performing a ritual from a book or an online source is effective; while a rite may be valid, it is not the basis of any true success. They do a disservice to themselves if they do not also seek an understanding of how magic works and the practical discipline required to develop the necessary skills.

Today it is much easier to find examples of magical rituals than it has been in the past, and naturally a consequence of such proliferation is the desire of the curious to experiment. Such experimentation will occasionally produce incidental successes that might seem to confirm the legitimacy of magic and encourage the user to further experimentation. While intuition and natural talent can go a long way, magic demands a consistent ability to control subtle power. Therefore, irregular accidental success is not actually evidence of being a good magician; taking it as such risks unintended side effects that only knowledge and authentic experience can mitigate.

For a ritual to be successful, you must have the conviction that your intention will be made manifest. This implicit trust cannot be imposed simply by believing in the efficacy of magic; it must be based on skill and experience in the execution of magical principles that truly work. Ritual is not simply wishful thinking enshrined in a ceremonial form—it is a wonderfully reliable art that can give you confidence when you are confronted with a spirit event.

Ritual formulas almost always consist of three fundamental components: the focus of intent, reciting of words, and performing of actions. Enacted together these elements—thought, word, and deed—serve to engage and stir the imagination to imprint an intelligence upon phasma and thereby effect a desired transformation. It is a complex and ever-shifting landscape that demands flexibility of mind and a disciplined regimen of practice.

ORATIONS

Language and the considered use of words are the very essence of human communication and are therefore crucial in attempting to engage an entity. Every magician knows that words express power—recitation of divine names, traditional orations, and the use of magical languages are integral to many magical systems. It is of equal importance to contemplate how language and words are employed in a sciomantic investigation so that the effect on a disturbance is somewhat controlled to limit a spirit's negative or intrusive reactions.

Magical orations are historically heavily laden with religious symbolism or constructed in the form of prayers. While traditional religiosity may not always be appropriate for some investigators, a formulaic approach to orations will allow you to define your interaction with the spirit and help maintain professional detachment. If religious language is preferred, a suitable prayer or invocation in accordance with your personal faith may precede the initial oration.

As a sciomancer, you must be cognizant of other people who may be present during the investigation. Overtly esoteric or archaic phraseology may make some people uncomfortable and exacerbate their fears of the unknown. It is therefore better to employ neutral and modern language not only to protect personal sensitivities but also to encourage clarity to all present regarding what is being said. The inspiration in all investigations should be compassion and rendering aid to both the living and the dead; to that end, always endeavor to bring certitude and confidence to those who have asked for help.

The practice of medieval magic makes use of specific and sometimes lengthy orations as components in a complete method of interacting with spirits. Understanding this systemized approach, we can adapt these usages to the art of sciomancy, where they are conditioned on the immediate need. Orations therefore tend to be shorter and more flexibly employed. The following list shows some of the uses traditional to medieval magic and that are most helpful in an investigation.

- Annunciation: A declaration of your identity and authority
- Application: The proclamation of the intent for the operation
- Evocation: An oration that stirs a spirit to approach for the purpose of interacting with them
- Interrogation: The prepared set of questions put to a spirit
- Placation: An oration that attempts to calm or put a spirit at ease
- Abjuration: A renunciation to threaten or coerce a belligerent entity when placation is inadequate
- Adjuration: Extracting an obligation from an entity
- Dismissal: A formal verbal closing to the interaction with a spirit

Annunciation

When entering a location that is supposed to be inhabited by a spirit, paranormal investigators may begin with an introduction wherein they verbally state why they are present and what they hope to achieve. In magic, this is known as the annunciation, a prescribed recitation that proclaims your identity and authority in the practice of your art.

Application

The declaration of intent with regard to the magical operation is known as the application, and in sciomancy it may be appended to the annunciation. Applications are usually constructed in a terse and unambiguous style. A modern adaptation based upon the ancient formulae of annunciation and application might look similar to the following:

> My name is (name of investigator) and I have been asked by (name of client or occupant) to investigate the spirit disturbances that have occurred in this place. I hereby directly address the spirit abiding herein and would have you know that my hope is to bring peace to you, not conflict. I ask that you communicate with me, requiring that you do so patiently and affably without deceit, terrifying visions, or causing harm to anyone here, neither to their bodies nor spirits. Therefore, come and approach me.

Evocation

Initiating communication begins with verbally requesting the spirit to interact. In magic, this process is called evocation, which means "to call out to" or "rouse." Strictly speaking, "evocation" refers to the method of eliciting a first contact with a spirit but is also used as the general word for the various complicated arts that involve deliberately calling up spirits, such as necyomancy. In sciomancy, we use the term "evocation" in relation to individual orations, not in the broader sense of an evocative art.

When you make an evocation, it should be respectful, clear, and specific. Be cautious of confusing the act of evocation with either conjuration or summoning. Evocation refers explicitly to magical techniques of rousing a spirit for the first time and beginning an interaction. Conjuration, however, is a process of contracting or negotiating a reciprocal action with an evoked spirit that is confirmed in the adjuration. Summoning is a simpler form of oration to draw a spirit back to you for periodical interaction after setting a time and place for further collaboration.

The equivalent to evocation employed by current paranormal investigators is sometiems called "calling out," and it is often indiscriminate in the use of language, seeking to encourage any activity rather than interaction with a specific entity. This may be deemed acceptable when the goal of the paranormal investigator is to incite and record evidence as to the veracity of spirit phenomena. However, when the aim is to compassionately resolve an incident, such indiscriminate language can entice the interference of spirits other the specific entity you wish to engage. When other spirits become involved, the aggregate information gathered during the investigation will become contaminated with extraneous data and hinder the success of the analysis necessary to strategize a resolution.

The use of evocation to attract spirits into communication is a cornerstone of medieval magic, ranging from a simple repeated oration to prolonged and intricate recitations. All evocations should be spoken with a confident voice that resounds with a commitment to draw the attention of the entity and incites them to approach. The emergent nature of sciomancy relies upon short and uncomplicated evocations as you may need to move from place to place while attempting to track and interact with the spirit. Every time the evocation is said, take a moment to observe the area. Note any anomalies that may have originated with the spirit that could signal responses to the recitation.

Precision in language is key to initiating contact with an individual entity as demonstrated in the following example of a simple evocation:

> I call upon the human spirit who frequents this place and whose disturbances have been witnessed herein; who in the day or night of (date), about the hour of (time), had appeared in the form of (state of manifestation) at this place. I invite you, spirit, to approach and communicate with me.

Important Note on Communicating with Spirits

During an investigation, you may wish to invite a spirit to communicate with you to learn more. You should only proceed if it is safe to do so and you have the proper protections in place. If you are certain the entity is a eudaemon (that is, a lares or a manes), you may decide to use a direct method of communication depending on your abilities and what you are comfortable with.

If the spirit is a cacodaemon, you should avoid direct communication until a strategy for resolution has been prepared and you have all the safeguards in place, which are described in more detail in chapter 13. If you wish to communicate but are uncertain as to the classification of the spirit, it is advisable to take full precautions. It is possible that the spirit will reveal themselves in their interaction.

Remember that during an inquiry, you should never make offerings to a revenant or do anything that might imply a contract. Offerings are reserved until the resolution stage, and only after the obsessing spirit has been bound by oath.

Interrogation

The process of verbal interchange with a spirit is known in magic as interrogation. Despite the modern negative connotations of the word, it simply describes the method of making queries. The rationale of establishing a dialogue with a spirit is to elicit pertinent information which will lead to uncovering the identity of the entity, their attachment, and the means to ameliorate their distress. The inquiries put to the revenant should be carefully considered and a general list of questions may be prepared before the interaction takes place. When establishing a discourse, it is important to convince the spirit to identify themselves and avoid using preconceived names. It is not unusual for a spirit to feign the identity of the entity you wish to speak to just to have an opportunity to interact with the living. Although disingenuous, this behavior is not necessarily a sign of maliciousness. Likewise, general curiosity should be precluded as the collaboration is likely to be of a limited duration and you must prioritize the inquiries to serve the overall objectives of sciomancy.

Ultimately, entering a dialogue with the spirit is the best means of accumulating the information you need to resolve the incident. Apart from directly hearing and seeing, there are many means of communicating with a spirit; some are traditional while others are more modern.

When selecting the method for speaking with the entity, consideration must be given as to whether you can directly confirm that the spirit you wish to speak to is indeed the individual with whom you are interacting. Try to avoid methods that rely upon a yes-no response, such as employing a flashlight or K2 meter, as it is better to have a process where the spirit can offer a more explanatory answer.

For centuries, necromancers have used scrying (gazing at a reflective surface) coupled with the faculty to hear spirits, which has proven incredibly effective. In modern paranormal methodology, discerning use of short-burst EVP sessions or spirit boards can also be adequate means of communication provided the necessary protections are in place and the methodology of their employment serves the ultimate purposes of the investigation.

Interrogation usually begins with questions designed to reveal the identity of the spirit: asking their name, where or when they were born, and about any events they may remember from their previous life. Next are inquiries that seek to establish the attachment the spirit is suffering, such as the cause of the revenant remaining in Qarth Arqa or what they need to resolve the issues of their mortal life. Finally is the attempt to elicit from the entity a prearranged sign that any resolution has been successful, as the subtlety of success may be overlooked.

Secondary questions germane to the investigation may be put to the spirit if the dialogue can be prolonged. Appropriate topics include whether other spirits are present, who they may be, where the spirit is entering into the location, or any other subject deemed relevant.

Queries should be limited and precise, as communication may be fleeting or achieved only once. If the initial communication is brief, any secondary questions can be reserved should other dialogues occur later in the investigation. At the conclusion of the interrogation, the spirit should be shown gratitude for interacting with the investigation to foster a climate of mutual respect and trust.

A good example of the interrogation process is recorded by Wirt Sikes (1836–1883) during which he received from his Welsh informants regarding interrogating spirits:

> … the spirit's business must be demanded; three times the question must be repeated unless the ghost answer earlier. When it answers it speaks in a low and hollow voice, stating its desire; and it must not be interrupted while speaking, for to interrupt it is dangerous in the extreme. At the close of its remarks, questions are in order. They must be promptly delivered, however, or the ghost will vanish. They must bear on the business in hand: it is offended if asked as to its state, or other idle questions born of curiosity.[31]

---

31   Wirt Sikes, *British Goblins: Welsh Folklore, Fairy Mythology, Legends and Traditions* (London: Sampson and Low, 1880), 148–149.

Placation

It is far better to alleviate the tension in a situation long before it rises to the level of conflict. Sciomancy does this through the process of placation, which is a systematic verbal method of calming the spirit. In sciomancy, placation depends upon the individual circumstances that you may find yourself in and therefore there cannot be a one-size-fits-all approach. You should be motivated by compassion to orally calm the entity and do so without appearing conceited. There is no room for exercising the ego in placation; the objective is to soothe unease and assist the spirit in understanding that you are truly there to help them. Placation serves the secondary purpose of developing a relationship of trust with the entity that will aid in establishing communication and ascertaining the attachment that initiated the obsession.

Abjuration

Traditionally necromancy has not been immune to discord caused by spirits. Occassionally, there are spirits who are predatory or aggressive, and the art has developed magical combative methods for application when necessary. Disputes with spirits should always be avoided whenever possible, yet it is equally important to realize that being steadfast in the commitment to resolution may bring you into conflict with an entity. When hostility looms as a real possibility, a necromancer may engage in abjuration or the magical use of threats, but this should be reserved as a final attempt to defuse the tension. Needless to say, you should not level a threat that cannot be executed with conviction; unless you are trained in the proper methods, abjuration should be utterly eschewed.

A trend among modern paranormal investigators that superficially resembles abjuration is the controversial use of provocation, which attempts to incite an immediate response from a spirit by employing accusative and combative language. The theory runs that aggression can garner an emotional reaction from any spirit present that may be observed and instrumentally recorded as evidence of the entity's existence. While some among paranormal researchers abide by the theoretical value in provoking, there are many who refute its use, believing that it is generally distasteful and may lead to potentially dangerous consequences emanating from the entity's induced rage. There is a fringe element within the paranormal community that engages in provocation for the thrill and notoriety it can bring and you should be cautious of engaging in an investigation with irresponsible people such as these.

Adjuration

"Adjuration" means "to swear." Simply put, it is extracting an oath from a spirit, or having the spirit swear to behave in a particular manner. Oaths hold greater weight with spirits than they do among the living. Should you manage to encourage a revenant to accede to an obligation, it is a very effective means to contain infestation activity or, in some cases, resolve the event. The oath you hope to administer should be constructed in such a way that the effect and conditions are plainly laid out in a simple and conclusive form. Some spirits understand the effect of obligations and won't hesitate to exploit a perceived loophole in the language.

Dismissal

Some sciomantic investigations are conducted over an extended period. If you need to leave the site of investigation and return at a later date, the living occupants may have no choice except to remain at the location of the obsession. In an endeavor to obviate any disturbances that may occur in your absence, you must end your magical operation with a dismissal, also called a license to depart. A dismissal is fundamentally an oral agreement in which the spirit is required to not harm or upset anyone and that the entity will receive further attention from you. Here is an example of a dismissal appropriate for sciomantic investigation:

> I am speaking to the human spirit who frequents this place. Be
> patient and calm in behavior, without danger or injury to any
> living person who enters herein. There is no need to unsettle
> anyone or anything. At a future time, I will return. Approach
> only me and I promise that I will seek resolution for you and
> attempt to bring you peace.

In many of the suggested orations, you may have noticed that you draw the attention of the revenant to yourself alone. Being familiar with the reality of both magic and the needs of human spirits, you must endeavor to insert yourself as a boundary between the sufferers of a disturbance and the obsessing spirit. In effect, you become a temporary attachment for the entity that protects the emotional sensitivities of the living and may provide hope to the revenant that someone is willing to hear them and help them find resolution. A sciomancer is essentially a spiritual negotiator and facilitator of communication, which has proven the primary means of solving obsessions.

PROTECTIVE SPACES

There are many instances in which you will need to make a space free of spirit influence as part of your investigation. When preparing the space where you intend to work, make sure that all necessary precautions have been taken and protection is in place. The use of talismans, amulets, and other precautionary measures should be taken advantage of, and personal spiritual forms of protection should be performed immediately before entering the space. The following rites allow you to make a secured space and set any protections you may need in the field.

- Exorcism of a Place: A two-step formula to cleanse and protect an area to make it free of spirit influence.

- Creating a Sanctuary: Preparing an enduring space to serve as your base of operations when working on-site.

- Place of Communication: Preparing a small secure area to safely communicate with entities.

- Emergent Protection: A quick method to establish a protected space as the immediacy of the need arise.

Formula for the Exorcism of a Place

Following are the two distinct steps for creating a protected space. The cleansing of the place removes spirit and residual influence, and the magical protection prevents the spirit from reentering the area.

1: Cleansing of the Place

This step refers specifically to the act of neutralizing the magical influences therein. This process efficiently transitions the location from one in which attachments and intelligences have impressed themselves upon the dense phasma to a place where the phasma has been elevated into a state of pneuma and any intelligence is dissolved. For the purpose of investigation, you should take care when using incense to ensure that you do not rarefy the phasma outside of the immediate area and thereby mitigate any spirit manifestation that you are seeking to record elsewhere on-site.

1. Mark out the space that you intend to protect.

2. Declare your intention to exorcise the space, and encourage entities to leave.

3. Asperge the area with consecrated water to cleanse the space. Pay attention to closets, cabinets, and corners.

4. Suffumigate with an incense to rarefy phasma.

5. Make recitations that reinforce the intention of transmuting a disturbed space into an environment of peace and tranquility.

2: Magical Protection of a Place

After the space has been cleansed and rarefied, it will need to be sealed against further spirit influence. If you are protecting a room, again pay special attention to liminal spaces such as doors, windows, vents, and fireplaces. These areas can be magically sealed using several methods, including a warding oil or wash applied above entryways, marking them with crossed lines, or placing amulets or protective talismans over them. Prayers and orations consistent with your faith or traditions are also beneficial in creating a sense of sanctity and spiritual defense that can reinforce the boundaries of your cleansed area.

1. Visualize a barrier of protection surrounding the space.

2. Traverse the boundary to reinforce your intent. (You may use a consecrated knife or iron.)

3. Declare your purpose to make a safe place; use prayer or orations.

4. Seal each entryway, strengthening them with visualization and appropriate orations.

5. To dismantle the protection, remove the seal with intent, words, and action.

Formula for Creating a Sanctuary

During an on-site investigation, an appropriate space within the location with little or no spirit activity should be identified to set up a sanctuary. It should serve as a center of communications and operations as well as a safe zone where participants can repeatedly retire to recenter themselves, log data, and adjust their investigatory tactics. In the formula that follows, we have employed a technique of moving through the space from corner to corner which can be found in medieval protection rites.[32]

This operation is a type of apotropaic working, meaning that protection is derived from either deflection or concealing the subject from harm. The benefit of this method makes a spirit unaware of your sanctuary; therefore it will not try to overhear or interfere when you return to its boundaries to strategize.

In performing this formula, maintain the visualization that any spirit observer will only see mist and that the sanctuary is obscured to their sense.

1. Prepare four talismans of protection.

2. Visualize a barrier of protection surrounding the space.

3. Traverse the boundary to reinforce your intent using a consecrated knife or iron.

4. Return to the center of the space. Raise the intentionalized iron above your head and proclaim an oration to make the space both protected and concealed.

5. Walk toward the first corner of the place with the iron still aloft. When you reach the corner, lower the iron until it touches the ground.

6. Place your first talisman in this corner and repeat the oration.

7. With the iron held low, return to the center and again repeat the oration.

8. When you have finished speaking, raise it up again and proceed to the corner opposite to the first.

9. Repeat steps 5 to 7.

· · · · · · · · · · · · · · · · · ·

32   Claude Lecouteux, translated by John E. Graham, *Traditional Magic Spells for Protection and Healing* (Rochester, VT: Inner Traditions, 2017), 246.

10. When you have finished speaking, raise it up again and proceed to the third corner of the room.

11. Repeat steps 5 to 7.

12. On returning to the center, place the iron on the ground.

13. You may now make any religious invocations, prayers, or recitations that reinforce the sanctity and security of the space.

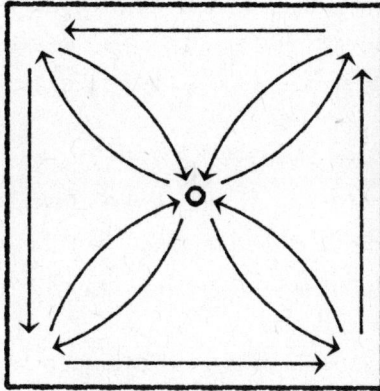

Sanctuary Procedure

Formula for the Place of Communication

The approach most used in the art of laying ghosts is to create a circle of protection to stand in and allow the spirit to remain outside its boundaries. A nine-foot circle of protection can be made simply by placing a consecrated knife or intentionalized iron in the center point. For the purpose of communication, it is better to also reinforce the perimeter and sanctify the space inside. Although circles were traditionally marked with either consecrated chalk or charcoal, a circle does not need to be drawn on the ground; you can keep its boundary in your mind. If you do want to mark it, one way is to use a length of rope that marks the circumference when its ends are bound together.

It may be helpful to have a small table inside the circle for the candle, incense, and any other item you will need while communicating with the spirit. A traditional Scottish method is to place a chair inside the circle for you to sit in addition to another chair placed outside the circle as an invitation to the spirit to converse.

1. Place your iron in the center of where you will form your circle and intentionalize it.

2. Visualize your circle as a sphere, not as a two-dimensional plane.

3. Walk the circumference of the circle to reinforce its boundary.

4. Return to the center and make any oration that confirms the boundary and invokes aid in protecting and sanctifying the interior.

5. To dismantle the protection, deactivate the iron with intent, words, and action. (Note: even after the iron has been deactivated, the effects of an active circle will take up to twenty-four hours to fully dissipate).

Method for Emergent Protection

Conditions can change very quickly in an investigation. At times, you will need to immediately create a space to work in that is free of any direct spirit influence. The simplest way to do this is to employ intentionalized iron so that an entity cannot directly interfere with you.

Intentionalized iron not only creates a barrier nine feet (2.7 meters) in diameter that a revenant is unable to cross, it can also bind a spirit within its confines, making it a deterrent. The only ritual action required to create a protective space is to actuate the iron, which is done using the same method to activate an amulet. It is wise to provide the spirits in the area some warning so that they have an opportunity to remove themselves. Otherwise, you can inadvertently trap an innocuous spirit or, more worryingly, bind a dangerous spirit in the space with you.

Conjurations or orations related to the purpose of your work in establishing a safe enclave can be greatly beneficial and will help you to focus intention. Remember to deactivate the iron when complete.

The effects of intentionalized iron are instantaneous and very useful to create protected spaces in an investigation or as part of an exorcism. Here are some methods:

+ Place an intentionalized item such as a knife, rail spike, nail, or cauldron in the center of a space to create a temporary circle of protection up to nine-foot in diameter (2.7m).

+ Arrange several iron nails or spikes within nine feet (2.7m) of each other pointing outward to protect a larger space.
+ Drive an iron spike at the corners of a fenced perimeter or the external corners of a building to reinforce an enclosed area.

Ritual is both a tool to facilitate your work and a sacred practice, and it should be embraced with confidence but also humility. When performing your rites, you must ready yourself by fostering an authoritative yet respectful demeanor, be mindful of remaining professional and emotionally detached, and maintain an honest and compassionate motivation. You should seek to embrace the responsibility of becoming a source of compassion and wisdom to both the living and dead, a wielder of the magic of words and a guardian healer of the veil.

CHAPTER TEN

MODEL FOR INQUIRY

Historically, when help was sought to lay a ghost, a sciomancer would gather the tools of their trade and travel to the obsessed location. Sometimes they would be accompanied by a seer and their close companions in the art. These inquiries were impromptu affairs where the necromancer was provided very little information prior to their arrival and compelled to rely entirely upon their skills and understanding of magic to react to emergent conditions in the field. The sciomancer's primary resources were their personal qualities, training, and natural talents to ensure successful outcomes. Any systematic elements in the methodology of examination were either received from tradition or developed through the individual practitioner's accumulated experiences.

FOUR ESSENTIAL OBJECTIVES

Good inquiry methods are the backbone of sciomancy. Even though our venerable predecessors were not availed of modern investigative models, they were pioneers in discovering the essential information needed to facilitate and implement effective solutions. The rudiments come down to four targeted objectives:

- Confirming who the active entity or entities are and their classification
- Understanding what type of infestation activity is occurring
- Revealing why the spirit is acting out and the motivating attachments
- Discovering where the spirit enters the location

A REASONED APPROACH

Medieval magicians applied classically inspired logic models to their procedures to answer these questions based on their education in the liberal arts and sciences according to the curricula of the Trivium and Quadrivium.

Fundamentally, an investigation in situ demands abductive reasoning, which relies on observation, previous experience and acquired knowledge to infer probable conclusions. However, when analyzing evidence, a more deductive approach is required to render certainty and order an overwhelming quantity of data. The result should be a series of sensible conclusions which are based on an understanding of necromantic principles.

Ideally, a modern necromantic investigation, while fueled by the accumulation of centuries of magical knowledge and techniques, should be equally reasoned and formed into a rational methodical procedure.

For the benefit of the modern reader who may not be familiar with these methods of logic, we have divided the gathering of information and analysis into two separate phases of an inquiry, although these will become more fluid with practice. This information will become the basis of an informed and therefore reliable strategy.

Stage One: Gathering Information

In the first phase of an inquiry, pertinent information is amassed through research, interviews, and the examination of the location in which the obsession is taking place. Careful collection of information to answer the four targeted objectives is the lifeblood of a proficient investigation. Ignorance or shortcuts can have the unwelcome potential to bring about adverse consequences to all involved.

Stage Two: Critical Analysis

Analysis should be a rational procedure performed with a sense of diligence and professionalism. Once information has been assembled, being able to ascertain the patterns of spirit behavior and areas of manifestation can allow reasoned deductions that may answer your questions and determine if some level of intervention is required. (This stage is also the subject of the next chapter.)

Stage Three: Strategy

Stage three focuses on developing a strategy based on the findings of the analysis, which may include a resolution to lay an unquiet spirit. In sciomancy, this requires a magical approach and proficiency in the necessary skills to achieve a desirable outcome. (This phase is discussed further in chapters 12 and 13.)

Let us turn our focus to gathering information; in particular, the practices of on-site investigation. While a full and complete process is described, the reality is that most sciomantic endeavors are emergent. The luxury of gathering a full team, setting up technology, and examining results in minute detail does not always exist. You may be called to respond to an event that has escalated and is at the height of its activity wherein risk might be a consideration or where the inexperienced activities of others have caused harm. Action may be required immediately without the personnel or instrumentation you would prefer, and you must rely instead on your magical experience and knowledge base.

The methodology presented here is intended as a guide and resource that can be adapted to the emergent conditions on the ground. We encourage you to understand the reasons for each element and then apply what you deem relevant per your resources and the unique characteristics of the disturbance you have been called to resolve.

PRELIMINARY RESEARCH

It is best practice to begin a thorough inquiry with a period of preliminary research to form an initial cache of information that may later contextualize or corroborate data gathered at the location of the obsession. Standard research will incorporate what is known about the history of the location, including previous owners, residents, visitors, deaths, and significant events that may be germane to the investigation. It should never be assumed that a spirit is historically connected to a place, as there are many reasons for an entity to be attracted to a location, but it often occurs that such a relationship plays a part in the spirit's attachment.

It can also be beneficial to examine any legends and ghost stories local to the site of obsession. Folklore cannot rise to the level of evidence, but it can depict how a community understands the supernatural and reveals elements of valid spiritual history within its narrative. Urban legends should not be ignored either as they can be the source of phasmata.

You should also explore magical groups that have been active in the area now or historically and whether there are any findings from previous paranormal investigations. Misuse of magic, evocation or summoning of spirits, and errant practices can affect the subtle environment in ways that require the skilled eye of a magician to identify.

Environmental Assessment

A general survey of meteorological and topographical influences can provide you with indicators regarding the likelihood of EMF activity and potentially phasmic-rich areas near and around the property. Remember that you are assessing the environment based on the factors that influence spirit manifestation. Places where unstable EMF and dense phasma coincide are more conducive to phenomena; they are also the cause of many false reports of spirit activity. As you progress in your inquiry, this distinction will be one of the factors you will need to determine. Another consideration is the proximity to wild and desolate places that may attract nonhuman terrestrial spirits. Following are some environmental factors to consider.

Topography

+ Phasma coalesces in depressions and near still waters.
+ Moving waters cause phasma to dispel near the water's edge.
+ Moving water can wash phasma upward to settle in depressions on elevated banks and appears to contribute to EMF disruptions.
+ Heavily vegetated areas can produce abundant phasma.
+ Additional phasma is released and intensifies in areas of material decay.

Geology

+ The presence of quartz, granite, and silicates increases EMF.
+ Underground streams are natural pathways for spirit migration and the production of phasma.

Meteorology

+ Heavy atmospheric conditions are associated with dense phasma.
+ Thunderstorms can drive spirits indoors and into enclosed spaces.

Built Environment

+ Electrical transformers and other powerful sources of electricity can agitate the spirit environment.
+ Granite buildings, tunnels, and roads promote spirit activity due to the ebb, flow, and containment of phasma.

Architecture

+ Basements, cellars, and lower levels hold dense or stagnant phasma.
+ In upper levels and attics, phasma is more fluid.
+ Passages, doorways, hallways, and stairwells enhance activity.
+ EMF from electrical appliances, Wi-Fi, and microwaves agitate phasma.

Role of Divination

As magicians, we have recourse to divination methods to gain insights that would otherwise remain concealed. Best practice would suggest that information derived from divination should be filed immediately as a theoretical resource and reserved for later review. You must be careful not to place too much reliance on divination prior to further investigation, as it could create preconceptions that can interfere with earnest examination. Having said this, we should never underestimate the value of divination. After all, it has been an important element in sciomancy for centuries simply because it works.

INTERVIEWS

By the time you have been called in to assess an obsession, it is possible that the people involved are feeling some distress, even if they do not display it. In some cases, their sense of normalcy may be shaken, the unknown rising to usurp what they have always been certain of, their spiritual faith possibly tested. Their emotions may be strained to the point of spiraling into anxiety because they have witnessed spirit activities that are outside their commonly held worldview. These people were and may still be on the front line of the merging of worlds and therefore possess incalculably valuable information pertinent to your investigation.

Just as you must diligently cultivate your magical faculties, you must develop proficiency in interview techniques. Moreover, the process of interviewing provides the opportunity to ameliorate the witnesses' fears, calming and comforting them.

Initial Interview

Interviews not only collect records of spirit experiences which occurred prior to an investigation, they also help establish a professional relationship. Initial interviews require an atmosphere that builds trust. It is a matter of offering a sympathetic ear and allowing the witnesses to share their stories. An interviewee who feels vulnerable and embarrassed can be reticent to recount information that makes them uncomfortable but may be vital to the investigation. The witness must feel assured that they will be protected from judgment and their testimony will be used for the purpose of investigation only, and any confidential admission will be inviolably kept private.

The ability to patiently listen to an agitated witness is fundamental to success. You must be careful to collect information without prejudice, whether confirmed or unconfirmed, and not to appear conceited or disinterested. You will need to be both gentle and instructive without appearing to demean the intelligence of the interviewee and always show sensitivity to their beliefs. While compassion and sympathy for a person in distress is appreciated, real solace will come from the reassurance you can offer with your unique understanding of sciomancy.

With your guidance, the witness will no longer need to accept being a helpless victim of unseen entities. Those things that appear to be unknown to them actually can be known, understood, and resolved.

Further Interview Techniques

As all memory is permanently stored as a faculty of the soul, it should therefore be accessible under the proper conditions. People process extreme experiences in very different ways that are always susceptible to emotional stimuli. Reactions can lead to unintended exaggerations and assumptions that make eye witness accounts appear inconsistent.

Memories are not stored as isolated and unconnected events nor as defined sequences, rather they are stored as a network of associations, like a web of relevancies. Therefore, comprehensive interviewing is not as simple as asking a witness what happened—it is about how we ask that question. We must apply techniques to tease out important information from the interviewee's sometimes scattered, emotively charged, and confused recall.

You should not consider testimony as the singular key that explains an event; it is an aggregate that needs to be somewhat deconstructed, and the relevant data extracted. What follows are some simple interview techniques that encourage the witness to shift their perception and recall elements that were previously over-looked. They can help you navigate through the web of associations that the witness is often unaware of, attempting to access the critical information necessary for your research.

Sensory Account

We usually process experience through the five senses: sight, hearing, smell, taste, and touch. Encouraging the witness to mentally relive an event through an environmental or personal context can reveal additional details. This type of recounting is done through mentally "setting the scene," asking the witness to recall the circumstances, feelings, sights, sounds, and environment leading up to and including the actual event. Context in memories can reveal chains of association because unlocking one point will naturally recall related particulars.

Detailed Focus

In this technique, the witness is asked to provide any detail, no matter how irrelevant it may seem. Such elements may be recognized as pertinent based upon your own experience and knowledge base, but a single recollection may reveal other details to the witness that can begin to uncover new strands in the web of connectivity. While the first interview technique may be viewed as assessing the general environmental context, this technique focuses upon the minutiae of the event.

Altered Sequence

When accessing the memories of a witness, the emotive power of the most recent events is more likely to be immediately called to mind. This can obscure other elements that may be more relevant. You should ask the witness to chronologically reverse their recounting of the occurrence from the latest to earliest events or have them relate the sequence entirely out of order in a random manner. Having the interviewee shift the narrative order has the potential of accessing the otherwise hidden elements of their memory.

Perspective Shift

When a person suffers an emotionally charged or traumatic event, they mentally entrench themselves as a defense mechanism. This reaction can cause them to focus only on the details that adversely affected them, replaying them in their minds and reinforcing any defensive reactions. With an awareness of this proclivity in the human mind, you can instruct the witness to shift their outlook and recount the incident from the perspective of other witnesses or even from that of the obsessing entity. This perspective change serves to draw the interviewee out of their cerebral defensives and can reveal dormant details that have been suppressed by the natural desire for mental security.

Misinformation

While these techniques can mitigate the interference of natural exaggeration or omission, you should be aware that there are people who will intentionally perpetrate hoaxes. There are paranormal researchers dedicated to scientific exploration of the supernatural who apply rational skepticism to their examination and deem it their responsibility to expose fraudulent impostors to further serious investigations.

As sciomancers, we have a mandate to resolve spirit disturbances. We are not specifically responsible for exposing hoaxes and confronting frauds. It is our purpose to uncover the cause of purported obsessions. If during the course of our inquiry we discover that fraud is in fact the cause, we have successfully done our job.

Deception can be motivated for a variety of reasons. Some hoaxes are clearly obvious while others may be more nuanced. There are occasions when creating false phenomena provides the subject with a defense mechanism to deny the reality of events they have witnessed and project some personal control amid chaos. Over the years we have found that the best policy is to professionally pursue an inquiry regardless of suspicions, trusting in the procedure and esoteric understanding to reveal the truth.

THE WALK-THROUGH

The first time that you are likely to physically enter an obsessed location will be during a cursory walk-through that familiarizes yourself with the layout and identifies the places where previous incidents had been reported. Viewing areas of reported activity can give context witness testimony and provide inspiration for any follow-up interviews. You should also be looking for any environmental conditions where phasma can potentially coalesce that are likely to become the focus of activity. Pay attention to sounds, lights, and reflections, and take note of anything you think you may need to come back and document. During your cursory walk-through, identify any potential safety hazards, the best places to set up recording devices and other instrumentation you intend to use, and where you will stage your sanctuary or base of operation.

Place of Rising

One of the phenomena that you will need to detect is the area where the spirit has found entrance into the location. This is known traditionally as the place of rising, as revenants appear to rise out of the ground when they enter a space. You should be aware of locations where the conditions favor a place of rising and record them for further investigation. This place will usually be seldom frequented and often in shadow, like the corners of a room or an enclosed space. If you have experience using dowsing rods or a pendulum, they can greatly assist.

During an investigation, do not attempt to disturb a place of rising. Only after a resolution has been reached and the spirit has departed can the place of rising be sealed with crossed lines or intentionalized iron.

Innate Observation Skills

Beyond an understanding of magical and environmental factors, you should seek to adopt methodologies that enhance your proficiency in observational skills. We are generally taught that good observational skills rely on the ability to focus on details that can be sequentially assembled and interpreted through the application of deductive reasoning. In sciomancy, we must also develop our heuristic abilities, our innate faculties to assess our environment on the instinctual level.

Over the course of evolution, human survival has depended on a subconscious process of recognizing changes in the environment. When a threat is distinguished, the limbic system in our brains sends out an immediate instruction to freeze, fight, or escape. With practice, we can learn to hone these natural propensities to recognize not only threats but also whatever anomalies we are seeking in our environment, such as when observing a location in a walk-through. In particular, pay attention to the way your body and instincts react to the presence of phasma, to high levels of EMF, and when an entity is present. With practice, other anomalies will begin to stand out as your senses start to zone in and pinpoint clues essential to your inquiry.

Our institutionalized education systems generally condition us to devalue our instincts. However, people who suffer extreme survival circumstances for long periods of time, are skilled in detective work, or who hunt or engage in dangerous activities often develop a reliance on these heuristic instincts. But for those others, attempts must be made to reeducate themselves to develop and trust their own innate assessments.

Carefully applying both rational and innate intuitive methods of observation during a walk-through will provide you with a rich resource of preliminary data. It will elevate the walk-through from simply familiarizing yourself with the location to an investigative process that establishes foundational data that will contextualize any accrued information.

A mindful walk-through can also provide an understanding of the environment and influences upon the everyday lives of any residents, giving you indications of the beliefs, interests, and relationships among the people involved; a reminder of the normalcy that a successful resolution seeks to restore.

WORKING IN A TEAM

As mentioned above, the early sciomancers often arrived at an obsessed location accompanied by their companions, usually apprentices and a seer to facilitate communication. These people worked as a rudimentary investigative team, and good sciomancers would have availed themselves of the individual talents of their companions.

Today some paranormal investigators also form teams, preferably arranged according to the specialty skills of the members. A technology expert, researcher, medium, and skeptic are some of the common roles found in these groups. Sciomancers can be inspired by our paranormal cousins in assembling a team to aid us in our endeavors. The only caveat to adopting the paranormal model is that when arranging a team, you must do so in accordance with the aims of sciomancy wherein the collection of evidence is solely to enable a resolution. It is also prudent to have access to a magician or expert with advanced skills whom you can call upon to lay an unruly spirit should it become necessary.

While a team of experts is ideal, the lack of one should not obstruct you in your endeavors. At the very least, have a support person who can assist you during an on-site investigation for reasons of safety.

Keeping an Open Mind

While most common roles assumed by paranormal investigators are self-explanatory, a word on the use of a skeptic is warranted. Healthy skepticism is essential in all inquiries, and every sciomancer must have a strong sense of rationality. Sometimes that which first appears to be a spiritual phenomenon is the result of natural or physical causes, so an honest investigator must uncover and eliminate that phenomenon from their final analysis. Skepticism should never be elevated over reason and understanding. Ironically, the desire to clarify the spiritual with a preconceived "rational explanation" can become an irrational fixation and will fundamentally interfere with the correct interpretation of a disturbance. Instead, we should approach an inquiry with an understanding of the unseen world and how it functions, referring to the arcana to guide us toward a broader picture of what is likely to be occurring.

Another loaded term to address is "debunking" in paranormal circles. When a phenomenon is reported by a witness, the designated skeptic will sometimes attempt to re-create the event to systematically disprove the supposed supernatural cause. The word "debunk" carries with it the meaning of exposing a fraud, hoax, or nonsensical event and implying a deceit on the part of the witness. This word can appear to be derogatory and may offend the very people we are seeking to help. It should be reserved for use according to its meaning and not simply because we were able to provide an explanation for events which did not involve a spirit presence.

Working with a Medium

While employing the talents of a medium or a psychic during an investigation is clearly an advantage, any information should be recorded in its raw and immediate form so that it does not create preconception or bias. When interpretation is needed, it should be done later by someone other than the person who received the initial impressions. This precaution is not intended to denigrate the important service of talented sensitives, rather it is simply a matter of compartmentalization that allows for maintaining the clarity of individual datasets by limiting contamination between them.

There can also be a strong emotional connection between the seer and the impression they have received that can naturally lead to assumptions that may not be accurate. For these reasons there is an old and pertinent maxim in our tradition that a prophet should never interpret their own prophecy. Likewise, if you intend to fill the role of a medium, you should step aside and let someone else lead the active investigation. In our experience, this is necessary not only for the integrity of the information revealed but also for the medium's health.

Staying Professional

All members of a sciomantic team must adhere to maintaining a calm, emotionally detached but compassionate demeanor. Participants should be trained in how to behave and follow operational procedures, with practical duties and responsibilities assigned.

At all times you should act with a balance of humility and authority that projects an aura of authenticity so that those who have asked for your aid can feel confident in placing their trust in you. Overemotional or dramatic reactions can fuel the flames of fear, especially among witnesses who are already suffering from the terror of their experience. The role of a sciomancer is to provide inoculation against the contagion of dread and be a shield behind which the uninitiated can find some succor and security. Your conduct and behavior have a real effect on the conditions of the investigation, and you must be cognizant of the consequences that a lapse in composure can create.

ON-SITE INVESTIGATION

An on-site investigation will allow you to gather pertinent information that will ultimately lead to a strategy for resolution. An investigation does not need to be a grand affair, nor does it need to occur at night. A full-scale operation as presented here is not always required, but no matter its length, the process is essentially the same. It must be remembered that first and foremost this is a magical procedure, and you should set your mind and protect yourself accordingly.

Preparation

The priority in any fieldwork is safety. Mitigate any potential hazards identified in your walk-through and establish safety protocols, emergency contacts, and clear emergency exits. Secure the area to prevent entry to the location from intruders, and ensure that you have adequate first aid, supplies, lighting, and a means of communication. Your kit should include your magical tools plus any botanicals you may require. If you are using electronic devices, always carry backup power and a low-tech alternative.

Sanctuary

Following the walk-through, an appropriate space within the location should be identified to set up a sanctuary, which will serve as a center of communications and operations. Where possible, try to choose a location with limited entry points and where running water is available for the treatment of EMF exposure. Depending on the location's layout, it may be necessary to establish more than one sanctuary.

There are numerous magical practices to cleanse and seal a spiritually safe environment; we would encourage the use of those tried and true methods, such as the example given in chapter 9.

Witnesses and Occupants

When there are witnesses or occupants present on location, it is good practice to appoint a team member to be their liaison, answer any questions they may have, and check on their well-being. If they wish to be involved, use your discretion to determine if it is appropriate. All participants will need to undergo cleansing and protection before and after any investigation or spirit activity.

Any person vulnerable to spirit attack should not be part of an on-site investigation, nor should they directly communicate with spirits. If any are present, they should remain in the sanctuary or another protected location. This may include:

+ Someone who has recently undergone trauma or surgery or has open wounds
+ Children, unborn babies, and people who are pregnant
+ Pubescents or other individuals who demonstrate uncontrolled psychic influence
+ Anyone who has previously experienced an obsession by a spirit at the location
+ Anyone who is considered mentally or emotionally at risk

Baselines

The optimal time to establish baseline information about the site is before your investigation commences. Always try to think ahead and record information so that you have something with which to compare your findings, such as photos, sounds, temperatures, and so on. If you have an EMF meter, you can check readings with appliances turned on and off. Avoid touching and moving objects unnecessarily; if you do, take note of them.

Monitoring Equipment

Any monitoring devices or instruments you intend to use should be installed in the strategic sites identified during the walk-through. If you want to take advantage of infrared technology or are operating in dark conditions, you will need to ensure that adequate lighting is available to safely investigate. Items that have been reported to move can be marked with chalk or tape where possible, and a thread can be placed across closed doors. Other techniques such as hanging ribbons to indicate a draft or thinly spreading a powder such as talc can be used to show movement. After setting up, be sure to secure the area so that it cannot be disturbed by living people or animals.

Regrouping

Prior to the operation, regroup with your team in the sanctuary. This is an opportunity to center yourself, reinforce protection, and empower your spiritualization. Any plans or analysis concerning spirits should only occur within this safe retreat. You will return to the sanctuary regularly to log information and consider results.

Operation

When you conduct your practical investigation, move systematically and strategically through the location, gathering pertinent information that will be needed to resolve the event. You should attempt to observe where activity is more prevalent, where infestation events have taken place, and where dense phasma is present. Technology may accumulate periphery and environmental evidence such as EMF spikes, EVPs, and photographic images that can prove invaluable during the analysis phase.

Likewise, if a medium or psychic is present during the operational portion of the investigation, their impressions can be recorded for later review. If a critically important piece of information is intuited, it should be shared, but generally impressions should not be revealed during the investigative process as it may unduly influence the gathering of raw data.

Log Events

Due to the dynamic nature of events, it is advisable to keep detailed notes of your observations and experiences and collate them during intermissions. Even in a brief investigation, you will be bombarded with information that you may not realize the importance of during the immediacy of the experience. When collecting information, try to fully describe any activity or manifestations witnessed. Whether you employ a personal journal or digital log, note the time and location of any event you experience in the field so it can be reviewed later.

Clear Communication

While on site during an investigation, your team should engage in a focused economy of communication, eschewing idle chatter or nonessential conversation. You should speak clearly and pertinently, never whispering, especially when recording equipment is being used. Respectfully pursuing a calm and rational inquiry will not only facilitate the gathering of relevant information but will also build a reputation for your team that transcends a single investigation.

Investigation Discipline

An investigation may present opportunities to witness spirit activity firsthand. It is important to follow procedure and stay composed and open-minded. There can be a temptation to rush toward the places where activity has been witnessed or instrumentation has captured potential spirit events. Only when more about the identity of the spirit has been ascertained should any attempt be made to communicate or interact with them. It is better to focus on the acquisition of information at this stage of the investigation and proceed through the location in a methodical and logical manner.

SPIRIT INTERACTION

When a spirit is seen with the naked eye or on camera, it is usually because the phasmic conditions are favorable. Over the course of your investigation, you may be confronted by the undeniable presence of the spirit; their manifestation should not be cause for fear. A sense of foreboding and chills are a natural effect that accompanies revenants.

Humanoid shadows and apparitions are a stage of spirit manifestation, not an attempt to cause terror. Likewise, red eyes are indicative of native terrestrial spirits that are typically not harmful.

Do not assume that a spirit is aware of you or means to harm you. Spirits do not have the same sense of judgment or proximity. What feels like a scratch could simply be a spirit trying to reach out to you. Objects that are thrown or fall may not be meant to hurt or target you, and touching and pushing can be a sign they are near you.

An entity who is acting furtively may simply not wish to be discovered. A spirit may shy away, especially if you exude dignification as a magician.

Making Contact

When you have deemed that sufficient raw data has been accumulated, the investigation may shift focus to the initial interaction with the spirit itself. If the investigation indicates that the spirit activity is human and not harmful (eudaemonic), it is safe to communicate with them during the investigation phase. If the spirit is suspected to be harmful (cacodaemonic), direct communication should be avoided until further analysis and a strategy for resolution has been prepared.

Most cases you are likely to investigate will be caused by manes having innocuous reasons for their attachments; when revealed, they will provide a path to resolution. Manes are not naturally aggressive or predatory and simply desire to fulfill the conditions of their attachments. For this reason, they may prove susceptible to amicable communication if they believe the sciomancers are there to truly aid them.

If you become aware of a manes that you would like to safely communicate with:

+ Be safe: Spiritual protection should precede any contact with unknown spirits.
+ Stay focused: Learn about the identity and cause of the disturbance.
+ Be vigilant: Maintain mental and spiritual fortitude.
+ Be diligent: Record responses and observations for further analysis.
+ Be discerning: Guard against a lemur trying to misrepresent themself.

- ✦ Keep control: Employ mediumship cautiously as it can present unique risks.
- ✦ Be smart: Do not try to banish a spirit, make offerings, or do anything to imply a contract during an investigation. Offerings are reserved until the resolution stage, and only after the obsessing spirit has been bound by oath.

Spirit Evocation

Instructions for evoking spirits and orations are more fully explained in chapter 9. Be careful to address the entity directly, and do not make open-ended invitations or presume their identity. If they claim to be someone you know, seek confirmation. It is possible that many spirits will be attracted to your work who just wish to be noticed; if this happens, you can respectfully ask those who are not relevant to your inquiry to move on.

A Flashlight Experiment

To establish first contact, you may choose to cede some modicum of control to the entity by encouraging them to select the investigator who will serve as the spiritual ambassador and primary contact in the interaction. The following description shows how the primary contact was chosen by a spirit in a case of laying ghosts.

> A jury of seven parsons was convoked, and each sat for half-an-hour with a candle in his hand, and it burned out its time with each, showing plainly that none of them could lay the ghost … The spirit could afford to defy them; it was not worth his while to blow their candles out. But the seventh parson was a stranger … In his hand the light went out at once. He was clearly the man to lay the ghost, and he did not shrink from the task …[33]

When time is of the essence a more modern approach may be needed. Today's paranormal investigators attempt to communicate with spirits using an experiment with a flashlight operated by twisting the base. The flashlight is placed on a sturdy surface where it cannot be disturbed with the barrel twisted to the point of

....
33   Henderson, *Notes on the Folk-Lore*, 337.

balance between on and off, so that a spirit can easily manipulate it. Questions are then put to the entity that can be answered by turning the light on or off.

This method is not reliable as a direct means of communication because it relies on yes-no answers but can serve in the same capacity as the candles of the archaic ceremony to let the spirit indicate their preferred point of contact. If the chosen person accepts the role, they should verbalize their willingness so that the spirit is aware of the agreement.

Spirit Dialogue

Once a dialogue has been established, the spirit should be allowed to communicate anything they wish to say. You may then ask simple questions pertinent to the investigation. While they may be reticent to answer these questions at first, there should be no reason to use abjuration or threat when communicating with a eudaemon. Be courteous and respectful. In some circumstances the spirit's answers may be recorded as an EVP or using your preferred method of communication. Be clear with your words and be careful not to ask leading questions or jump to assumptions. Do not ask the entity to repeatedly exhibit activity in the name of curiosity or evidence. We should always respect the spirit and never expect them to perform for our entertainment.

Before you dismiss the spirit, make sure you establish a means to recognize them and negotiate any options for further communication. Always employ the practice of ars remissionis following spirit discourse.

FINALIZING THE INVESTIGATION PHASE

Many times, an investigation can be completed in a few hours, but it can frequently consume days, weeks, or even months. If it is likely the inquiry will last more than one trip, you can lock down the site if you plan to return within twenty-four hours with permission. Otherwise, you should deactivate the protective sanctuary and restore the property to its original state. Do not take away any items belonging to the property when you leave. If you suspect an item is obsessed, you can magically secure it on location until you return.

If you need more time to conduct an analysis, censing the property with a rarefying botanical—for example, juniper—can give the occupants a reprieve while you formulate a resolution. In the meantime, continue to supply protection and support for the occupants and consult with them both to assure them and to learn more about their experiences.

A good investigation is only one phase of resolving a spirit disturbance. Every unique situation requires a unique approach but at its core, the procedure is consistent. Sometimes an investigation may need to be repeated until enough information can be gathered, allowing you to proceed to a suitable resolution. On the other hand, there are times when the case is potentially dangerous; in those circumstances, the emergency may need to be immediately addressed and a lengthy investigation is rendered impossible.

In this chapter, we have addressed some of the practices of the investigative process and how to avoid common pitfalls. In the next chapter, we will explore how to keep an inquiry focused and interpret findings to determine whether a situation requires intervention.

Chapter Eleven

Model for Analysis

The image of paranormal investigators spending hours staring at screens and listening to audio recordings to catch one or two pieces of elusive evidence does not really apply to sciomancy. Analysis is a fluid process that should occur parallel to your inquiry. The entire experience of investigation is gathering information, and a good investigator will be continuously evaluating.

However, at some point, you will need to come to a final assessment so you can identify the cause of the disturbance and determine whether a resolution is required. This transition may be precipitated by the need to take immediate action or because the avenues of inquiry have been exhausted.

To keep an inquiry on track requires a level of structure to your analysis. In this chapter, we will walk through the process of organizing your information to reveal relevant data and analyzing it to distill evidence. At the end of the chapter is a chart for identifying the appropriate action to resolve a spirit disturbance when both the spirit's classification and their pattern of activity are known.

Organizing Information

The procedure of conducting an analysis can appear complicated but is necessary to solve a spirit crisis in an efficient and conscientious manner. A disciplined approach to organizing data will lead to a clearer solution. Should intervention be needed, the information gained from this process will be crucial. In the case of sciomancy, information can be arranged and prioritized according to four essential categories: who, what, why, and where.

Who

When a disturbance is suspected to be spirit-related, the first question to resolve is who. That is, who is the entity responsible for obsessing the location? Discerning whether the cause is a human spirit and their classification will go a long way toward understanding the nature of an event.

If a revenant is obsessing a person, object, or place, it is imperative to attempt communication and ideally lay them to rest. A verifiable name or historical records may be difficult to ascertain, but any information regarding the entity's distinctive character should be collated to create a composite portrait of the spirit and to choose appropriate affinities or, if you're fortunate, pertinent relics.

Six Steps of Spirit Classification

Learning to recognize sublunary spirits is fundamental to sciomancy. The step-by-step process illustrated in the accompanying flowchart can be adapted to reveal the type of spirit, and their behavior.

1. Is the Activity Sentient?

The first step is to review any infestation events to identify if the cause of the disturbance is self-aware. A resolution regarding a sentient spirit will be very different from one that deals simply with phantasms and phasmata. Phenomena may include voices, noises, apparitions, objects moving, touching, and so on. Nonsentient activity can be managed by cleansing the space or dispersing the phasma. If there is supernatural phenomena you suspect is caused by a living person in the location, you will need to proceed with sensitivity, as it could be related to repressed trauma. If the cause of a disturbance is sentient, further classification is required to determine the type of spirit.

2. Is the Entity Human?

Next, confirm whether the entity is human. There are several types of nonhuman daemones that may occasionally be encountered in an investigation, the most common being terrestrial spirits. They can be recognized by their red glowing eyes and a multitude of orbs. (For a full classification, see chapter 4.)

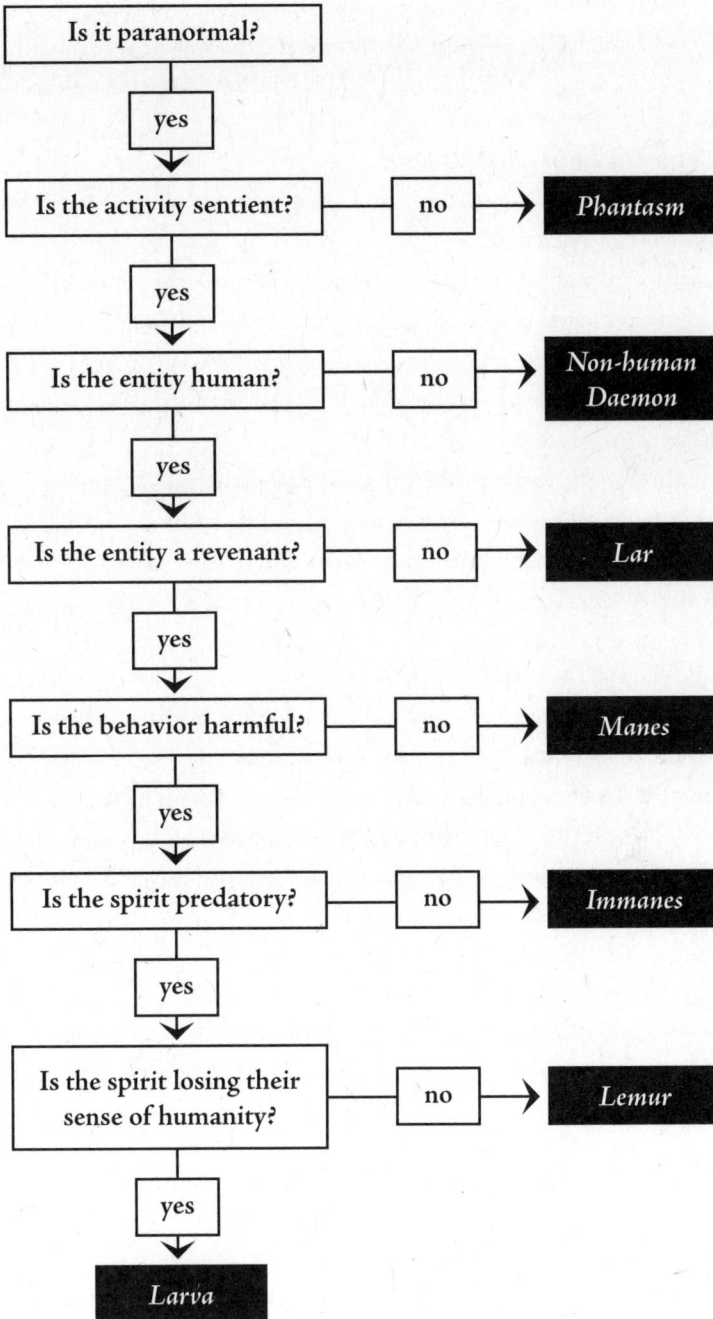

Six Steps of Spirit Classification Flowchart

If the spirit is not human but one of the other daemonic classifications, the interaction and resolution will not fall within the purview of sciomancy, and any associated phenomena can be eliminated from your investigation.

3. Is the Human Entity a Revenant?

Once the spirit has been identified as human, it is necessary to ascertain whether the spirit is a lar or a revenant.

If a lar is causing a disturbance, it may be because they have a message to impart or have returned to offer guidance and comfort. A family may need reassurance to accept the presence of a lar but there is otherwise no need to intervene. If there is still further cause for investigation, a lar may aid you and can protect against other active entities.

Revenants can be distinguished from lares by the accompanying feeling of dread and isolated cold spots. The remaining steps discriminate between the four types of revenants—manes, immanes, lemures, and larvae—based on their behavior and purpose.

4. Is the Revenant Harmful?

For the purpose of sciomancy, revenants can be separated into two groups, eudaemones and cacodaemones. If a revenant spirit is a eudaemon, they will be classified as a manes. Most revenants you encounter are likely to be manes, and there may be an opportunity to help them find resolution. All other types of revenants are considered cacodaemones (harmful spirits) and are most likely to cause an infestation i.e., immanes, lemures, and larvae.

5. Is the Spirit Predatory?

If a revenant is potentially harmful but not predatory, they can be classified as an immanes. Immanes may often go unnoticed until an infestation occurs. Indications can include:

+ Outbursts of spirit activity that is random and uncontrolled
+ Fixation on certain events, places, people, or objects
+ Signs that the spirit is in a state of distress or confusion
+ Experiencing arbitrary empathic thoughts and emotions
+ An apparition showing their state at death e.g., wounded, and so on

In contrast, lemures and larvae are both predatory spirits. They are strongly motivated by a need for phasma. Signs of predatory behavior include:

+ Spirit activity that is controlling, menacing, and focused
+ Targeting of an individual and symptoms of oppression
+ Patterns of infestation that incite fear and excite emotion
+ Appearing larger to intimidate, or diminutive to escape attention

6. Is the Spirit Losing Their Humanity?

The final step in the classification process is to distinguish between the two types of predatory revenants, lemures and larvae.

Larvae are predatory spirits who have remained in Qarth Arqa so long that they have started to forget their human state. They may involuntarily exhibit bestial features and behaviors. Larvae seldom enter the realm of the living or seek to cause disturbances. If a larva is the cause, assistance from an advanced necromancer is required.

Lemures are the most likely predatory spirit to be encountered. When a lemur is the cause of an infestation, a resolution is imperative. Lemures can learn the ability to manipulate their appearance and influence thoughts and emotions for the purpose of preying on an individual.

Distinctive Attributes of the Spirit

In addition to the classification, a review of all information collected during the investigation should be undertaken. Any details that can be learned about the entity causing a disturbance are potentially useful. This could include:

+ The era in which the revenant lived
+ Their unique characteristics or story
+ The name of the entity
+ Relics or a grave that can be used to evoke or summon and expiate the spirit
+ Affinities that provoke memories or interests to draw the spirit's attention
+ Actions that may provide validation or bring peace

This may not be a straightforward process, but it is imperative that you build the best profile of the spirit that you possibly can before proceeding further.

What

When there is a spirit disturbance, we need to see the pattern of infestation as a type of narrative or communication. We can learn a great deal about the spirit and their attachments from how they behave and the effect they have on the environment of a location. A spirit always acts for a reason, therefore it lies hidden in their actions. If events are escalating, it is important to consider these five things: What activity is taking place? How frequent is the activity? What is the intensity of activity? What conditions or stimuli exacerbate activity? What patterns and anomalies can be observed?

Activity

When comparing infestation activity, prioritizing the reliability of information is crucial. It is important to study every event in context of your understanding of the spirit world and avoid making assumptions. Not all activity will be spirit related, and not all phenomena caused by a spirit is deliberate. Phenomena can also be the result of your influence on the phasmic environment, or the impressions of others.

Frequency

From the moment you begin the interviews, start to recognize how frequent the incidents of infestation are and when they first began to escalate. Low level frequency may indicate that the entity is not particularly powerful or has no real interest in directly targeting the living inhabitants of a location. High frequency events can indicate the presence of an immanes who has difficulty controlling their emotive outbursts or a spirit who is trying to communicate. Sometimes, lemures will employ high frequency infestation to terrorize the target.

Intensity

Quantifying the intensity of events is important to identify if there is an acceleration and to better prepare yourself in case the spirit becomes agitated during the resolution phase. Harmful activity that is escalating will require prompt attention. If the occurrence of infestation has been previously more concentrated, it may indicate a period of dormancy in which the spirit is deciding the course of action they intend to take in the future, or a change in environmental conditions.

Stimuli

Reports about spirit disturbances may include many events the witness believes to be interrelated. You will need to determine which incidents are relevant and consider each in context. Isolating the actions that prompt an infestation can help to identify the cause. In some cases, the trigger will be directly related to the spirit's attachment. In other instances, it may be due to incidental circumstances, or physical phenomena that do not alone preclude a spirit presence. Theories can be tested to determine if an activity incites a reaction provided it is carried out with concern for the well-being of both the living and the dead. Some examples of stimuli include:

+ Construction or renovations that agitate a source of phasma
+ A change in the purpose, activity, or people at the location
+ A familiar event triggering a memory for the spirit, such as a wedding or birth
+ An occupant who has experienced trauma or recent emotional turmoil
+ Arrival of a new person or object with a spirit attachment
+ A recent death or accident in the area or connected to the location
+ The emergence of subtle faculties to perceive spirits by any of the occupants
+ Magical activity that might attract and/or threaten spirits

Patterns and Anomalies

Finally, you should attempt to identify whether the infestation incidents appear to have a pattern of occurrence, which might suggest whether an infestation is intentional and help you classify the spirit. Also pay attention to events that stand out from an established pattern. For example:

+ An apparition that is repetitive and unresponsive may indicate nonsentient phantasm or phasmata.
+ If the actions seem erratic and emotionally driven, the spirit is likely to be an immanes.
+ If the activity appears to be a targeted assault, it may indicate the presence of a lemur.

Patterns apparent in spirit infestation may reveal a message the revenant is unable to communicate directly. This may shed light on the attachment they are suffering and their current state of being. Understanding the spirit's motivations or any subtle communication is a distinct edge when planning a resolution and you should always be conscious of taking advantage of any information the revenant willingly offers.

Prolonged Activity

Discovering the answers to the persistence of patterns will determine if the level of activity is an infestation, obsession, oppression, or possession.

Table 8: Identifying Prolonged Activity

	Description	Causes
Infestation	Frequent paranormal activity that increases in intensity	Living person exuding uncontrolled or intense psychism Manes trying to communicate a message Immanes or manes unaware of their actions Lemur or larva inciting an emotional response to gain phasma
Obsession	A spirit becomes fixated on an attachment	Manes, immanes, lemur, or larva Phasmata in rare cases
Oppression	Focused, sustained spiritual and emotional attack on individuals	Predatory targeting of a subject by a lemur or larva
Involuntary Possession	The consciousness is set aside while a spirit inhabits the body, requiring permission or submission to the spirit	Lemur, usually connected to a subject of oppression Larva, in very rare cases Immanes, in rare cases, only if very desperate

Why

Discovering the motives of the obsessing spirit is arguably the most important question in an analysis that will determine the course of any future action. Attachments are the fetters which bind a human spirit within Qarth Arqa. This is the raison d'être of sciomancy and laying ghosts, and therefore the primary goal of collecting information during an investigation.

There are two types of attachment for a revenant: what binds them within Qarth Arqa, and whatever they have projected onto a person, place, or thing. The latter forms the anchor of the obsession and needs to be understood if successful resolution is to follow. These two types of attachment are not necessarily mutually exclusive. A spirit may be bound in the metacosmos by the same emotive link that inspires them to obsess; solving one may solve the other.

Attachments Binding a Revenant in Qarth Arqa

The roots of an attachment generally fall under one of the following categories:

+ Heavy emotions that weigh the soul down
+ Confusion from trauma, sudden death, or spiritual doubt
+ Unresolved issues or incomplete tasks
+ Holding on to their body or aspects of their material life
+ Family and loved ones clinging too tightly
+ Fear of losing themselves or facing what comes next
+ Lack of funerary rites and guidance
+ Satisfying urges and compulsions inherited from their former life

Obsessive Attachment to a Person, Object, or Place

For the purpose of alleviating a spirit disturbance, the more immediate concern is knowing what attracts a spirit to the subject of their obsession. Once the attachment is identified, an attempt can be made to understand its cause and potential means to mitigate its effects.

Person

First, take note of who is present when manifestations occur and if activity increases or decreases when certain individuals are present. A person who is the target of an obsession may show symptoms of oppression. Possible causes can include:

+ The person was known to the spirit during their life, or they have a likeness to a person of interest.
+ A spirit who is trying to communicate may focus on a person who has a latent ability to perceive spirits or is emotionally susceptible.

- If the person was recently exposed to a place of spirits or present at a death, they may have caught the attention of a spirit.
- A predatory spirit may be targeting an individual.

Object

If the spirit activity is focused on an object, it will persist even if the object is relocated. An obsessed object may exude a certain aura. Also pay attention to objects that have recently been acquired or have a history. For example:

- The object may have been owned or used by the spirit during life, or it has a resemblance to something familiar to the spirit. It may be related to an unresolved task.
- A spirit will be drawn to an object if it is used by the living as a focal point to contact the spirit.
- There is a magical connection forged between the spirit and an object.

Place

There are many ways and reasons for a revenant to be attached to a place. Sometimes a spirit can be observed moving about the space in a way that replicates the activities of their daily life. Some possible causes include:

- The location was frequented by the spirit during life or reminds them of a place significant to them.
- The site is connected to an unresolved task, impactful event, or trauma relevant to the spirit.
- The place provides a source of phasma which sustains the spirit.
- The spirit has been invited or enticed to the place, or they are bound there, e.g., by magic, a barrier of iron, or a predatory spirit.
- The place is where the spirit's grave or relics are located.

Where

Understanding where the spirit activity is likely to take place is a great advantage that permits you to focus your analysis in a more efficient manner. This can be done by mapping previous manifestations based upon witness accounts and your observations that are then compared to areas where activity is expected to occur—that is, places where phasma can naturally coalesce or sites where a significant event or emotion may have left an impression. Identifying where activity is more prevalent can be instrumental in understanding whether a spirit is sentient or what their intentions may be.

Place of Rising

If it is determined that the spirit obsessing the location is a cacodaemon, it is vital to discover their unique place of rising. All revenants who abide within a location will have one place of rising that serves as the stable point by which they can enter and leave the metacosmos to hide and rest while still retaining their phasmic form. The place of rising will always be in an unfrequented spot rich in phasma, most often in a corner or crevice. In the unfortunate case where exorcism of a location is warranted, the place of rising will be the last area cleansed and sealed so that an aggressive spirit may not reenter the location.

Characteristics

A place suitable for rising will be a natural tear in the fabric of the veil separating our world from Qarth Arqa. The location must be neglected and undisturbed because it requires dense phasma that would be diminished by agitation. Once established, occupants will naturally avoid the area, as being near it causes discomfort.

There will usually be a buffer zone around a place of rising that stays free of active phenomenon. When perceived with the subtle senses, it may appear as a small rend or tear surrounded by phasma; the feeling can be likened to the sensation of reaching into a funnel of cobwebs.

Appearance

When indoors, a place of rising is usually in the form an undisturbed corner, isolated crevice, or crack in the wall or foundation. While it is possible for a revenant to rise in a setting other than a corner, centuries of necromancy provide evidence that it is the most likely. Corners are liminal spaces composed of the meeting of three lines that define length, breadth, and height. These three dimensions symbolize our physical world, and in the subtle environment of spirits, symbolism can solidify into reality. The ability of these structures to harbor phasma makes them favorable environments for places of rising.

Outdoors, a rising place may appear as a hole in the ground, under tree roots or a rock, or in a tunnel. Historically, a grave is the primary place of rising or, if magic is involved, the depression where a revenant was first evoked.

Entry Points

Like corners, windows and doorways are liminal spaces that offer little resistance for a spirit to pass through. For this reason, they should be magically protected. Unlike corners, they do not retain phasma, so a spirit entering by this means must find a rising place within the location that can serve as an anchor to the metacosmos if they are to stay.

With few exceptions, the walls of a building constitute a spiritual barrier that is difficult for an entity to cross unless the activity is due to phantasm, or the layout of the building has changed and the spirit has a symbolic entry point that no longer resembles the structure. Another exception is when a spirit is invited into the location. Under these circumstances, the walls of the structure offer no real resistance to the entity. Unhindered entry could occur if the spirit arrives with a person to whom the spirit has an attachment. It can also ensue with the misuse of a spirit board or if a spirit attends an indiscriminate prayer or evocation.

Motivation

When a spirit enters a location, it may be due to a variety of reasons, some more purposeful than others.

+ Drawn by an obsession: Revenants can feel compelled to be near attachments from their incarnate life or an affinity to something or someone familiar.
+ Seeking subsistence: A revenant will search for places of dense phasma to sustain themselves or take refuge from a rainstorm. A lemur or larva may enter a location to seek out prey or when they have been exorcised from another place.
+ Accidental: A spirit can simply discover a place to rise out of curiosity or attraction. They can also follow or be lured by other spirits.

Place of Burial

If the identity of the spirit is known, their grave or the place where their physical remains are interred can sometimes be located. This is extremely valuable information, as the tomb or resting place of the physical remains form both a symbolic representation of the underworld and the location where powerful relics of the spirit reside. A revenant can be called back to their grave at any time, and they can be laid far from the location they had been previously obsessing. This option allows the obsessed location a reprieve from activity and the time to reestablish security using remedial measures. Once the spirit is removed from the location and they are laid at their grave, they may not be able to find a way to reenter the previously obsessed space.

Speculation

In paranormal investigation, there is some conjecture about the nature of portals and vortexes as how spirits enter our world. Sometimes a team may identify a location of active EMF spikes as a portal or believe it is a permanent gateway. A true place of rising will be often be close to the ground or floor. It forms when there is a small rift between the metacosmos and our reality that has some stability. These rifts are not permanent; they can heal naturally, be assisted with repair, or be forcibly closed. Another misunderstanding is that ritual of any kind creates dangerous portals that remain open. In reality, most cultural and magical practices that have a means to open a passage to the dead also have a means to close it.

AN ANALYTICAL METHOD

The word *analysis* comes from Greek, meaning "to loosen throughout," which implies breaking a complex subject down into its composite and simple elements.[34] Successful analysis is built upon deductive reasoning and pattern recognition, it is an application of logic that moves from the general to the particular. While your experiences as a sciomancer are very often powerfully emotive, analysis must be an intellectual exercise. Forming a methodical approach may vary for everyone, as we all process information differently.

Some people find it helpful to employ matrices and mind mapping techniques, but this is not always necessary. Whatever method you use, it should lead you to a reliable set of conclusions from which you can draw a possible solution.

· · · · · · · · · · · · · · · · ·

34 "Analysis," Online Etymology Dictionary, https://www.etymonline.com/word /analytics#etymonline_v_44313.

Distilling Evidence

The point where an investigator can often be led astray is in determining which pieces of information they have gathered are the most relevant. Organizing your investigation into who, what, why, and where will go a long way toward preparing your information. The next important step is to filter the large amount of material you have reviewed and draw from it a selection of only the most reliable evidence that will form the basis of your conclusions. Arriving at this concise set of evidence is an important step that should not be missed.

Deciding upon what is and is not evidence should not be an arbitrary process based on what you think is the most important or what you hope the answer will be. Distilling evidence is a process in which consistent pieces of information are drawn together and considered in context. A single piece of information on its own does not support any conclusion; but when various data are found consistent with each other, a small piece of the narrative emerges—*this* is what is meant by "evidence."

Processing Evidence

The following method of refining evidence is adapted from investigative techniques and offers a logical approach to the needs of sciomancy. Information is prioritized according to its reliability under three headings: primary, secondary, and tertiary.

- Primary data is that which is proven and cannot be disputed. It takes three or more supporting primary data to form a piece of evidence.
- Secondary data is likely to be authentic. If there are three consistent items of secondary data, they can be promoted to become a primary datum.
- Tertiary data is deemed unproven or circumstantial. When three or more tertiary data support each other in a logical manner, the conclusion may then be elevated into the secondary class as a datum.

Evidence must only be drawn from primary data, but the remaining classes of data may be examined in context of the overall narrative. Where there is internal support, a datum can be elevated from one class into another. Information received from a medium, divination, and third-hand accounts should always be considered as supportive, never as indicative of primary evidence.

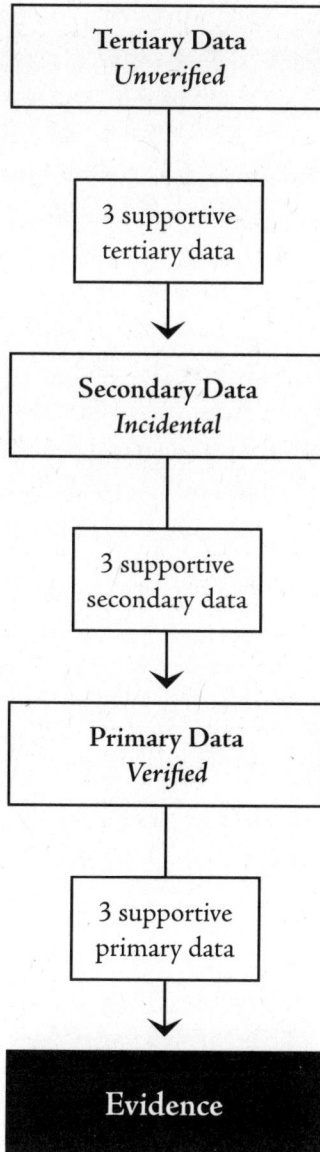

Method to Extract Evidence from Data

When this exercise is complete, you should have a small packet of reliable evidence. From this evidence, you will be able to form conclusions to the questions who, what, why, and where. If the evidence is true, any deduction will always lead to a true conclusion.

Not every investigation requires the same detail of analysis. Knowing the classification of a spirit and the level of activity is enough to determine whether intervention is required. If it is determined that a cacodaemon is causing an infestation, a more formal resolution will be needed (the focus of the next chapter). In these instances, it is imperative to also determine the place of rising, the focus of the obsession, and enough information about the identity of the spirit to call them forth.

A GUIDE TO INTERVENTION

The following chart is intended to provide a starting point to identify the appropriate resolution to a spirit disturbance when both the classification of spirit and details of obsession are known. There are six types of intervention listed, represented by letters A through G. Suggested methods for each type of resolution are described in the text following the table. Practical methods for the resolution of revenants are detailed in the next chapter.

Table 9: A Guide to Intervention

Type of Spirit (Who)	Confirmed Spirit Activity (What)				
	Occasional	Infestation	Obsession	Oppression	Possession
Nonsentient	A	A	A	G	-
Nonhuman Daemon	B	C	C	G	-
Lares	C	-	-	-	-
Manes	D	E	D	-	-
Immanes	D	F	D	F	G
Lemures	F	F	F	F	G
Larvae	G	G	G	G	G

Key to Resolutions	
A – Control the space	D – Make peace
B – Coexist	E – Eudaemonic resolution
C – Pay attention	F – Cacodaemonic resolution
	G – Seek expert advice

Methods of Intervention

The following methods relate to the list of solutions outlined in the key to the above chart.

Solution A: Control the Space

Occasionally, nonsentient phenomena can be easily settled if the source is identified. Sometimes a place is so rich in phasma and history that phenomena will always reoccur.

+ Cleanse the space: Asperging with salt water or savory can cleanse a nonsentient phasmata from the immediate space.
+ Protection: If the phasmata is intentional, the source of the intelligence may need to be identified and protected against.
+ Rarefy phasma: Use botanicals for ligation to reduce the concentration of phasma and prevent phenomena manifesting. If phasma density is environmental, suggest ways to circulate and disperse phasma regularly.
+ Reduce causes: If the behavior of an occupant is contributing to the activity, try to address the matter with sensitivity. The source may be latent subtle abilities or repressed emotion.

Solution B: Coexist

Infrequent phenomena related to nonhuman spirits do not require interference. In most cases, the spirit will be indifferent to human presence. The exception is terrestrial daemones, who sometimes take a curious interest.

+ Diversion: If terrestrial spirits cause disorder, try to direct their attention outdoors.
+ Compromise: If terrestrial spirits seem upset, it may be an issue of territory. One approach is to dedicate an area of land to them that remains undisturbed.

Solution C: Pay Attention

Activity that is benign but persistent may be an eudaemon trying to convey a message.

+ Communication: Acknowledge the spirit and establish a method for interaction.
+ Divination: Use a reliable method to reveal the message.
+ Observation: Watch and listen. Ask for a sign to confirm your findings.

Solution D: Make Peace

It is quite normal for manes or immanes to be attached to a location. Mostly they remain unnoticed except for mild activity. In some cases, gentle intervention may be desirable.

+ Offerings: Cultural and religious offerings for the dead help sustain spirits and bring clarity. Botanicals such as frankincense and basil can serve the same purpose.
+ Communication: A manes or immanes may be inclined to communicate with you. Be patient. Do not challenge or provoke.
+ Cleanse the space: Lift the atmosphere if there is a buildup of negative emotion impressed on the phasma within the location.
+ Modify phasma: If spirit activity is distressing to the occupants, affective incense can be sparingly employed. Circulating phasma will also help prevent visible manifestation from occurring.

Solution E: Eudaemonic Resolution

Infestation by manes is rarely harmful but may be distressing to the occupants. It often indicates that the spirit is trying to communicate.

+ Offerings: Offerings outlined in solution D can soothe the spirit.
+ Communication: Dialogue with the spirit may lead them to expiation, or peaceable agreement. (Refer to the following chapters.)

Solution F: Cacodaemonic Resolution

If an infestation is caused by a cacodaemon, refer to the following chapters. Obtain as much information about the identity of the spirit as possible, including the place of rising and the nature of their obsession.

Solution G: Seek Expert Advice

These events require magical expertise beyond the scope of this book. If you suspect any of these outcomes, gather as much information as you can. Use your discretion to seek trustworthy, experienced guidance.

+ Oppression resulting from a nonsentient presence
+ Targeted harmful behavior by a nonhuman spirit
+ Possession by a revenant

As a sciomancer, you must comprehend the balance between gaining knowledge and acting, and make the best decisions open to you. An approach to analysis subsumed with pursuing a perfect understanding will never attain the ideal. The purpose of sciomancy is to create a strategy of resolution that best answers the needs of the crisis, and that purpose cannot be overwritten for the desire to understand minutiae.

An obsession won't take a break while an in-depth and absolute analysis takes place. There is not always a perfect solution or time to gather more information. Decisions often need to be made and acted upon based on what is known and then adjustments made as new evidence is revealed. In time, experience will allow for a favorable juxtaposition between knowledge and action, but until then, you must be aware of grasping the moment when it presents itself and gather as much knowledge and understanding as possible before that critical time arrives.

CHAPTER TWELVE

PATHWAYS
TO RESOLUTION

Once you have evaluated your evidence and reached your conclusions about the nature of a disturbance, you will need to determine what actions will be required to reach a resolution.

If you conclude that the nature of a disturbance is an infestation caused by a revenant, there are four primary types of intervention presented in sciomancy: expiation, ligation, exorcism, and misericordia, each of which are explored in this chapter. Knowing how to choose the right interventions and implement them is the subject of the following chapter.

Obviously, any resolution you decide on should be the best option that you can conceive of with the available information that serves firstly the people who need help and secondly the concerns of the spirit. There is no one-size-fits-all when it comes to sciomancy, but there are guidelines and processes. Ultimately it is your commitment to compassion along with your clarity and confidence in your knowledge base that will guide you to the correct strategy for resolution. Resolution is, after all, both the goal and culmination of laying ghosts: "…and thus after the ghost was appeased by the proper ceremonies, the house was haunted no more."[35]

. . . .

35   Pliny the Younger, *The Letters of Pliny the Younger*, vol. II, books VI–X, trans. William Melmoth, rev. F. C. T Bosanquet (New York: Hinds, Noble & Eldridge, 1900), 251.

PERMANENT AND REMEDIAL RESOLUTIONS

Too often people think that resolution always comes to a conflict between a practitioner and the spirit, but this view is erroneous—most resolutions are found in compromise. When a spirit becomes acrimonious or rebels against negotiation, the interaction can certainly become contentious. However, a sciomancer must rise above the emotional desire to enter dispute and dispassionately remain true to the goal of accomplishing the best resolution possible for both the living and the dead.

Compassion and understanding must always be the guiding factor, even when you are engaged with a belligerent entity. It must be remembered that the rationale of sciomancy is to bring peace to an otherwise disturbed location. It is not an arena for displays of ego or to prove individual prowess in confronting spirits. You must galvanize yourself against taking offense from entities that can distract from your objective. As such, you must steadfastly hold true to your purpose and not allow yourself to fall into mission-creep due to an emotional reaction.

To act compassionately requires a certain level of altruism, and to do so dispassionately means setting aside personal feelings and emotions. While cooperation can often solve the obsession, you must be prepared for times when confrontational measures are necessary to achieve resolution. To ensure a successful outcome, you must be able to implement both remedial and permanent solutions.

Remedial Solutions

Remedial solutions are measures that reduce the effect that the spirit or spirits can have within a location. Their purpose is to create a state of reprieve to lessen the emotional pressure upon the living occupants. They can also encourage the spirit to communicate more directly. There are times when remedial solutions are the only (and sometimes even preferable) option. They fall under two broad headings: ligation and exorcism. Ligation consists of procedures that directly disempower the influence or actions an entity can utilize, while exorcisms are methods of breaking the attachment an entity may have formed with a person, place, or object.

Permanent Solutions

Permanent solutions are those which bring the revenant spirit to a point of closure, passing through the Gates of Death to continue their natural journey. Permanent solutions can also be classified under two headings: expiation and misericordia.

Expiation is always the most desirable method of resolution. It occurs when the entity voluntarily relinquishes their phasmic body. This is the true goal of laying ghosts, and it is your role as a sciomancer to guide, encourage, convince, or placate the spirit to take the next step on their journey. In modern spiritualist and paranormal circles, it is often called aiding the spirit in "crossing over" and is easiest when the spirit already has doubts about their attachments.

Misericordia is only reserved for the most extreme circumstances where physical danger demands an immediate and severe response. While it too causes the spirit to relinquish their phasmic body and move through the Gates of Death, it is accomplished through coercion and force. This is no trite subject; it is always a serious and solemn consideration for any necromancer to take the accountability on themselves of abrogating a being's personal choice or will. Circumstances must be dire to even contemplate the necessity of performing misericordia.

FOUR METHODS OF RESOLUTION

The following table outlines the four primary types of intervention sciomancers practice to resolve an infestation. Knowing the right approach is governed by rules of engagement which are explained in the following chapter.

Table 10: Methods of Resolution

Resolution	Meaning	Effect	Result
Expiation	Atonement	Guide the spirit to willingly release all attachments and enter the Gates of Death	Permanent
Ligation	Binding	Mitigate the effects of infestation by controlling the environment, by oath, or by magic. Some forms are more lasting than others	Remedial
Exorcism	Expulsion	Separate an undesired spirit influence from a person, object, or place	Remedial
Misericordia	Mercy	Compel a spirit to enter the Gates of Death	Permanent

PRACTICES OF EXPIATION

In the language of religion, expiation is synonymous with atonement, taking responsibility for one's personal errors and making amends to become a better and more spiritual person. This sense of responsibility also lies at the heart of the term's usage within necromancy, where it has the specific meaning of resolving the errors that bind a revenant within the metacosmos and impede their progress through the Gates of Death.

Necromancy views expiation not as a moral cleansing but rather as an inner process of integration that severs the emotional and intellectual ties to the recently concluded life and frees the soul to prepare for a new existence. To take part in guiding or aiding a soul in their own catharsis toward divine unification is a humbling experience—in effect, you become an agent of natural universal law. There are few philosophies or religious doctrines that offer such clear proof of the promise of an afterlife as laying ghosts, and it is an honor to be both a witness and a participant in that truth.

Expiation should remind and encourage us to resolve the attachments that bind us in life and not wait until physical death. The process should hopefully ease the burden of our own transition toward that world our soul truly longs for. This drive to achieve integration while living should create sympathy for the plight that spirits who have yet to find expiation endure and inspire us to bring them consolation.

Process of Expiation

Communication and reasoned negotiation are the only true means of encouraging expiation, and it must be the revenant's voluntary choice. The method of expiation consists of three basic stages:

1. Establish dialogue with the spirit.

2. Reveal the attachment.

3. Guide them to release their attachments and enter the Gates of Death.

Establish Dialogue

Once communication has been established, you should attempt to bring the entity into a cognitive recognition of those attachments which bind them. The spirit may feel they have left things unfinished and request that a task be performed before they can move on. In other negotiations, communication resembles therapy, easing emotional burdens and guiding the spirit to the realization that expiation is the correct course for their progress.

Reveal the Attachment

The spirit may not be consciously aware of the emotive hooks that anchor them within the metacosmos, so you must illuminate them before they can be resolved. Focus firstly on the attachment causing the immediate disturbance; if expiation becomes a possibility, then the spirit's attachments that bind them in Qarth Arqa will need to be reviewed and understood if they are not the same. Some themes of attachment include:

- ✦ Recognition: Some manes simply wish to be seen and heard. Acknowledging their presence can bring them a sense of calm. If their death was not reported, or they desire for their story to be known and remembered, there are many ways their memory can be honored. It may be possible to learn their name or introduce them to the living occupants. If the spirit is uncertain of their deceased state, validation may be all that is required for them to expiate.
- ✦ Salvation: A manes may seek spiritual aid if they carry heavy emotional burdens, feel they died without forgiveness, or did not receive proper funerary rites. A spirit may accept spiritual counseling from you. To that end, consider the belief system that the spirit themself may adhere to. Understanding how the spirit perceives religion or the afterlife can open avenues of building trust and advantageous negotiation. If it is not possible to administer the rites of faith specific for the spirit, offerings to the dead may suffice.
- ✦ Warnings: The spirit may be trying to alert the living about a situation or imminent danger. It may be personal to the spirit, or it may be related to the unseen realms, e.g., visitors with negative connections, the proximity of a predatory spirit, misuse of magic, activities causing harm to spirits, or phasma being disrupted.
- ✦ Constraints: The spirit may be bound to the location by others. If loved ones are clinging to the deceased too tightly, it may be possible to guide the family toward releasing a manes. Sometimes a revenant can be accidentally

trapped by protective boundaries. If the spirit is restrained by a predatory entity or they were magically evoked but not dismissed, further examination will be required.

+ Elapsed task: A spirit may be focused on an errand that is no longer relevant, because too much time has elapsed, the circumstances have changed, the people concerned are deceased, or the situation has been resolved. You may be able to explain that it is no longer their responsibility or that completing the task is now not required. If they accept this, they may be able to move on.

+ Incomplete assignments: In certain circumstances, the entity may have an expectation that their unfinished business can be concluded; for instance, to find something that was lost, solve a question or mystery, bring some awaited information, or deliver a message to someone. In such cases, you may choose to take it upon yourself to pursue those tasks and encourage the spirit to release their connections.

Release the Attachment

The next step is to bring the spirit to the realization that they can and should release their attachments voluntarily. When the spirit is ready to do so, they often find their own way to progress on their natural journey. This can be a beautiful and spontaneous event to witness, and of course no further action is necessary when a spirit willingly passes through the Gates of Death.

However, revenants whose only knowledge of what comes after physical death is their experience of being bound in Qarth Arqa may remain in a slight state of confusion as to where they are to go, or whether there is any direction. You must be prepared to gently guide the entity toward the next step and encourage them to pass through.

You will need to remain open-minded and intuitive when guiding a spirit and help them to identify their own path to the Gates of Death as it appears to them, rather than to a preconceived notion of what you think it should look like. In some reports of near-death experience there is a vision of light or an illuminated tunnel, and this has become a very popular image for modern paranormal investigators and spiritualists when helping a spirit "cross over." In our experience, a revenant in this condition will see the next step in a form that is both inviting and familiar to them, such as a childhood home or a field of flowers. Sometimes there may be someone whom they can trust to guide them or symbolism which is culturally significant or meaningful to them.

Whenever a soul takes these steps toward the Gates of Death it is cause for a solemn moment. The first part of the journey of expiation may be tenuous for an uncertain spirit, and you must be careful not to call them back. However, sometimes the feeling of expiation is immediate, met with joyous exultation emanating from the entity that is emotively tangible. When a spirit has passed, violets or pasque flowers can be laid, and any lit candles or lanterns can be extinguished.

Results of Expiation

When a spirit expiates, there is no need for any other remedial measures beyond counseling the living. The obsession and infestation cease, the soul is safely pursuing their destiny, the dust of the experience can settle, and closure can be found.

If the revenant was a loved one of the occupants, it helps to remind them that the soul has found their home and that they are not gone permanently but can return as a familiar lar and offer their love and guidance without the confusion and fear associated with obsession. A healing reconnection between the living and dead is made possible and a loving relationship may be renewed.

When the spirit is unknown to those who have undergone obsession, helping them to understand why the entity has behaved the way they have can bring its own serenity to the living. However, if the obsession has been hostile, expiation provides the sufferers with a certainty that it will never be renewed and that their security is returned to their own control.

Refusal to Expiate

Expiation must be voluntary, and we must respect that some revenants will choose not to. To do this work, we must see the process that follows death as sacred and value the role that personal choice and independence play in an entity's resolution. Although the natural order of spiritual progress is preferred, we cannot become conceited and repudiate a revenant's choice to not move on. Necromancy teaches us that this progress will ultimately happen, that no spirit can survive indefinitely in Qarth Arqa, and it should inspire sympathy in you rather than a callous disregard of innate liberty.

In cases of refusal, try to extract a promise from the spirit that they will desist in causing further disturbance. When revenants choose to exercise their prerogative to turn their face from the divine journey, it should only be of concern if that choice brings harm to others.

PRACTICES OF LIGATION

Ligation refers to methods of binding; that is, actions that limit the revenant's means to cause a disturbance. If a spirit cannot be expiated, most resolutions require ligation as a remedial solution. Ligation can bring much-needed relief to an environment and people who feel overwhelmed. In that respite there is an opportunity for you to be more deliberate in action rather than simply react to the dynamic changes that can occur in an active spirit crisis.

Affective Ligation

The very first form of ligation is to control emotional factors that exacerbate the disturbance. This can be as simple as reassuring the living, bringing them into a state of calm, or temporarily removing an individual from a location that agitates the entity.

Managing emotional extremes can reduce the intensity of raw phasma that feeds predatory spirits and fuels infestation activity. It may also benefit individuals targeted by spirits to decouple their relationship.

Controlling the emotional environment is essential but difficult to maintain and is best used in combination with other methods of ligation for sustained effect, such as regularly exorcising the space. Placing a clear quartz crystal in the room can work to some degree in removing excess phasma, and censing with frankincense or sandalwood can bring balance to emotions.

Environmental Ligation

The next form of ligation affects the environment, such as rarefying phasma into a state of pneuma. The easiest way to do this is with botanicals such as sage and juniper, or other plants and gums that have a temporary effect, lasting usually about two to three weeks. These botanicals do not repel spirits nor exorcise them; they simply make it difficult for an entity to act.

Drastically reducing the availability and density of phasma mitigates the spirit's means to interact with the physical world. Ligation can be used between attempts to expiate the spirit or to control an infestation for a period until specialist help arrives.

Instructing the occupants in methods of ligation can return some amount of control to their hands. You should help them understand the importance of upholding their emotional and mental courage.

If a spirit is determined, they may still find ways to continue to act, such as trying to interfere with the thoughts or dreams of the living. Although this can be disturbing, the occupants can better endure these minor interferences if you explain to them the very minimal limits in which a revenant can now operate. It may not be pleasant, but it is also not dangerous or physically threatening.

Environmental ligation requires regular attention to maintain. Circulating the phasma to prevent buildup also has the benefits of dissuading other casual spirits desirous of a phasma-rich environment and reducing the likelihood of false reports of spirits and nonsentient spirit activity.

Adjuration

When communication has been undertaken during the resolution phase, the revenant can either be encouraged or coerced into giving their oath to cease their disturbances of the location, or to safely leave and never return. This form of ligation is called adjuration.

Having its roots in the evocation rituals of medieval European magicians, it is a very effective tool to control infestation. Historically, it has been known to magicians that when a spirit makes a vow, that oath is binding in a way that a verbal contract in the physical world is not. The spirit is constrained by the rules and conditions of the subtle realm where they abide, and when forced or stirred to engage in an obligation, the power of that oath is indissoluble.

Any negotiation should only be done when deemed appropriate and to the advantage of your goals—that is, the best resolution for all concerned. Any contract made with an entity is binding; you should define how long and under what circumstances the agreement should last. If the spirit complies, the agreement can be sealed with an incense offering to the dead.

Magical Ligation

The last form of ligation is to bind the spirit directly through magical means. Like the inviolable rule that an oath given is absolute, identity and names have a unique power. There are advanced techniques and procedures which a necromancer can use to call and bind a spirit if their name is known. Entities can be cognizant of (or at least sense that) their identity may be a threat to their independence and will do anything to avoid sharing it. This is one of the reasons your inquiry should attempt to identify the revenant acting on the location in case such an action is needed. Receiving a name can allow a sigil, or a symbolic representation of the revenant's core identity, to be formed that can then be acted upon to influence the spirit directly, such as binding them from acting in certain ways.

In a similar manner, any relics that have been discovered to belong to the spirit in life or photos can be used as a conduit to achieve the same effect as the use of a sigil. When a sigil and relic are combined there is an even more potent link. Magically binding a spirit from acting in a particular way can be an efficient means of ligation but should be reserved for situations when a revenant cannot be negotiated with. However, such operations properly fall under the practices of necyomancy and are not the focus of this book.

Practices of Exorcisms

The word "exorcism" is usually considered to mean a casting out or the banishing of something. However, the etymology of the word is far from certain. The most common explanation is that it comes from the Greek *exorkismos*, "to swear an oath," yet the root of this word has also been conjectured to be from *herkos*, meaning "fence," rather than *horkos*, "oath."[36] In magic, the theme of forming a boundary and clearing the space within is more aligned to the concept of removing something from within the confines of a fence than extracting a vow for whatever is being removed (which is actually adjuration).

In the arcana of necromancy, "exorcism" has become a convenient term used to describe actions designed to sever the attachments of a spirit to the place, object, or person they attempt to obsess. Orations, prayers, botanicals, and rituals can all play a role in achieving this end.

Exorcism is used extensively in magic, often referred to as simply cleansing or banishing. It should not be confused with a blessing, or the rarefying of phasma, which is a form of ligation. More specifically, exorcism is the magical removal of an influence from its subject. That is, any intelligence or thought impressed onto the phasma is erased, rendering it neutral.

. . . .
36 "Exorcism," Online Etymology Dictionary, https://www.etymonline.com/word /exorcism#etymonline_v_14073.

For the most part, exorcism is a simple rite with little repercussion. However, when it is used as a method to resolve an infestation there is much to consider.

Exorcism can be employed when a disturbance is caused by a cacodaemon to cleanse the focus of obsession—the object, person, or place of interest. In turn, exorcism eliminates the revenant's attraction to the location, and in some cases affects their ability to act.

Although exorcism can play a role in eradicating the link between a revenant and their obsession, it is not a panacea to the crisis an entity causes even though some religious bodies and paranormal investigators see it as such. It can only be a remedial aid since it does not resolve a spirit's attachment that binds them to the metacosmos.

Ascertaining when exorcism is necessary is a critical skill, and you must assess the situation and take precautions against any potential risks. A cacodaemon can react adversely to losing their connection to the core of their obsession. Also be aware that when you sever a cacodaemon from their subject of obsession by exorcism, the tie that binds the entity is also removed. If you are not careful, a revenant motivated by desire, such as a lemur, will now be free to cause further disturbances elsewhere.

Exorcism of a Place

The exorcism of a place refers to cleansing a physical area of phasmic impressions and spirit influences. It is regularly used in magic as a step within a greater process, such as before the dedication of a temple or during the casting of a circle for magical operations.

In the practice of sciomancy, the exorcism of a space has a twofold objective: cleansing the space of residual influence and at the same time making the space unfit for revenant spirits, thereby keeping them at bay. The exorcism of a place is usually accompanied by practices of protection to prevent the spirit from reentering the area once the effects of cleansing have worn off.

Cleansing a Multiroom Space

In sciomancy, we often need to exorcise a location with multiple rooms, making it a matter of cleansing one space at a time in a systematic process. A warding wash or talisman can be set at liminal areas, such as windows and doors, as you move into each room, expanding your area of protection. (The method to exorcise a space is given in chapter 9.)

Exorcism of a place can be used strategically to safely steer a hostile spirit toward the controlled area where you will attempt to communicate with them for the purpose of expiation, or, if this is not possible, to their place of rising. Thought should be given to the size and complexity of the premises to decide the order in which each room will be cleansed. An example of how to interpret this method is explained more fully in the next chapter.

Exorcism of an Object

When a revenant attaches to an object, it often follows that the object becomes the epicenter of the infestation. In such cases, exorcism of the object may cut the obsession off at its source.

Cleansing an object is probably the easiest form of exorcism. An object that is emotively important to a spirit can serve as an anchor in an environment that is otherwise unfamiliar to them. In most cases, if their attachment is disbanded the spirit will feel disadvantaged and desist infestation activities, or at least be more willing to be compliant. When dealing with a threatening spirit, exorcism of an object should be done in a controlled way to ensure the spirit is not empowered or released without restraint.

Precaution against Burning

There is a popular theory that an object that has a spirit attachment should be destroyed by burning it to stop the entity from having any power. This hypothesis is not supported by magical arcana and there are several good reasons to pause and consider before taking this action both on a practical and magical level:

+ The effect on the person who possesses the item, especially if the object has some sentimental or monetary importance.
+ The release of toxins that may be unsafe or can cause damage to the environment.
+ The act of burning an object serves to unleash the bonds that tethered the spirit and, as mentioned, allows a dangerous entity to continue unimpeded.

+ Burning an object obsessed by a revenant serves only to empower the spirit with phasma.

Sacrificial, burning has an extremely specific ritual purpose in the history of magic. The practice of ceremonially burning an object was usually reserved as a sacred offering to celestial deities and to carry and empower a prayer, and modern practitioners still use it in this way. A lemur will sometimes try to influence their subjects of oppression to perform similar rites as a form of subversive worship to them and therefore should be avoided in all capacities.

Methods of Exorcising an Object

A very simple exorcism frequently used in magic is sprinkling the object with consecrated or salt water using hyssop or other herbs as an asperger. The effect of water that has been properly sanctified and empowered can be very successful in removing the intelligence or attachment imposed upon an object. It is useful for general cleansing, for example, to wash away influence when a preowned item is brought into an environment, to neutralize an object that has become intentionalized, or as a preparation for other magical acts.

However, this method is limited. When a more permanent medium is required, a savory wash can be applied that has the advantage of completely removing the intelligence from the phasma of the object so that no vestiges remain.

The method of exorcising an object described here can be used to safely control the negative consequences that can occur when an object is either magically cursed or obsessed by a revenant. This action should take place after the spirit has been exorcised from a place. The formula requires three steps: contain the object, proceed to sever the intelligence from the phasma and transfer it to another form, and finally disable the remaining materials.

EXERCISE
METHOD TO PERMANENTLY
EXORCISE AN OBSESSED OBJECT

In the example given here, clear quartz is used for its ability to store the transformed phasma in a neutralized form. Red thread is used in Scottish practices to symbolize the transfer of power.

1. Contain the object in a magic circle or circle of salt.
2. Recite an oration to clearly state the intention of removing the negative intelligence and restoring the object to a neutral state.
3. Employ a savory wash to sever the intelligence from the phasma. If a wash is not appropriate, cense with savory and mugwort, allowing the smoke to infuse and surround the object.
4. Bind a clear quartz crystal to the object with red thread to absorb remaining phasma.
5. Leave the object bound in the circle overnight.
6. Unbind the crystal and wash with consecrated or salt water and wrap in a dark covering.

Exorcism of a Person

The exorcism of a person described herein is for the remediation of spirit influence when an individual has been targeted by an oppressive spirit or is exhibiting other signs of influence. Do not attempt these techniques if there are signs of possession as it will aggravate the situation. Genuine involuntary possession by a spirit agency is a rare and specific condition that requires expert training to diagnose and treat. Not only can a mismanaged exorcism cause greater harm to the subject but there can also be potential legal ramifications to consider.

For a spirit disturbance to be successfully resolved, any obsession of a living person must be addressed. Otherwise, the individual may inadvertently invite the spirit back on a continuous basis. This is important for any individual who has been targeted by a revenant, whether during this instance, or anytime previously. You will need to pay especial attention to determine if the attachment with the spirit or spirits is reciprocal, in which case remediation will require patience and vigilance.

EXERCISE
METHOD TO EXORCISE SPIRIT INFLUENCE FROM A PERSON

Much like what is used to cleanse a place or object, consecrated water and botanicals that rarefy phasma can be used on a person provided they are willing and cognizant of what they are undertaking.

1. Cleanse or asperge a person with consecrated or salt water to temporarily dissuade the spirit's interest.
2. Say prayers or orations specific to the purpose.
3. If the person is not part of an on-site investigation, you may cense the person with ligation incense to weaken the spirit's influence.
4. Give the person intentionalized iron or an amulet to wear.
5. Move the person to a protected space free of spirit influences and help them regain their spiritual balance and empowerment.
6. The subject must regularly practice a regimen of ars remissionis, phasmic cleansing, protection, and spiritualization to stay free of spirit influence.

The same procedure can be used at the conclusion of any stage in the inquiry or for anyone who had been directly engaged with a spirit. It also is a beneficial practice before leaving a location to exorcise anyone who has entered the place. However, never do this during an on-site investigation if the person intends to reenter the location. The aromatic remains of the cleansing will affect the environment being obsessed and interfere with the delicate balance between security and negotiation that you must attempt to achieve for the investigation to be successful.

PRACTICE OF MISERICORDIA

The word *misericordia* implies an act of mercy but despite its amiable name, it refers to coercing or forcing a spirit to pass through the Gates of Death. In the age of medieval chivalry, knights carried a dagger called the *misericorde* that was used to strike the coup de grâce upon mortally wounded foes so that they did not have to suffer. The term "misericordia" carries a similar import in necromancy.

The practice of misericordia is reserved for larvae. It can also be applied to lemures when the safety and sanity of living people are threatened by violent behavior *and* all other options have been exhausted. Ultimately, such predatory spirits will benefit in their soul's progression once they have been forced to pass through the Gates of Death; in this regard, misericordia is considered an act of compassion on the part of the necromancer when reason and sympathy are wanting in a rapacious spirit.

Lemures can be destructive and avaricious in targeting living people. If threat has escalated to the point where the potential for real damage has been actuated and attempts at communication and abjuration action have failed, there may be no other recourse. Larvae, on the other hand, are impossible to communicate with, and their dedication to predatory behavior means that remedial action will just encourage them to find their prey in another location. When facing a larva, there are no other responsible or ethical options open to the necromancer—misericordia is the only reasonable choice.

Simply knowing methods to conduct misericordia does not represent a full understanding of its responsibilities. By the very nature of the act, a necromancer forced to execute misericordia must remove choice and responsibility from the entity, imposing an experience that can be likened to the physical death they have already suffered.

For ethical reasons, we have decided not to include methods of misericordia in this book. If you find yourself in circumstances as a beginning sciomancer where misericordia is the only option, attempt all forms of remedial action that you think are appropriate to mitigate the spirit's aggression. If possible, refer the case to someone who has knowledge and skills in performing ethical methods of misericordia. There is no shame in reaching out to others with differing knowledge of the esoteric. Referring a case to a specialist is the timeworn recourse for any professional.

Of the methods of resolution described, exorcism and ligation are practical skills that you can develop in simple ways such that should the time come, you will be well practiced to use them to remediate an infestation. Expiation, the goal of laying ghosts, is an experience that we hope you will have the opportunity to know. It can be greatly enhanced by developing your ability to see, hear, and feel spirits.

Regardless of how prepared you are, success in sciomancy is never assured. You cannot always make perfect decisions. In the final analysis, the right action usually consists of an accumulation of more good decisions than poor ones, and action rather than inaction. Of course, there are cases where an absolute solution is imperative, but in truth most obsessions find their resolution in less-than-perfect circumstances.

Chapter Thirteen

Methods to Lay Ghosts

Not every spirit disturbance is an incursion. A crisis in the eyes of the inhabitant of a location may be as innocent as a deceased relative trying to gain their attention or the echo of an event in a chamber of phasma.

At the conclusion of the analysis phase, we presented a chart designed to determine the nature of a solution and possible remedies. If it is determined that a location is the target of infestation by a revenant, an appropriate and ethical method of resolution will need to be considered. In this chapter, we will outline the acceptable practices you can employ to mitigate these events, referring to the methods of resolution already discussed—expiation, ligation, and exorcism of a place—along with some brief recommendations on what to do in a situation where misericordia is the best option.

Before moving into the resolution phase, you should have in your possession some essential knowledge to define the parameters of your operation. This information should be acquired as part of your inquiry process:

+ The spirit is classified as a revenant
+ The activity is indicative of infestation, obsession, or oppression
+ Sufficient detail is known to evoke and communicate with the spirit
+ The focus of the obsession has been identified
+ The place of rising has been located

STRATEGIES FOR
IMPLEMENTING A RESOLUTION

Although every resolution will be unique, there are certain methods, strategies, and tools that can always be of use (and at times necessary) to a sciomancer when resolving an infestation, including how to prepare the location and what will be the best means of communication with the spirit. Throughout this chapter, we refer to eudaemonic and cacodaemonic resolution. For consistency, we have used this in the strictest sense, relating manes to eudaemonic resolution and all other types of revenants as cacodaemonic. In practice, the lines between what is benign and harmful are subjective and dependent on the circumstances. The importance of this distinction is procedural, to provide options you can employ depending on your assessment of the situation.

Dynamic Strategy

The dynamic nature of dealing with an infestation firsthand cannot be overstated, especially when there is a potential for danger. Understanding how to make good decisions in unruly surroundings is vital, and the faculty of discernment must be honed as a primary skill. Your stratagem will need to be naturally responsive to allow for emerging circumstances, but you should not lose sight of the task. You must remain confident in your proficiency and precommitted to executing your plans without wavering and see them to their conclusion. Caution may be called for to judge the right action to take, but there are times when hesitation becomes prevarication and the critical moment to act passes with adverse consequences.

An Ethical Approach

As sciomancers, it is imperative to understand the ethical consequences of our actions. Ours is an art in which we deal with the human condition as it permeates the border between life and death. You must avoid the trap of perceiving spirits as different from the living, no matter their state of being. Encountering a spirit who means to cause harm is not dissimilar to confronting a living aggressor. Similarly, it can be easy to vilify a revenant rather than to try to understand them and why they exist.

Like any study of behavior, classifications of revenants are not rigid. During events, you must pay attention to changes in the conduct of an entity and reassess as needed. For example, an immanes who can be calmed and regains their lucidity can be considered as a manes. Equally, an immanes whose behavior escalates to become menacing can be deemed a lemur for the purposes of enacting a resolution.

RULES OF ENGAGEMENT

Before you attempt to make any strategy of resolution, you must first consider these crucial rules of engagement. These rules are based on the classification of a spirit to guide you in knowing which path of resolution is available to you. For example, it is never permissible to exorcise a manes, though exorcism may prove the most valid option for a lemur. Expiation is preferable to all other methods but if expiation does not ensue, most resolutions require ligation.

We encourage you to take note of these rules and hold to the ethical foundation a sciomancer should hope to evince. Necromancy should be a noble endeavor, as should the practice of magic in general.

Table 11: Rules for Engagement with Revenant Spirits

	Expiation	Ligation	Exorcism	Misericordia
Manes	Only option	Not acceptable	Not acceptable	Not acceptable
Immanes	Best option	Acceptable	Last resort	Not acceptable
Lemures	Best option	Acceptable	Acceptable	Last resort
Larvae	Not an option	Not acceptable	Not acceptable	Only option

Strategy for Manes

Expiation is the only resolution that can be applied in the case of a manes, but it is not necessary to achieve peace. Manes are eudaemones who usually quietly coexist with the living. If a manes is causing disruption, asking the spirit to desist may be all that is needed. Unless they have an attachment to the location, they may willingly vacate or quieten their activities. Further intervention may be required when persistent activity indicates the spirit is trying to convey a task or message or the activity is causing distress to the occupants. In both cases, communication is key.

Convey a Message

Communication with a manes may reveal a message they wish to impart. It may be related to themselves, their death, or because they are known to the occupant or are trying to alert the living about a situation.

Try to obtain the subject of the message and the intended recipient. Repeat the message back to the spirit for verification, but carefully consider any consequences before choosing to relay it. In some cases, the message may be for you, the sciomancer, being either pertinent information to the case at hand or something related to the unseen realm they feel you can act upon.

Unresolved Task

The attachment a manes suffers is that of unfinished business. One central theme to the old stories associated with laying ghosts is aiding a manes to complete their task. If the spirit has a request they want your assistance to resolve, you must decide if you are willing and able to accomplish it. As with any negotiation, define terms describing how long and under what circumstances the agreement should last. If the manes complies, you can confirm the alliance with an incense offering to the dead. For example:

1. You agree that you will attempt to complete the task on behalf of the spirit.

2. You will return to report if the task is completed within a certain period.

3. During this period, the spirit will agree to desist disruptive activity.

4. If the task is completed, the spirit agrees not to resume disruptive activity.

Adjuration for Manes

If the manes is not ready to expiate, you may encourage them to make an obligation to refrain from alarming the occupants, as they are usually open to the effect they have on the living. By way of compromise, it may also be necessary to advise occupants on how to coexist with a manes. Certainty regarding the nature of the spirit and its harmlessness can settle the fears and concerns of the people who must share their space.

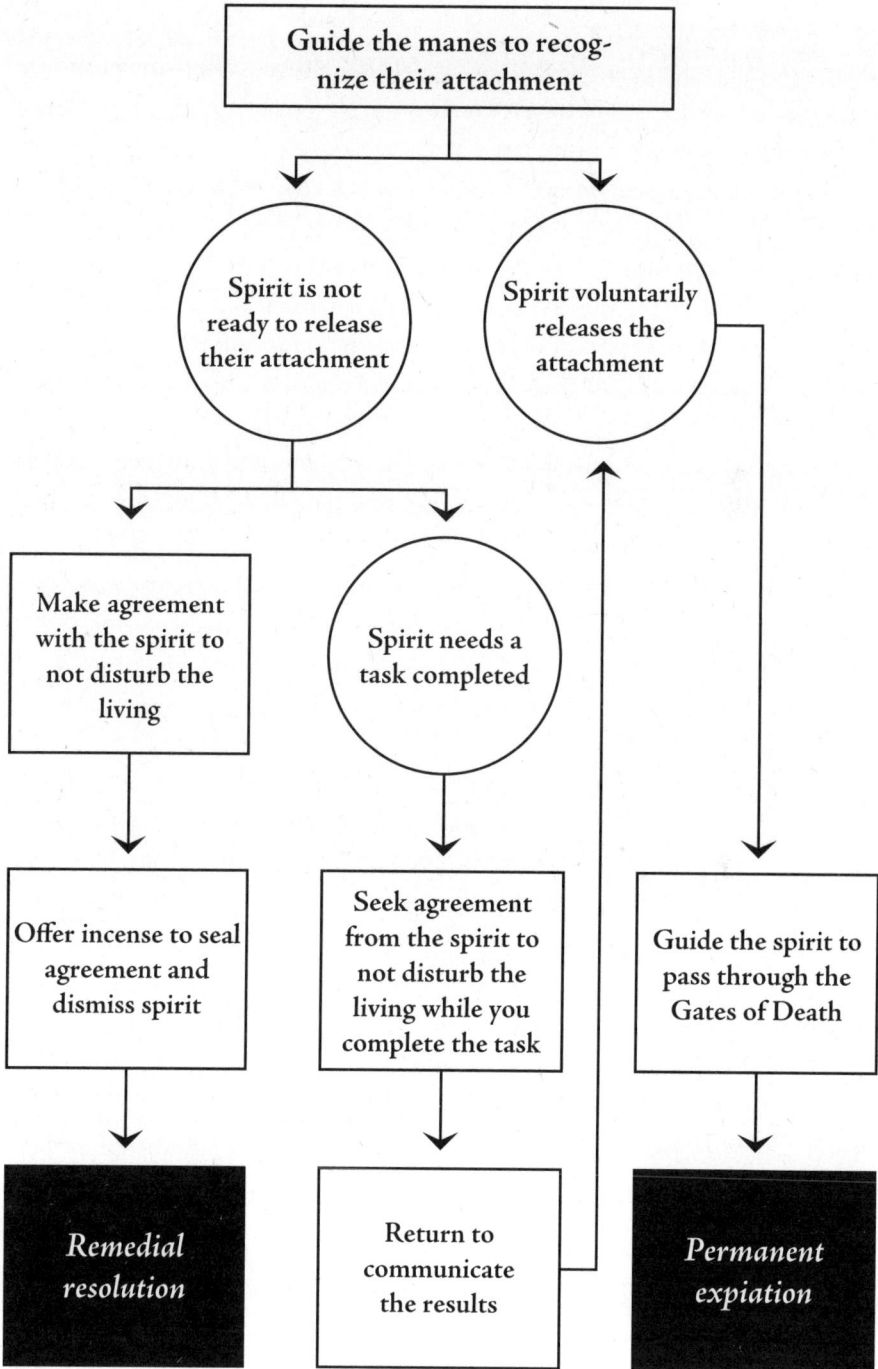

Flowchart for Manes Resolution
Expiation is the most desirable outcome.

Strategy for Immanes

Immanes can be unpredictable and vary widely in behavior. Some may be near to being a manes, while others may verge on becoming a lemur or a larva. A gentle and compassionate approach is needed, but at the same time you should put all precautions in place for a cacodaemonic resolution in anticipation of an erratic reaction.

Expiation of Immanes

Expiation is always the preferred method of resolution, but in the case of an immanes, they may not be susceptible to negotiation or guidance due to their confused condition. They may not even be aware that they are dead, possibly lost in a dreamlike delusion.

Attracting the attention of an immanes can require some creativity. The light of a candle and clear resonant sound are traditional methods. Singing or speaking to them can also have a calming effect.

The presence of St. John's wort can bring an immanes to a state more lucid and open to dialogue. You can also suffumigate with expiation incense, which may aid them in recognizing the Gates of Death.

Ligation for Immanes

In the absence of an option to expiate an immanes, you may need to resort to remedial measures to obviate the spirit's effect in the location. Do nothing that will cause harm to the spirit or exacerbate the infestation. Rather choose any ligation responsibly. Wherever possible try not to push the immanes entirely from the location. The obsession the immanes is attached to is ironically the conduit of their healing. If the entity loses their connection to their former life, it may lead to more dire conditions for them.

It is also important not to prevent an immanes from retreating to their place of rising or completely restrict their movements. If an immanes feels trapped, they can become desperate and act erratically. It is better to regularly apply ligation to limit the immanes's influence on the physical environment of the space, and counsel the living inhabitants on how to live with the presence of a traumatized spirit. Reinforce the notion that compassion and understanding can go a long way in bringing the immanes back from the brink, returning them to the state of a manes and opening the possibility for expiation in the future.

Try to establish dialogue
with the immanes

Spirit is lucid and
can communicate

Guide the spirit
to overcome their
attachments

Spirit retains
their attachment,
but gains clarity

Spirit releases
the attachment
voluntarily

Immanes
remains in a
fugue state

Spirit can be
approached as
a manes

Guide the spirit to
pass through the
Gates of Death

Employ a regime
of ligation to
control phasma

Refer to
manes

Permanent
expiation

Remedial
resolution

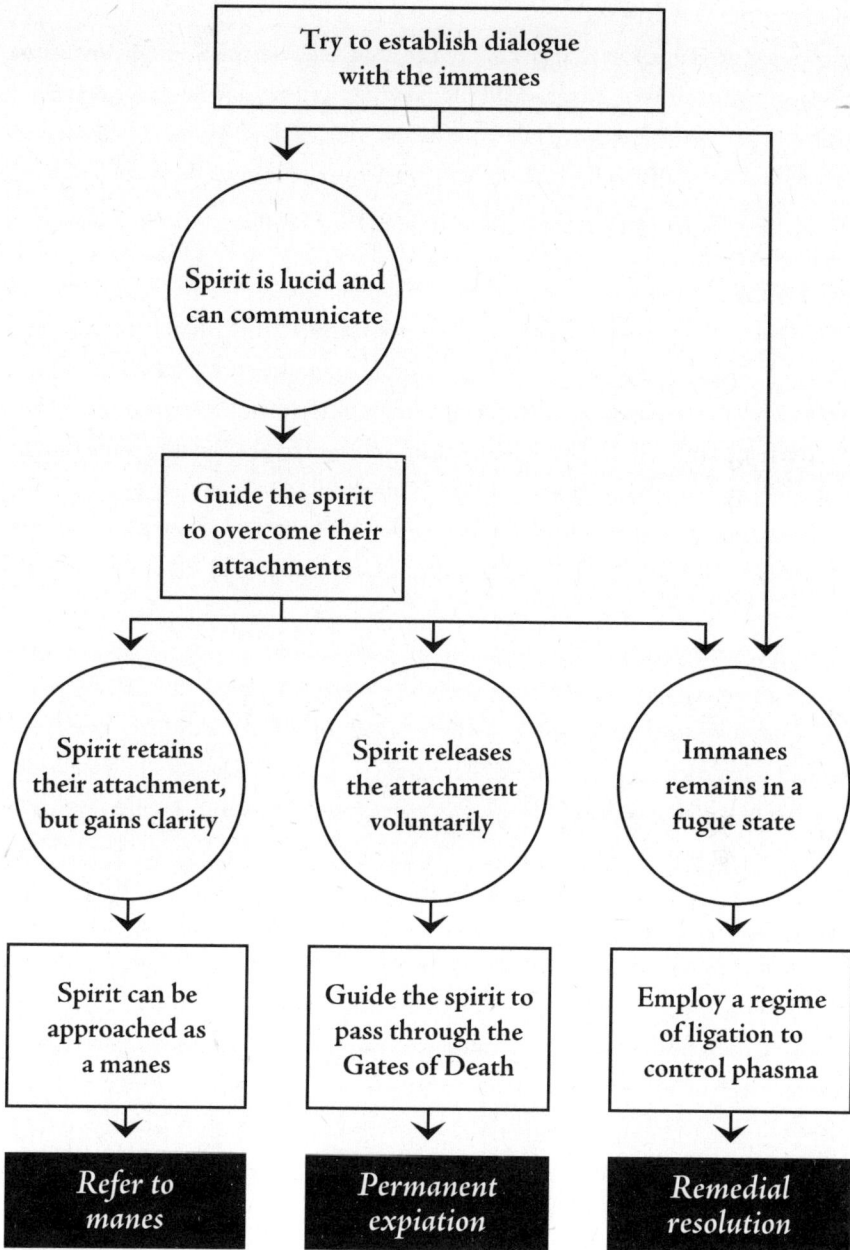

Flowchart for Immanes Resolution
If an immanes spirit cannot be expiated, ligation is an option.

Strategy for Lemures

Lemures are predatory by nature but are not always powerful. Some are homeless scavengers, while others are seasoned hunters. Regardless, it is never wise to allow a lemur to stay in the vicinity of living people due to their potential for mental and spiritual harm to a vulnerable person. If a lemur cannot be persuaded to expiate, remedial measures need to be taken to protect the living.

Expiation of a Lemur

Despite their propensity for vice, lemures are cognitive beings and may be persuaded to find expiation. Your firm conviction may cause the entity to choose expiation over a prolonged dispute they cannot win. In circumstances like these, your spiritual authority and sciomantic skill set can be formidable tools in convincing belligerent entities that expiation is preferable to the ramifications of continued resistance. You must consistently provide the option of expiation for the revenant to take advantage of, explaining what it is and why it is the most suitable resolution.

Throughout your interface, you should be wary of a lemur feigning compliance, seeking pity, or trying to elicit other emotions from you and only use tools of communication that cannot be manipulated. You must also be cognizant to not push a lemur into a situation of desperation. If they do not willingly expiate, simply move to the next phase of your strategy. In most cases this will be remedial practices of ligation.

Ligation for Lemures

If you feel that you would benefit from reattempting the expiation process, you may decide to implement a period of environmental ligation in which you prevent the lemur from any activity until you can try again. Under these circumstances, you may be able to negotiate with the spirit. You must be very cautious in your dealings and not allow yourself to be tricked or betrayed. A lemur will try to avoid committing themselves to any form of obligation wherever possible. They may play games to try to elicit concessions from you. Do not be tempted to win their assent by softening your terms. It is important to be firm in your communication and conscious of an entity's potential desire to manipulate the exchange. Only after the revenant concedes to expiate in a method that is clear and unmistakable can you make an offering of funerary incense to confirm the deal.

If the lemur will not expiate, you may seek adjuration if it is safe to do so. The goal of this adjuration is to acquire the lemur's solemn and binding vow that they will immediately leave the premises via their place of rising and permanently return to the metacosmos.

If you can verify that the entity has left the premises, immediately seal their place of rising and other entry points, reinforcing the outer protections. Just because you have resolved one spirit does not mean that others will not try to fill their place, especially if they sense rich phasma or vulnerability to exploit.

At this point, if you cannot negotiate with the lemur to leave, you may opt to force them to leave through the process of exorcism. If you do not think you can achieve this, you may employ ligation incense and protection to mitigate the entity's ability to act until specialist help arrives.

Exorcism for Lemures

Exorcism is a remedial method of resolution reserved for situations when a lemur cannot be expiated or adjured. When banishing a lemur from a location, it is unwise to simply force them to leave without any restraint, as then they will be free to obsess other living people and cause more harm. It is better to coerce them to exit from the place in a controlled way.

We recommend exorcising the location by strategically pressing the lemur to retreat to its place of rising, compelling them back into the metacosmos and out of our physical reality. When the spirit has exited, the place of rising must be sealed with crossed lines to prevent reentry. Any objects or people to which the lemur has an attachment should also be exorcised of influence.

To return to the world of the living, the lemur would have to discover another tear in the veil. Until that possibility can be exploited, the lemur must survive as best they can in the chaotic milieu of Qarth Arqa.

Misericordia for Lemures

In extreme cases where the lemur is particularly dangerous and immediate action must be taken, misericordia may be the only viable solution. This should never be an easy decision. It demands grievous circumstances, and a necromancer should try to avoid it at all costs.

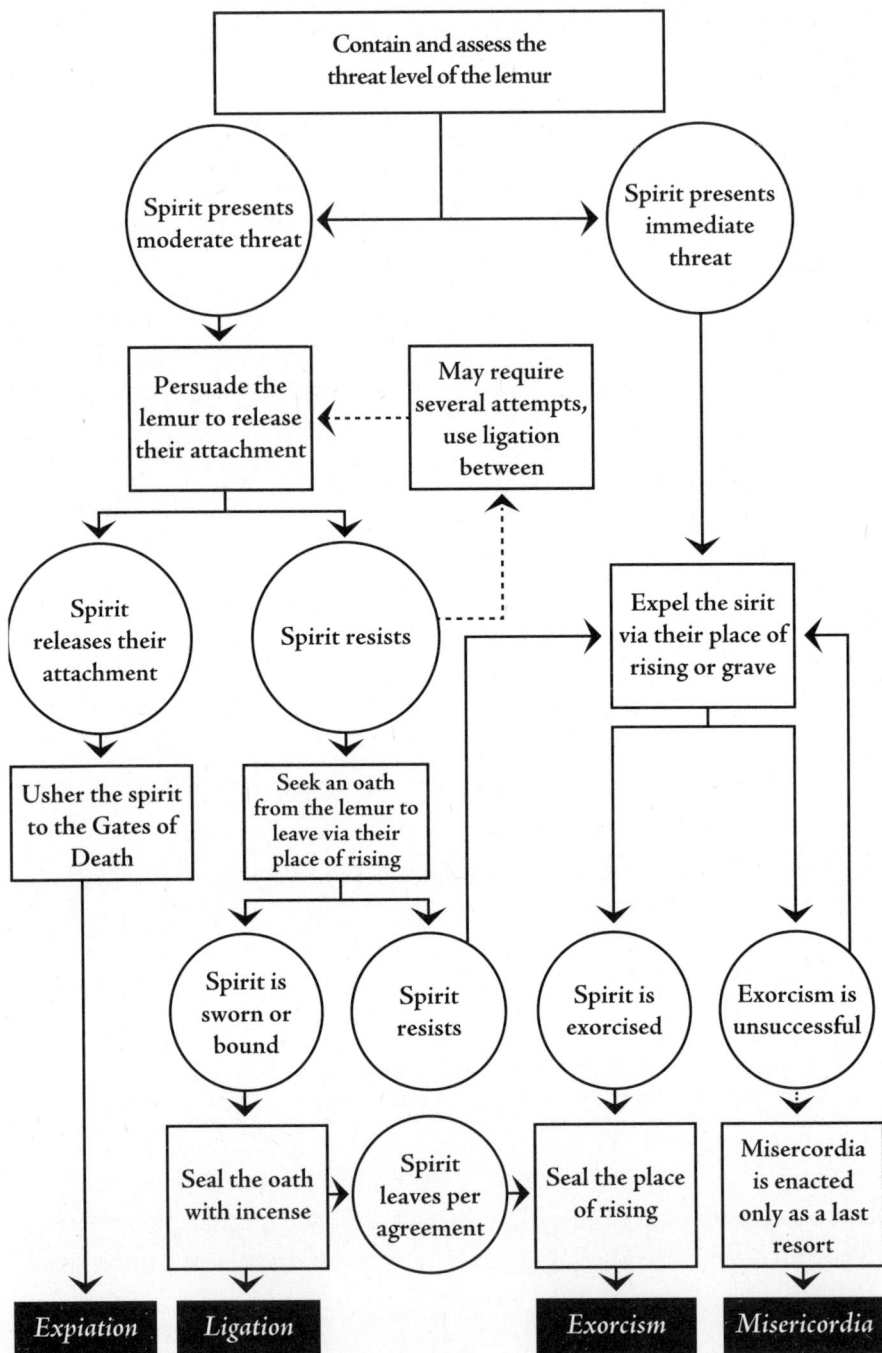

Flowchart for Lemur Resolution
Any harmful activities of a lemur should be mitigated, whether by expiation,
ligation, or exorcism from the location.

Strategy for Larvae

Unfortunately, in the case of dealing with a larva there is no opportunity to negotiate or communicate with them. Larvae are by their very nature incapable of cogent intellectual thought; they are purely driven by intense survival instincts and predatory behavior. In the unlikely event that you discover a larva or any spirit that you are not confident dealing with, you should not try to make contact or engage with them. Urgently seek a trained and experienced priest or magician. If they cannot deal with it themselves, they may know someone who can. In the meantime, provide protection for all people and gather your information together. You may cleanse and rarefy the phasma in your immediate vicinity, but do not attempt to exorcise the entire premises or disturb anything unless you are instructed to do so.

PROCEDURAL ACTIONS

As already discussed, the classification of the spirit causing the disturbance will help you to outline possible strategies for resolution based on rules of engagement. You should also have in your possession some essential knowledge to define the parameters of your operation, including the severity of the obsession, the identity of the spirit responsible, and their place of rising.

There are many variables you will need to consider. It is important to have procedural guidelines in place to safely control the spirit environment. When you understand the principles involved, you can learn to apply them as needed.

Planning Checklist

+ What is my strategy or plan of action?
+ Do I have the right team and experience to execute the strategy?
+ Do I have the resources and commitment to see the resolution to the end?
+ What tools and aids do I need to bring?
+ How will I ensure that everybody involved is safely protected?
+ How will I control the space where the spirit is active?
+ Can I confidently evoke and recognize the spirit causing the infestation?
+ Do I know how and when to execute the right method of resolution?
+ What are the possible contingencies and outcomes I need to prepare for?
+ How will I know if the resolution is successful?

Safety and Protection

Eudaemonic resolution requires very little setup and may simply progress directly from an investigation. You should secure the physical location to ensure there will be an uninterrupted environment and always take a moment to check on the well-being of all participants and reinforce protection. Importantly, before any spirit interaction, imbue your spiritual empowerment.

Cacodaemonic resolution naturally requires more preparation. Although lemures and immanes differ in intention, their propensity to cause harm requires equal precaution. A situation can very quickly escalate if processes are not in place.

Participants

Only those who absolutely must be present by necessity should be there; those who are present must follow the lead of the sciomancer and avoid interfering in the process.

If possible, relocate nonessential and vulnerable persons from the premises. As they leave, they should be cleansed and protected to ensure they are free of spirit influence. If they choose to stay on the premises, they should remain in the sanctuary. Any participants who are not present but are connected to the case should also be spiritually protected. Prior to and after spirit contact, have the team practice ars remisionis to reinforce their personal protection and spiritualization. This includes after a resolution or before reentering an exorcised space.

Assessing the Location

It will be imperative to control the environment from the outset and remove the entity's ability to dictate the conditions. If you are progressing directly from an investigation, you will need to pause to appraise the physical location using knowledge gained to identify key strategic areas, including the place of rising and the best location to evoke or summon the spirit.

Confirm the Sanctuary Location

The sanctuary set up during the investigation can continue to serve as your base of operations if practical. This is a space that is cleansed and protected from spirit influence. It will need to be moved if you discover it contains the place of rising or blocks access to it.

Locate the Place of Rising

During your investigation, you should have identified the place of rising, the liminal point where the spirit first entered. This is the small fissure where the veil between our realm and Qarth Arqa is compromised, allowing a spirit to temporarily slip in and out of the metacosmos. A spirit will be protective of this space, and it is not wise to prevent them from accessing it. If a spirit is aggressive, they can be maneuvered to this point of exit.

Define Perimeters and Boundaries

For cacodaemonic resolutions, you will need to magically reinforce the outer perimeter of the area where the spirit is active, limiting all opportunities for escape, except the place of rising. This will allow you to control where the spirit is and prevent them from leaving the premises if they are harmful. (This step is not required for eudaemonic resolutions.)

Choose a Site to Call the Spirit

Using the knowledge gained from the investigation, determine the best place to evoke and communicate with the spirit. This should be somewhere the spirit has been seen or is known to be active, or in the location of a relic or affinity.

In cacodaemonic resolution, it is best to bring the spirit to a space adjacent to the place of rising so that if exorcism ensues, you will be able to better control the environment. However, you may prefer to call an immanes to a space where you feel you have the best chance of attracting their attention. As a precaution, you will need to ensure there is a clear pathway that has not been exorcised extending between the area for communication and the place of rising. Ensure that spirit entry to the space has not been prevented by any forms of protection or intentionalized iron, etcetera.

EXERCISE
METHOD TO COMMAND THE SPACE
Successful implementation of a resolution relies on your ability to methodically limit the space where a spirit can be active and direct them to the place that is most advantageous to you. The following procedure is one way to bring a cacodaemon to a designated place for the purpose of communication. The same

principle can be applied to bring a lemur directly to a place of rising for exorcism. In the case of eudaemones, you may bypass this step and call them directly to the place where you wish to communicate with them.

1. Magically secure the outer perimeter of the area you identified. Walled areas can be protected by placing iron at each corner or side. Seal each window, door, and entryway. If the boundary comprises outdoor areas, you may actualize inherent perimeters such as fences and property lines by placing a nail or talisman where the boundaries meet. Waterways and iron rails are natural deterrents. Where no boundary exists, you can make one with intentionalized iron spaced nine feet (2.7 meters) apart.

2. Withdraw to a protected space free of spirit influence. This will usually be the sanctuary where you set up your base of operations, or you may create a space furthest from the place of rising if that is more logical.

3. Using the technique of exorcising a multiroom space described in the previous chapter, expand the protected area. Move through the space systematically, cleansing a room or section at a time. You may burn incense to rarefy phasma or place magical deterrents as you go. Pay special attention to corners, doorways, and enclosed spaces.

4. Cleanse the entire area within the perimeter except for the spot you allocated to call the spirit, the place of rising, and the passage between them.

5. As you limit where the spirit can feel comfortable, they will naturally gravitate toward these unprotected spaces. The presence of relics or affinities will draw them to the place you allocated to communicate with them.

6. If the spirit is agitated, be prepared to mitigate their activities. Whether you drive them into the space or gently entice them will depend on the spirit's condition and how willing they are to be persuaded.

SPIRIT COMMUNICATION

Whether it is with an eudaemon or cacodaemon, the space where you intend to communicate can usually be prepared in advance. Good preparation leaves nothing to chance, so think very carefully about any recording devices, tools, or items you may need on hand for a successful contact.

Preparing a Space to Interact with the Spirit

The approach most commonly used in the art of laying ghosts is creating a circle of protection to stand in that allows the spirit to remain outside its boundaries (described in chapter 9). Another traditional method is to create a magical circle that you wish the spirit to move into, allowing them a single entry point you guide them toward. When you see a sign confirming that the spirit has entered, you can close them inside the circle while you remain on the outside. In the case of a manes or immanes, the first method is preferable, but if using the second method, you should at the very least leave a gateway open so they do not feel trapped.

Convocation for Resolution

Ideally, you will make the space inviting to the spirit rather resorting to coercion.

+ Affinities and relics specific to the spirit should be presented in the manner most appealing to them, be they objects, activities, or music.
+ An anointed candle or lamp and a small bell can serve to guide the dead to you.
+ St. John's wort or parsley are specific funerary botanicals that communicate to the deceased that you are there to bring peace.
+ Convocation incense can be used to intensify phasma for communication. If uncontrolled phenomena occur, you can reduce phasmic density.

Evocation or Summoning

Specificity in language is a necessity when dealing with spirits, especially a cacodaemon. The protocol to call forth and communicate with spirits is explained more fully in chapter 9 with examples.

+ Prepare any orations or other recitations that you might need beforehand and commit as much as you can to memory. Make sure to bring notes or books in which your orations are written with you into the space.

+ Speak clearly and precisely to announce yourself, your dignification, and your purpose.
+ Call upon the specific spirit you wish to speak to. Make an oration using their name (if known) or identifying information.
+ Speak to the spirit calmly and respectfully. Try not to provoke, threaten, or abjure. If a spirit is being acrimonious and you cannot placate them, it is better to seek the help of an expert than to enter a discord you do not have the skills to undertake.

Dialogue

Once there is an indication that the spirit is willing to interact, you may proceed with the interrogation. The person for whom the spirit has shown a preference should lead the talking. Remember to stay focused—the goal is to build trust and learn why the spirit is causing a disturbance and how it can be resolved. We have found the simple method of our forebears effective:

+ Ask the spirit up to three times what it is they wish to say.
+ Allow the spirit to respond without interruption.
+ Ask relevant questions only after they have responded.
+ Be brief and focused, as the communication may not last long.
+ Do not ask questions about being dead or idle curiosities.

CONCLUDING A RESOLUTION

Depending on the outcome of the interaction, several possible actions could follow. If the spirit is not yet ready to expiate, you will keep moving on to the next step in your strategy until you come to a peaceful resolution, whether that is ligation or exorcism. Each method of resolution is a magical operation and should be attended with the proper intent, words and action.

Acknowledging Expiation

When you have verified a spirit has expiated you can conclude the event by honoring the spirit's passing. Traditional ritual gestures usually include the following:

+ A relevant prayer or oration marking the expiation of the soul
+ Request for guides to help them on their journey
+ An offering to the dead, such as funerary incense or an alternative

- ◆ Extinguishing the lantern or candle
- ◆ Laying of a pasque or violet flower

Procedure for Ligation by Adjuration

You may achieve a peaceful resolution by making a truce with a coherent spirit. For a manes, you might agree the spirit will desist activity that disrupts the living for the duration of their tenancy or until you make further communication. For a lemur, you should require an oath they will leave the location by the place of rising forthwith and never return. If the spirit is an immanes, you might not be able to extract a promise but you may be successful in instructing them to act peaceably.

1. Define the terms clearly including what you expect from a spirit and what you will do in return, such as an offering of funerary incense.
2. When the spirit shows you a clear sign of acquiescence, acknowledge it verbally.
3. At the conclusion of the communication thank the spirit and dismiss them.
4. Burn an incense offering to the dead if you have not already done so.
5. Extinguish the lantern or candle.

Procedure for Exorcism

In the case of a lemur, you may need to progress to exorcism if they pose imminent threat, or if neither expiation nor adjuration is successful.

1. Using the same method to exorcise a place, proceed to cleanse the final room, driving the entity toward the place of rising. Ensure there is no other option for the cacodaemon to escape.
2. Point intentionalized iron at the crevice or corner to ensure they do not flee.
3. Once you sense the spirit has vacated, seal the place of rising by drawing or laying a binding symbol or crossed lines.
4. Strew a handful of violets or pasque flowers across it.

5. You should then quickly move on to perform other measures of exorcism if needed, if you have not already done so. This may include:

◆ Objects that were the target of obsession should be exorcised with savory wash using the method described in the previous chapter.

◆ Anyone who has been on the premises can be cleansed with consecrated water.

◆ If known, the grave should also be sealed with crossed lines to prevent the spirit rising there.

VERIFYING THE RESULTS

Following any resolution, it is necessary to gauge the success of the operation, especially when dealing with a cacodaemon. It is imperative to do this prior to any activities or cleansing that could mask the results.

Confirming Departure

When a revenant has left either by expiation or returning to their place of rising, the atmosphere will feel significantly different. Look for signs of spirit departure. These may be specific to the culture of the deceased or the practitioner. Some traditional signs that we have witnessed include an unmistakable feeling of release, a sudden gust of wind, a candle flame being extinguished, an apparition of smoke evacuating, or the sound of ravens calling. The departure of the dead can also be verified by practices of divination or an omen from a trusted spirit guide.

Prevent Reentry of a Lemur

Once the spirit has departed, you should take measures to protect the premises. This is especially important if the spirit was a lemur, and to hinder access from other offending spirits. Cleanse the space, people, and objects of residual impressions.

In the days following, whatever temporary methods were used can be replaced to make them more lasting. Reinforce the protection of the premises with iron, amulets, or talismans. Permanently seal the place of rising with fixed cross lines; if it is a crack or crevice, block it if possible.

Restore Balance

Only after the protection has been fully reinforced and you have confirmed the cacodaemon has departed should you allow for the censing of any botanicals other than to rarefy phasma. This is an appropriate time to make an offering to ancestors. In the meantime, prayers and orations to higher powers, ancestors, or guardians should continue.

Confirming Spirit Ligation

If the resolution resulted in environmental ligation, success can be indicated by the feeling of pneuma, a light atmosphere that is not rich in phasma. Infestation activity should have subsided and feelings of oppression abated. This effect is temporary, based on the method used to rarefy phasma. The situation will need to be monitored after the initial resolution and reinforced on a regular basis. However, continued ligation can cause the spirit's interest to diminish over time.

If ligation was achieved by adjuration there should be no signs of obsession or spirit influence upon occupants. The success of ligation can also be further verified with methods of divination and guidance.

EVALUATION AND FOLLOW-UP

A sciomancer has a duty of care to mitigate reinfestation. After a resolution, there is much to do to monitor events and ensure the safety of all involved.

Postassessment

During and after the event, you should debrief your team and evaluate the outcomes. You will need to consider the ongoing protection and spirit environment and prepare a plan for follow-up with clear objectives.

Handover

Once the cause of a spirit obsession has been addressed, you can focus all your attention on the needs of the occupants. Being on hand to answer any questions, provide specialist knowledge, and counsel those who have endured the disturbance is as much a part of a sciomancer's job as resolving the crisis itself. Success should be measured by the peace brought to the location. If you leave without comforting and supporting the living inhabitants, they have not achieved true closure.

Experiencing a spirit infestation can take a toll on individuals and affect their confidence, so you must gauge the status of their well-being. We encourage you to work within their existing beliefs to restore their spiritual fortitude and remain free of infestation. Reinforcing their faith and principles can often provide strength and comfort to those who have endured a spiritual crisis, and it may be the only pillar of stability they have to lean upon. Sciomancy is not an art in which the ego is celebrated. Attempting to present yourself or your own beliefs in the way you wish to be seen rather than empowering theirs will only make resolution even more elusive.

Healthy Spiritual Practices

It is essential to work with the affected occupants to ensure they know how to maintain a protected environment and prevent further infestation. This will include a regimen to renew protection as well as education to change daily habits. If someone has been the target of oppression, the reality is that they will need to learn how to establish their spiritual and mental courage to prevent a similar thing from happening again. It requires some vigilance, but with the right support and commitment on their part, they can be stronger than ever. Some good habits in which you can instruct them include:

+ Maintain a routine of spiritual cleansing and personal protection
+ Practice spiritualization to prevent becoming a target for entities
+ Honor relationships with lares and guardians who protect people and places
+ Employ spiritual protection for the home, place of work, and while traveling
+ Exorcise preowned objects brought into the home suspected of attachment
+ Be selective about inviting people in beyond a designated protected area
+ Proactively cleanse residual phasma after events, high emotions, and visitors

Renewing Protection

Most methods of protection require renewing on a regular basis. The table in this section can be used to develop a routine to maintain the optimal phasmic environment for protection. Ideally, occupants will learn to implement it for themselves in a way that is comfortable for them and works with their system of belief.

It can be beneficial to choose a time to renew annual protection to coincide with a holiday or cultural event so it becomes second-nature. For instance, in Scottish customs, May Day is a time to protect the home and livestock, Lammas to protect boundaries and contracts, all Souls Day to protect the dead, and Candlemas the unborn and newly arrived.

Table 12: Regimen for Renewing Protection

Remedial Action	Time of Expiration
Personal protection	Twenty-four hours
Exorcism with sanctified water	Two to three days
Ligation incense	Two to three weeks
Protection of entry points	Reinforce every twelve months
Talismans	Recharge as needed
Amulets	Recharge if not worn for a period
Crossed lines	Indefinite unless dismantled
Intentionalized iron	Indefinite until removed or deactivated

Follow-Up

We recommend you follow up with the participants regularly to monitor their progress and check for signs of infestation. It is advisable to prepare a list of consistent questions for each contact so that you can identify new patterns and anomalies should an infestation reemerge. During this time, you can also remind them to renew their protection at appropriate intervals, depending on the regimen you have set up with them.

When you engage in sciomantic work, you are continuing an ancient tradition of both guarding and healing the veil. It doesn't matter whether you are applying modern technology or investigatory methodologies—your intention and practice are part of a stream of magical art that has its source in prehistory. The living need your help, and equally the spirits of the unquiet dead require your compassion. You are, in effect, an agent of divine progression and a critical influence that will change lives. This responsibility may seem like a burden to some, but the realization that you are an essential cocreator of the universe is a fundamentally profound personal liberation.

CONCLUSION

Sciomancy is a complex subject, but it is also relevant and fulfilling. In this book, we have presented a range of information pertinent to understanding spirits of the dead and the invisible realms they inhabit from a magician's point of view. We have introduced arcana explaining the passage of the soul and the manifestation of spirit phenomena, and we have dug into the vaults of occult knowledge to provide methods to classify and recognize spirits.

For those interested in a hands-on approach, we have advised how to safely conduct an inquiry; including tools, botanicals, procedures for on-site investigation, and how to analyze your results. And finally, in the event of a spirit disturbance, we have explored magical techniques to bring about a resolution and guidelines to know what action is appropriate.

Practices like laying ghosts are found among many living traditions, performed by the individuals or organizations that maintain those venerable wisdoms. These caretakers of tradition have always known that the dead and the living are not separated and that we never truly lose the ones we love. They are links in a long chain of history, treasured knowledge throughout the centuries that has been delivered into our hands. Every culture has these living traditions and magical practices. They are far from lost to the modern world and can inspire us in our own contemporary attempts to continue in our task.

Living traditions are much more than simple examples of folk magic or cultural sentiment. Many of these traditions are initiatory and deeply esoteric with well-defined philosophies and alternative faiths. Several are also syncretic, incorporating classical and medieval magical ideas within a native cultural expression of the occult. True cultural traditions are nuanced; modern attempts to connect to those cultures can be too romanticized or based primarily in academic theories.

It should be said that living traditions are not calcified in the past; they too grow and evolve. It is normal for living traditions to refresh themselves and undergo internal revival. After all, the old ways would die off if they didn't reflect the changes of the community in which they serve. They can renovate themselves because magic is principle based, founded on arcana, which serves as anchors so that the essential mysteries can be maintained even when society changes.

Magicians and initiates learn from one another, and in the current century we have entered an exciting time of esoteric exploration. In the case of British esoterica, so many traditions have relocated to the UK in more recent times. The same is true in other countries that consider themselves to be multicultural. We would encourage respect for living traditions as custodians of unique wisdom and seek to build an awareness of their presence in your own part of the world.

Historically, much of the lore of necromancy has been obscured by fear, suppression, and persecution. Yet it remains, scattered in the writings of theologians, philosophers, and esotericists as well as in fragments in magical literature. We were in a fortunate position to have had the context of a cultural means of laying ghosts, which enabled us to look through the scattered remnants of necromancy and bring them together to better our practice of resolving spirit disturbances.

So long as spirits of the dead walk in the shadow of life, the laying of ghosts will remain relevant. In this way, sciomancy is a practical art that answers the needs of the moment. With just a fundamental understanding you can immediately start to apply the principles outlined in this book. Whether you are simply curious, already working with the spirits of the dead, or actively engaged in paranormal investigation, the material presented herein can bring clarity and direction to your endeavors.

Due to the nature of the subject, it has been necessary to focus on emergency situations, such as predatory spirits and harmful infestations, and so on. In reality, the vast majority of interactions with human spirits are innocuous and often beneficial. We the living have always abided with spirits; it is a natural coexistence.

In our busy, prepackaged modern world, people can often view the presence of a spirit as an inconvenience that challenges their fabricated sense of normalcy, something "paranormal" and therefore something to fear. As magicians, we have a different perspective. We accept the reality of spirits sharing our world and remember that we will all pass through the same transition; we will all inevitably face death and what comes after. Only understanding will clear the clouds of fear by making the unknown known and ignite our hearts with compassion for those souls confused in their journey.

In a similar manner, this understanding can remind us of the importance of actively resolving our issues during life, before we too are met with the challenges of the pathway to rest. We can seek for ourselves a good death, a process that should breed in us a sense of responsibility to make things easy for our loved ones and others. We can confidently and lovingly undertake funerary rites and ancestral ceremonies, knowing that our actions and intentions have a real effect on souls that may need our support or guidance.

Where danger from a spirit incursion or a crisis looms, the same understanding helps us comprehend what is needed and calmly take action to bring peace to the turmoil and tranquility back to the people and places previously disturbed.

Occult philosophy teaches that all manifest existence originates in the metacosmos. Through the application of magic, we shape ideas and bring them into being, drawing on the natural processes which actuate creation in its evolution. The metacosmos is therefore malleable and impressionable. As cocreators of the universe, it behooves us to use magic responsibly and be conscientious stewards of the borders between our world and others interacting with our own, including the realm where unquiet spirits reside. To this end, we can not only protect the living but bring healing to lost.

All souls are of a single family, resonant sparks of divine light seeking comprehension of the greater all. Therefore, our souls share the same journey to unlock the wisdom and power of our divine selves. To have sympathy for unquiet spirits is to show compassion for another soul on the road in the grand adventure of being. If we stumble, we all would hope that a hand would reach out to steady us, and we should wish to do the same for others.

Each one of us can be a conduit of ancient tradition, passing the knowledge and wisdom of being guardians of the veil to future magicians. We don't have to be perfect, just sincere, and we must allow evolution to take its natural course as the next generation receives possession of the torch from our own weary hands.

The reality is that spirit investigations are occurring all over the world. People are finding ways to engage in seeking the truth of the unseen realms. Paranormal investigation and research have become a common aspect of modern life. Originally such investigations were purely designed to prove the existence of the paranormal but as the years have passed, some of these investigators have begun to question how they can assist in those events. We are seeing the coming together of the old and new worlds, a juxtaposition of purpose; we can learn from one another.

There is a view among some investigators that they need to rediscover the unseen worlds, that there simply is no certain knowledge about spirits or how we can help them. In truth, there is no need to reinvent the wheel; there are many systems for understanding and working efficiently with the dead. What paranormal research brings to us is an exponentially growing field of ars nova, new technologies and investigative methods that can enhance and advance the art of sciomancy.

In our vocation, we have worked alongside sincere and incredible paranormal investigators. We perceived at an early period that, while they lacked the ars vetrus in their methodology, their enthusiasm and ingenuity was inspiring. We didn't hesitate to incorporate elements of paranormal investigation into our methods as ars nova. We can only hope that any paranormal investigator that reads this book will be equally inspired by the ars vetrus.

Arguably one of the most important contributions of this book to the field of paranormal research is the classifications of daemones, specifically human spirits. These are observable realities and can easily be proven by experience in the field. The language and terminology might be particular but the actuality of their existence and effects are universal. With that in mind, we have chosen to end this work with some key takeaways that address some common misunderstandings.

- Spirits and the invisible worlds *can* be understood.
- A phenomenon is more likely to occur when there is dense phasma.
- Many false reports of spirits may be attributed to the effects of EMF.
- Phenomena can be observed and classified to identify the types of spirits.
- An orb can indicate a sentient spirit, but not all sentient spirits are human.
- Humans are naturally prone to see, hear, and feel the spirits of the dead.
- Revenants are human spirits bound to the corporeal world by attachments.
- An haunting occurs when a revenant fixates on a person, place, or object.

- Involuntary possession is rare and usually due to a predatory human spirit.
- Revenant spirits appear to rise from the ground.
- Crossed lines and iron can be used to prevent their transit.

The journey to becoming a truly adept sciomancer is a long one, of knowledge, practice, and preparation. We encourage you to reread and become familiar with the content provided. However, there is no substitute for experience on the ground. This is an art that demands participation in real-life circumstances. It is not a purely academic or theoretical study; to that end, we have written this book to offer you the means to make a real difference in people's lives and aid souls in distress.

DEFINITION
OF ARCANE TERMS

Language is the cornerstone of systemizing and communicating the arcana of an esoteric tradition. There are many variations in the terms employed by different magical, cultural, philosophical, and spiritual systems. A comparative study of the etymology of terms used can shed light on the reasons certain ideas may have become adopted. This lexicon is derived from both written and oral sources. In sharing it, our hope is that it can assist people from diverse backgrounds to employ a common, defined language in their investigations.

A

Abjure, Abjuration: From the Latin *abiūrgarē*, meaning *to deny an oath*. In magic, an abjuration involves regular orations that coerce a spirit into a course of action or contract. Abjuration is posed in argumentative language and should be reserved to challenge a belligerent or threatening spirit. A magician should never make an abjuration if they do not have the authority or dignification to support it.

Adjure, Adjuration: Latin *adiūrāre*, meaning *to swear an oath*. In magic, an adjuration is a verbal oration designed to encourage a spirit to bind themselves to an oath. When sworn by a spirit under appropriate magical conditions, oaths and vows are inviolable and can serve to obviate future disturbances or serve as an element in a resolution strategy.

Adrastia: (Also **adrasteia, adrastea,** and **adrasta,** among others.) From ancient Greek, meaning *she from whom there is no escape*. Named after the goddess Adrastia, to whom it is said that even the gods must adhere, this spiritual process describes the inevitable nature of fate and the certainty that all choices and actions must be answered for in life. As such, adrastia is necessarily intertwined with the power of destiny and the progression of the soul, incarnating from one body and life to another, ever learning in the pursuit of understanding, enlightenment, and ultimately, apotheosis. (Synonym: **karma**)

Aerial Daemon(es): Also called spirits of the sun, these are nonhuman spirits inhabiting one of the seven recorded sublunary worlds. In their essential nature, they are driven by intellectual concerns rather than instinctual or emotional ones. In demeanor they can appear detached and haughty or proud.

Aether, Aetheric: From Latin and Greek *aither*, both referring to the pure air of the upper regions, therefore a symbolic reference to the rarest or least dense of the three states of hyle. It is most often associated with the substance of the celestial realms.

Affinities: In necromancy, things that may bear similarity or be familiar to a human spirit but have no actual or physical connection to their former life. Music of the period, style of clothing, smells, and so on are common affinities.

Agape: From Greek meaning *love* and *charity*; by extension, it bears the arcane sense of attraction. It is accompanied by the connotation of the sacred. Agape is the force in the universe that causes like things to attract to one another. Atoms are drawn to each other, spirits are drawn to their affinities or relics, and all matter is held together by the manifestations of agape. (Synonyms: **attraction, caritatem**)

Amulet: From the Latin *amuletum*, likely originating from *āmōlīrī*, which means *to avert* or *remove*. An amulet is a spiritual object that protects the owner from misfortune. The appearance of the amulet can vary considerably based on symbolism and method, but it always serves as a vehicle of intent for the purpose of protection.

Anima: From Latin, often associated with life and emotion. Originally from PIE *ane-*, meaning *breath*. One of two temporary adjuncts of the mens, the anima is the part of the self that interacts with phasmic realities during life. Its nature is to be drawn to the chthonic and its faculty is the imaginatrix. The anima is our instinctual and emotive self and thus stands in juxtaposition to its twin, the animus.

Animus: From Latin, meaning *mind*, and PIE *ane-*, meaning *breath*. One of two temporary adjuncts of the mens. The animus is the rational and intellectual part of our incarnate selves; its faculty is called *ratiocinatio*. It is of a celestial nature and stands in juxtaposition with its twin, the anima.

Apotheosis: Latinized, from Greek *apotheoun* meaning *to achieve deification*. Apotheosis is the state in which a soul no longer needs to reincarnate, having reached sustainable enlightenment, unity with divinity, or godhood.

Apparition: From Latin *apparitionem*, meaning *an appearance*. A term commonly used in medieval accounts to refer to the sighting of a spirit that has manifested in a translucent, recognizable appearance. (Synonym: **specter**)

Aqueous Daemon(es): A classification of sublunary spirits. Also referred to as spirits of Venus or sometimes marine daemones. They are of a like nature to humanity but are often more driven by their passions.

Arcana: The plural of the Latin *arcanus*, meaning *secrets* or *mysteries*. In medieval magic, arcana refers to the corpus of esoteric knowledge, principles, and laws regarding the occult arts and sciences.

Arqa: A term from Hebrew Qabalistic literature. Arqa is one of the seven earths and said to contain within it the Little Eden, the place where the souls of the dead who have successfully shed their earthy existence aspire to find rest and understanding between incarnations. Little Eden is the Hebrew equivalent to the Greek Elysium. Arqa is associated by medieval magicians with the planetary influence of Mercury. (Synonym: **Hades**)

Ars Nova: From Latin, meaning *the new arts*. Ars nova comprises those pioneering pursuits in the magical disciplines when new theories, experiments, and understandings are devised based on the arcana of the ars vetrus. Once tested, confirmed, and adopted, ars nova can be considered and included in the ars vetrus.

Ars Remissionis: From Latin, meaning *the art of remission* or *the art of release*. Ars remissionis refers to the essential practice of disengaging oneself from any spirit or magical operation. The purpose of magical release is to purge any lingering phasmic connection by which the magician may influence or be influenced by the subject of their working or call upon themselves undesired consequences after the magical operation has been completed.

Ars Vetrus: From Latin, meaning *the old arts*. Ars vetrus is the accumulated wisdom and arcana that have been tested and confirmed and thus most often handed down as tradition to the next generation of magicians.

Atom, Atomic: From Greek *atomos*, meaning *indivisible*. In magical arcana, an atom is the smallest building block of the universe. These atoms are imagined as sparks of divine light forming hyle or the universal substance from which all things are formed.

Attachment: The subject of a revenant's fixation on aspects of their former life that prevent them from shedding their phasmic body and binds them in Qarth Arqa.

C

Cacodaemon(es): From Graeco-Latin (Gr. *Kákos*, "bad" and *daímōn*, "spirit agency"). Refers to sentient sublunary spirits judged to be potentially harmful. In regard to necromancy, these include the spirit classifications of immanes, lemures, and larvae.

Celestial Realm: Of the three worlds predominating in Indo-European cultures and medieval thought, the celestial realm is the heavenly firmament, cognate with the superlunary spheres or realms in which aether is the predominant phenomenon. (Synonyms: **aetheric realm, astral realm, firmament, heavens, Ouranios, superlunary**)

Cleansing: Magical practice of removing residual and negative influences set upon phasma, whether from a body, object, or place.

Coagula: From Latin *coāgulāre*, meaning *to make thick* or *solid*. In arcana, it refers to the primordial modality that causes things to draw together. Of an esoterically feminine archetype, it is the faculty of nature that births new form into existence.

Conjunctio: From Latin *coniungō*, meaning *to join together*. One of the three primordial modalities, it is the proto-mercurial function in the universe, the stasis that exists between solve and coagula that holds forms together and is therefore present in all manifested existence.

Convocation: Originally from Latin *convocāre*, meaning *to call together* or *to call in assembly*. Convocation is the magical art of gathering spirits; that is, drawing them to you and actively creating the best environment for their interaction. Convocation often includes (but is not limited to) the use of botanicals, orations, affinities, and relics.

Crossed Lines: Found in many cultures, the ancient practice of using intersecting lines as a symbolic and magically potent barrier to prevent spirit access.

D

Daemon(es): Graeco-Latin, from the Greek *daimon* and ultimately from PIE **dai-mon-* meaning *a divider* or *provider*. Daemones are spirit agencies, those sentient entities that permeate the sublunary worlds, thus sitting in the animated juxtaposition between divine and phenomenal. As such, human spirits are also considered daemones.

Daemoniacs: A term used in magic to describe hallucinations or illusions imposed upon a person by a spirit or phantasm that therefore cannot be wholly trusted. Historically the word has been used to refer to any hallucination derived from an imbalanced state of mind.

Daemonology: The occult study of daemones. (*See* **Daemones**)

Dignification: From the Latin *dignitas* meaning *merit* or *worthiness*. In magic, dignification is used to describe the process of a magician attaining authentic spiritual authority in their art, considered essential when engaging with spirits.

Discarricare: From Latin *discarricāre*, meaning *to discharge*. Discarricare is the process of shedding accumulated or excess phasma through transference. In modern occultism and spiritual practices, it is often referred to as *grounding*.

Dismissal: The final stage of any formal communication with a spirit in which the magician respectfully bids farewell to the spirit and instructs them to leave the communication without doing harm to any. (Synonym: **license to depart**)

E

Ens: From Latin, meaning *being*. The ens is the eternal self-realized atom surrounded by a cloud of aether (numen) and impressed by its own unique genius. That is to say, the ens is the immortal that persists from one incarnation to the next. (Synonym: **soul**)

Eudaemon(es): From Greek, meaning good spirits. Sublunary entities not considered to cause harm and may be actively benevolent. In necromancy, it refers to lares, familiar lares, and manes.

Evoke, Evocation: From Latin *ēvocāre*, meaning *to call forth* or *to call in from*. Evocation is an oration in which a magician calls a spirit to them. It differs from invocation in that it is requesting the entity's immediate presence or that they appear before them.

Exorcise, Exorcism: From the Greek *exorkizein*. In occultism, it refers to the magical process of cleansing. It has come to refer to the expelling or banishing of a spirit or spiritual influence from a person, object, or place.

Expiate, Expiation: From Latin *expiāre*, meaning *satisfaction* or *atonement*. Expiation is a process of catharsis wherein the deceased successfully releases their attachments to their previous life and passes beyond Qarth Arqa. The expiation process involves the relinquishing of the phasmic body, which in turn releases the ens to complete their journey to Arqa.

F

Familiar Lar(es): Familiar lares are human souls who have successfully transitioned through Qarth Arqa and willfully return between incarnations to aid their still-living loved ones and are thus called *familiar*. They differ from other lares in that they are still bound within the cycle of reincarnation, not yet having achieved apotheosis. When familiar lares frequent their own family, they are called *domestic lares*—that is, the lares of the household. (*See also* **Lares**)

G

Genius: From Latin and PIE root *gene-* ("to give birth" or "beget"), translated as *generative power* or *inborn nature*. The genius is the eternal intelligence impressed upon the numen; the intelligence of the immortal soul.

H

Hyle: Derived from the explanations of Aristotle, the hyle is conceived as the universal substance from which all things are formed. It is composed of atoms, indivisible particles, or sparks of divine light. Hyle manifests in three states of spiritual matter based on density: aether, pneuma, and phasma. (Synonyms: **atomic fire, fire, philosophical fire, Prima materia**)

I

Imaginatrix: From Latin, refers to the faculty of imagination considered to be primarily of the anima. The imaginatrix permits for the creation of new ideas, conceptualization, innovation, and emotive expression. When honed, this faculty allows the magician to perceive and manipulate subtle forces. (Synonym: **phantasia**)

Immanes: Negative form of **manes**. Immanes is a classification of necromantic spirits describing those revenants who exist in a state of confusion or emotional distress. Unlike manes, they are incapable of taking the steps toward resolution, being lost in cycles of their own trauma or delusion after death.

Infernal Realm: From Latin *infernalis*, meaning *the lower world*. Commonly in Christianity, it refers to the doctrinal ideal of a plane of punishment identified in English as Hell. However, it is predated by the Indo-European concept of three worlds in which the infernal realm is the lowest or underworld, where chthonic gods reside. This understanding persists in the arcana, ascribing the infernal realm as a place where dense phasma predominates. (Synonyms: **chthonic, nether realms, underworld**)

Infestation: From Latin *infestāre*, meaning *molesting* or *disturbing*. The stage of paranormal phenomena in which spirit activities are perceptible to human witnesses and cause repeated disturbances. An infestation is characterized by frequency and intensity.

Intelligence(s): From the Latin *intelligentia*, meaning *power to discern*. In arcana, the intelligence refers to the function, purpose, or intent with which a subject, object, or place is imbued.

Interrogation (of a Spirit): From Latin *interrogāre*, meaning *to ask* or *inquire*. Interrogation of a spirit is one of the phases of formal dialogue in which a spirit is questioned or interviewed. It should include verifying the identity of the spirit and gaining any pertinent new information.

Invoke, Invocation: From Latin *invocāre*, meaning *to call upon* or *call out to*. An invocation is a magical oration in which one calls upon a spirit or deity. It differs from evocation in that it is petitioning an entity remotely and not asking the entity to immediately appear before you.

L

Lar(es): *Lar* was imported into Latin culture from the Etruscans and means *aristocrat* or *lord*. Lares are human souls who have no need to reincarnate, having achieved all they can upon the earth and secured a permanent place in Arqa. (Synonyms: **heroes, holy ones, honored ones, mighty ones, spirit guides**)

Larva (pl. Larvae): From Latin, meaning *a mask*. A larva is a revenant who has lost all memory of their human life, reason, and even appearance. Larvae are entirely driven by the instinctual desire to feed on the phasma they need to maintain their spirit body.

Laying Ghosts: A traditional practice of seeking a resolution to a disturbance caused by a revenant. Some use the term to refer to specific regional practices, but it is also broadly applied by antiquarians, folklorists, and ethnologists to a number of cultural practices.

Leluric Daemon(es): A type of inhuman spirit that permeates the uppermost sublunary world and as such is of a much rarer phasmic form than other types of daemones; they are also called spirits of Jupiter. (Synonyms: **atmospheric daemones, igneous spirits**)

Lemur(es): From Latin, used by the Romans to refer to evil spirits of the dead. These are revenants who purposefully refuse to cross through the Portae Mortis (Gates of Death), and in some form desire power to maintain their forms. Whether by creating fear or seeking adoration, lemures are defined by their willingness to be harmful and predatory in their pursuit of phasma. They differ from larvae because their actions are intentional and deliberate rather than being purely instinctual.

Ligation: From French into English, descending from Latin *ligāre*, meaning *to tie* or *bind*. Ligation is the magical process of binding a subject. In sciomancy it often refers to limiting the spirit's capability to interact with our world through methods inclusive of but not limited to altering the phasmic environment, binding them to a specific location or object, or extracting an oath from them.

Lucifugii (sing. Lucifugius): From Latin, translated as *ones who flee the light*. These are a type of inhuman daemones who are rarely seen, dwelling in the deepest and darkest of the sublunary worlds. Lucifugii are as powerful as they are instinctual and possess little to no cognitive reasoning capabilities of their own. They are also described as spirits of Saturn.

M

Manes: From Latin, meaning *good spirits of the dead*. In necromancy, manes are the most common classification of revenant, referring to those who remain in Qarth Arqa to complete what they perceive as unfinished business. They seem rational and can be communicative.

Memoratrix: From Latin, referring to the faculty of memory inherent within the immortal ens. Memoratrix is considered essential to both the practice of magic and esoteric thought, as it is conceived that when the soul returns to Arqa upon death, it takes with it the memories of life, integrating them into the eternal mystery of the soul's progress.

Mens: From Latin, meaning *mind*. The mens is conceived as the pneumatic balance between the aetheric ens and the phasmic spirit body. The soul projects the mens for the purpose of creating a personality to navigate a single incarnation. The divisions of the mens are the anima and the animus. (Synonym: **nous**)

Metacosmos (pl. Metacosmoi): From Greek, meaning *between the world(s)*. The metacosmoi are the border regions between sublunary worlds and are sometimes referred to metaphorically as waters or seas. Metacosmoi are of the nature of solve, and so any form therein is subject to a constant state of dissolution. Regarding necromancy, the metacosmos that lies between our world and the world of the dead is known as Qarth Arqa.

Misericordia: From Latin, meaning *mercy*. Misericordia is the magical process of forcing a revenant to relinquish their phasmic body, thereby compelling them to cross the metacosmos into Arqa. The use of misericordia means that the choice to resolve their attachments is taken from them. Misericordia should only be used in very specific and extreme circumstances.

Movement: Environmental phenomena that occur due to the interpenetration of our world and a particular metacosmos, therefore often suggesting the emerging presence of an entity. As a general rule, if they are perceived, movements proceed signs. (Synonym: **motion**)

N

Necromancy, Necromantic: From Graeco-Latin, originally from Greek *nekros*, meaning *death*, and *mantis*, meaning *one who prophesizes*, *divines*, or *is touched by divine madness*. Mantis (and manteia) have survived in the suffix *-mancy* and carries with it the connotation of a divine and magical art. Necromancy, therefore, can be seen as the sacred magical art of dealing with the dead.

Necromantic Daemon(es): Refers to any human soul or spirit. Also called spirits of Mercury in medieval and renaissance magic.

Necromantium: From Latin via the Greek *Nekromanteion*. A sacred place, tomb, or temple employed for the practice of necyomancy. Sometimes the term *necromantium* is used for a scrying mirror constructed specifically for operations to evoke human spirits.

Necyomancy: From Graeco-Latin, a practice within the discipline of necromancy that focuses on the art of evoking spirits of the dead, often conducted in a temple, tomb, or sacred space called a *Necromantium*. Necyomancy is the descendant of ancient Greek rites of communing with the dead called *Nekyia*.

Nigromancy, Nigromantic: From Graeco-Latin, meaning *dark* or *black arts*, was originally used as a derogatory term to describe the pagan and early medieval magical practice of engaging in commerce with spirits in daemonology. This later became a source of superstition and confusion, where necromancy was erroneously dubbed black magic or the dark art, due to similarity in names.

Nube(s): Latin for *cloud*, refers to the coalescence of phasma and one of the stages of spirit manifestation. A nube will look like a misty haze, the color of which will denote the type of sublunary spirit.

Numen: Latin meaning *divine will*, a sphere of aetheric light denoting the vehicle of the ens. A numen is the first state of spirit manifestation. When perceived, the numen may be described in essence as seeing the light of the soul. (Synonyms: **form of fire, orb, robe of light**)

O

Obsession: From Latin *obsidēre*, meaning *to beseige*. Obsession occurs when a place, person, or object serves as the emotionally intensive focal point of a revenant's attachment. (Synonym: **haunting**)

Offering(s): Gifts given to spirits or deities that include but are not limited to various foodstuff, certain flora, incense, liquor, ale, and phasmic-rich organic matter such as milk, eggs, and meat.

Oneiromancy: From Greek *oneiro*, meaning *dream*. Oneiromancy is the magical discipline of employing dreams and the dreamscape.

Oppression: From Latin *opprimere*, meaning *to press against*. As it is used in necromancy, it describes the malevolent targeting of a specific living person by a predatory revenant. During oppression, a lemur or larva will attempt to excite significant emotional responses from their subject such as fear, anger, love, or worship. The process of oppression is always taxing on the subject, as the predatory spirit will attempt to break down mental fortitude and exploit emotional insecurities.

Orations: From Latin *orationem*, referring to something that is spoken. In magic, orations are spoken words used for an operational purpose. They can come in many forms, such as prayers, invocations, evocations, abjurations, adjuration, and so on.

P

Phantasm: Related to the Greek *phantos* and *phainein*, meaning *to be visible*. A phantasm occurs when an impression has been made on the phasmic environment but has no consciousness attached to it. Labeled collo-quially as "residual hauntings" by modern paranormal investigators, a phantasm may be characterized as a memory made manifest. Examples include a form repeating the same action, echoes of past sounds, et cetera. (Synonyms: **phantasama, phantom**)

Phasma, Phasmic: From Greek *phaso*, meaning *light*. Phasma can be understood as a substance of light; it is a dense collection of hyle. It is malleable and necessary for ideas to become form; for example, the body of a spirit. When a magician does any magical operation, it is almost always done through the manipulation of phasma.

Phasmata: The artificial creation of a phasmic body or phenomena that can be crafted by a magician, sometimes created by accident through the projection of collective and emotive thought. In modern paranormal and occult circles, phasmata are often called *thoughtforms* or *tulpas*. The latter adopted by Theosophists, itself supposedly originating in Tibetan spiritual practice.

Placation: From Latin *placēre*, meaning *to appease, pacify,* or *quiet*. Placa-tion is a regular form of oration in which the magician diplomatically attempts to calm or assuage a spirit, often in order to achieve a desired accord. In sciomancy, for example, the necromancer may make a placa-tion to calm an agitated immanes in order to facilitate communication or lessen the intensity of the disturbance.

Place of Rising: Used to describe the liminal space where a revenant is usu-ally perceived to rise from the ground and through which they can enter in and out of the metacosmos.

Pneuma, Pneumatic: From Greek, meaning *wind* or *breath*. Pneuma is one of the three states of spiritual matter or hyle. Being a middle state of density, it is lighter than phasma but denser than aether, therefore acting as a stabilizing factor between the aetheric and the phasmic. (Synonym: **spiramen**)

Poltergeist: From German *poltern* and *geist*, meaning *a noisy ghost*. Refers broadly to any infestation events. Rather than being a classification or unique type of spirit, the term refers to the activity of spirits brought to the attention of witnesses due originally to their sound but also to the movement of physical objects.

Portae Mortis: Latin translation of the Hebrew *shaare-maveth*, meaning *the Gates of Death*. The stage of death referred to in the Seven Hells wherein all attachments to the previous life are relinquished, including the phasmic body, and the soul transitions into Arqa to rest between lives. (Synonym: **Gates of Death**)

Possession: When a spirit or other entity sublimates the consciousness of a living person. There are two types of possession, voluntary and involuntary. When voluntary, a trained practitioner enters an altered state in a generally positive spiritual experience and gives permission to an entity or deity to take temporary control. When forced or involuntary, possession is a violent intrusion that follows an intense period of oppression to wear down the victim's resolve and is never spontaneous nor instantaneous. Note that other altered states such as mediation, rapture, and so on can be mistaken for possession.

Q

Qarth Arqa: From Hebrew, meaning *the Cold of Arqa*. It refers to the metacosmos that lies between the realm of the living and the realm of the dead or Arqa. It is described as a sea or no-man's-land where revenants can be temporarily bound. (Synonyms: **Cartagra, Erebos**)

R

Ratiocinatio: From Latin *ratiōcinārī*, refers to the faculty of reasoning considered to be primarily of the animus. The ratiocinatio permits the animus to dispassionately apply discrimination and judgment. It contextualizes experience and provides for the communication of concepts. (Synonym: **Ennoia**)

Relic(s): Objects that hold a significant phasmic link to a subject, such as a lock of hair or sentimental possession that can therefore be used to call, draw, or evoke the spirit to which they belonged. (Synonyms: **object link, taglock**)

Resolution: From Latin *resolvere*. In sciomancy, it can have multiple meanings. One is the process a spirit undertakes to resolve their attachments to their former life and release their phasmic body. It is also the method of magical intervention that can bring a revenant to a resolution (e.g., expiaition, ligation, and exorcism). Resolution is further used to refer to the overall process of achieving a solution to a spirit incursion, which is measured when the wisest and most humane outcome available for both the living and dead is achieved.

Revenant: From French, meaning *one who remains*, itself from the Latin *revenīre, to come back*. It is the spirit of a deceased human being who has not shed their attachment to their earthly life and is bound in Qarth Arqa and may interact with the world of the living. (Synonyms: **ghost, undead, unquiet spirit**)

S

Sanctuary: Derived from the Latin *sanctum*, meaning *blessed*. Used here to describe a magically consecrated area that can serve as both a place of protection and refuge, established as a safe zone and center of operations within a sciomantic investigation.

Sciomancy, Sciomantic: *Scio*, from the Graeco-Latin *skia*, meaning *a shade*. Sciomancy is one of the two branches of necromancy along with necyomancy. Sciomancy focuses on communicating with manifest human spirits or "shades" of the dead in the location where they frequent. Most often these spirits are revenants, and sciomancy works to resolve the events caused by them. The necromantic use of the word "sciomancy" should not be confused with the divination practice of the same name, wherein the diviner prognosticates from the casting of shadows.

Second Death: This is the condition of a revenant in Qarth Arqa wherein they suffer constant dissolution due to the nature of the metacosmos working upon their phasmic form. It is called the second death in allusion to the similar decomposition of the physical body following the initial or carnal death.

Seven Earths: The earths are a Hebrew system of classifying the seven coexisting sublunary divisions or worlds that abut each other. These worlds are separated by their own metacosmoi and attributed with seven broad classifications of daemones. Entering European magic via Jewish mysticism but cognate with the concepts already present in local traditions, the seven earths offer a Qabalistic model to describe the universal ideal of the seven sublunary worlds.

Seven Hells: A conceptual model of the potential events following incarnate death described as seven divisions of Qarth Arqa in Hebrew tradition. Each division represents a psycho-spiritual state in the experiences of a deceased human spirit.

Sign(s): Objective phenomena indicating the manifestation of a spirit in near proximity. Unlike movements, which could be considered effects to the environment, signs are indicative of the immediate presence of the spirit themself.

Simulacrum: From Latin, meaning *a copy* or *imitation*. A simulacrum is a phasmic form or matrix, which can be formed naturally or artificially. The phasmic body of a spirit is one such simulacrum.

Solve: From Latin *solvere*, meaning *to disperse* or *to dissipate*. Solve is the primordial modality opposed to coagula and refers to when atoms dissipate, go outward, or shed. An esoterically masculine archetype, solve is the faculty of nature that facilitates dissolution and change.

Spirit: From Latin *spiritus*, meaning *breath* or *blow*. The term has a long history of usage and is defined in various ways. In magic, it refers to the actuated construct of a phasmic body or simulacrum. In a strict technical sense, a spirit is defined by having this animated form, and may be sentient such as a daemon, or non-sentient as in the case of phasmata.

Spiritualization: The practice of aligning oneself to the spiritual truth that permeates all things and being thereby empowered. Often accomplished by ritual, religious rites, meditative exercises, and/or prayer according to the magician's or spirit worker's culture or tradition.

Sublunary: Meaning *under the moon*, refers to the understanding that all things below the celestial realms receive the powers of the firmament filtered by the lunar influence. It refers to the realm of transformation and change, where magic is active and souls reincarnate. Its denizens are referred to as sublunary spirits or daemones.

Subterranean Daemon(es): A classification of sublunary spirits famed for their magic, craftmanship, loyalty, suspicion, and even hostility. Subterranean daemones are also classified as spirits of Mars.

Summon(ing): From vulgar Latin *summundre*, meaning *to call*, and *summonere*, meaning *to remind* or *advise privately*. In magic, after a spirit has been called by evocation and a relationship or contract has been established between them and the magician, to call them again is to summon them.

T

Talisman(s): An artificial magical construct with a material basis designed to create a desired effect. More particularly, talismanic magic refers to a specific discipline of the occult arts in which symbolic images are carved, drawn, or otherwise inscribed on a physical object such as stone, paper, wood, or wax to denote a magical intelligence or functional intention.

Terrestrial Daemon(es): Nonhuman sublunary spirits that permeate the terrestrial realm. Terrestrial daemones are numerous and varied, ranging from lonesome mountain spirits to daemones who assist in the growing of flora, etcetera. They are collectively described as spirits of the moon. (Synonym: **Nature spirits**)

U

Umbra (pl. Umbrae): From Latin meaning *shade* or *shadow*, one of the stages of manifestation pertaining to any class of spirits or daemones that appear as a dark and defined figure. Perceiving a spirit as an umbra is dependent on the conditions of the phasmic environment and does not imply any specific intention on the part of the spirit themself. (Synonym: **Shadow people**)

Bibliography

Agrippa, Heinrich Cornelius. *The Fourth Book of Occult Philosophy*. Whitefish, MT: Kessinger Publishing, 1992. Originally published 1559.

———. *Three Books of Occult Philosophy (Llewellyn's Sourcebook)*. Edited by Donald Tyson. Woodbury MN: Llewellyn Publications, 1992.

Apuleius. *The Works of Apuleius, Comprising the Metamorphoses, or Golden Ass, the God of Socrates, the Florida, and his Defence, or A discourse on Magic*. London: George Bell, 1853. https://archive.org/details/worksofapuleiusn00apul.

Campbell Thompson, R. *The Devils and Evil Spirits of Babylonia*, Vol. I. London: Luzac & Co, 1904.

Democritus Junior (Robert Burton). *The Anatomy of Melancholy: What It Is, with All the Kinds, Causes, Symptoms, Prognostics, and Several Cures of It*. London: William Tegg & Co., 1849. https://archive.org/details /anatomyofmelanch00burtuoft/page/116/mode/2up.

Glanvill, Joseph. *Saducismus Triumphatus: or, Full and Plain Evidence Concerning Witches and Apparitions; in Two Parts—the First Treating of Their Possibility, the Second of Their Real Existence, Second Edition*. London: James Collins, 1682. https://collections.nlm.nih.gov/catalog/nlm:nlmuid-2354009R-bk.

Greer, John Michael, and Christopher Warnock, translators. *The Complete Picatrix: The Occult Classic of Astrological Magic, Liber Atratus Edition*. (n.l.): Renaissance Astrology Press, 2011.

Gregor, Walter. *Notes on the Folk-lore of the North-East of Scotland*. London: Elliot Stock, 1881. https://archive.org/details/cu31924009599212.

Gregory of Nyssa. "On the Soul and the Resurrection." In *Nicene and Post-Nicene Fathers, Second Series, Vol. 5*, edited by Philip Schaff and Henry Wace, translated by William Moore and Henry Austin Wilson. New York: Charles Scribner's Sons, 1917.

Harper, Douglas. Online Etymological Dictionary. Last accessed August 13, 2023. www.etymonline.com.

Henderson, William. *Notes on the Folk-Lore of the Northern Counties of England and the Borders*. London: W. Satchell, Peyton and Co. 1879. https://archive .org/details/cu31924006726552.

Homer. *The Odyssey with an English Translation by A.T. Murray, PhD in two volumes*. London, W. Heinemann; New York: G. P. Putnam's Sons. 1919. https://archive.org/details/odyssey11home_.

Honorius of Thebes. *The Sworn Book of Honorius: Liber Iuratus Honorii*. Translated by Joseph Peterson. Lake Worth, FL: Ibis Press, 2016.

James VI and I. *The Demonology of King James I: Includes the Original Text of Daemonologie and News from Scotland 1597*. Edited by Donald Tyson. Woodbury, MN: Llewellyn Publications, 2011.

Karr, Don, and Stephen Skinner. *Sourceworks of Ceremonial Magic Series Volume VI, Sepher Raziel: Liber Salomonis*. Singapore: Golden Hoard Press, 2010.

Kirkpatrick Sharpe, Charles. *Historical Account of Belief in Witchcraft in Scotland*. Glasgow, UK: Thomas D. Morison, 1726. Reprinted 1884.

Lecouteux, Claude. *Traditional Magic Spells for Protection and Healing*. Translated by John E. Graham. Rochester, VT: Inner Traditions, 2017.

Maclennan, Malcom. *A Pronouncing and Etymological Dictionary of the Gaelic Language*. Edinburgh, UK: Acair & Aberdeen University Press, 1979.

MacTaggart, John. *The Scottish Gallovidian Encyclopedia*. Glasgow, UK: Thomas D. Morison, 1824.

Peterson, Joseph H., trans. *Verus Jesuitarum Libellus*. Esoteric Archives. http://www.esotericarchives.com/solomon/jesuit.htm.

Plato. *The Dialogues of Plato Vol. i, Translated into English B. Jowett M.A.* New York: Random Press, 1892. https://archive.org/details/dli.ernet.524833/.

Pliny the Younger. *The Letters of Pliny the Younger Vol II, Books VI–X*. Translated by William Melmoth, F. C. T. Bosanquet revision. New York: Hinds, Noble and Eldridge Publishers,1900. https://archive.org/details/lettersofplinyyo00plin.

Plutarch. *Moralia, On the Signs of Socrates, Volume VII*. Translated by Frank Cole Babbit, Harold Cherniss et al. Cambridge, MA: Harvard University Press/ Loeb Library, 1959.

Roberts, E. P. *The Isle of Gramarye or Tales of Old Britain Part I*. London: MacMillan Company Ltd, 1915.

Schaff, Phillip. *St. Augustine's City of God and Christian Doctrine*. New York: The Christian Literature Publishing Co., 1890. https://www.ccel.org/ccel/schaff/npnf102.i.html.

Scott, Reginald. *The Discoverie of Witchcraft*. New York: Dover Publications, 1972. Originally published 1587 by William Brome (London). https://archive.org/details/discoveryofwitch00scot/.

Skinner, Stephen. *The Complete Magician's Tables*. London: Golden Hoard Press, 2006.

———. *Michael Psellus' Dialogue on the Operation of Daemons*. Translated by Marcus Collisson. Singapore: Golden Hoard Press, 2010.

Sikes, Wirt. *British Goblins: Welsh Folklore, Fairy Mythology, Legends and Traditions*. London: Sampson and Low, 1880. https://archive.org/details/britishgoblinswe00sikerich.

Sepher Raziel–Liber Salomonis. British Library Sloane MS 3826, folio 19. (Also consulted edition by Don Karr, 2002).

Van Horne, Patrick, and Jason Riley. *Left of Bang: How the Marine Corps' Combat Hunter Program Can Save Your Life*. New York: Black Irish Entertainment, 2014.

INDEX

B

C

D

E

I

Q

R

S

T

U

V

W

Warding (See also Protection), 145,
146, 163, 219

Warding oil, 146, 163

Wash(es), 132, 144, 145, 163, 172,
219, 221, 222, 244

Water, 66, 67, 71, 73, 98, 101, 116,
118, 119, 129, 136, 143–147, 150,
151, 163, 172, 181, 205, 221–223,
244, 247

Wierus, John, 86

Welsh, 159

Witness(es), 27, 49, 69, 72, 98, 103,
105, 136, 174–176, 179–181, 183,
195, 198, 212, 214, 262, 266